THE ENTABLO MANUSCRIPT

Para Patricia,

¡Gracias por todo!

Sarah

 THE WILLIAM & BETTYE NOWLIN SERIES
in Art, History, and Culture of the Western Hemisphere

THE ENTABLO MANUSCRIPT

*Water Rituals and Khipu Boards
of San Pedro de Casta, Peru*

SARAH BENNISON

University of Texas Press

Austin

Figure 1.11 and a slightly modified version of figure 1.3 appeared in a book chapter by the author, "The Record Keepers: Maintaining Irrigation Canals, Traditions and Inca Codes of Law in 1920s Huarochirí," in *The Social and Political Life of Latin American Infrastructure: Meanings, Values, and Competing Visions of the Future*, edited by Jonathan Alderman and Geoff Goodwin (London: University of London Press, 223–251).

Unless otherwise indicated, all photos are by Sarah Bennison.

Copyright © 2023 by the University of Texas Press
All rights reserved
Printed in the United States of America
First edition, 2023

Requests for permission to reproduce material from this work should be sent to:
 Permissions
 University of Texas Press
 P.O. Box 7819
 Austin, TX 78713-7819
 utpress.utexas.edu

♾ The paper used in this book meets the minimum requirements of ANSI/NISO Z39.48-1992 (R1997) (Permanence of Paper).

Cataloging-in-Publication Data is available from the Library of Congress.

 LCCN 2023001751
 ISBN 978-1-4773-2542-1 (hardcover)
 ISBN 978-1-4773-2543-8 (PDF)
 ISBN 978-1-4773-2544-5 (ePub)

doi:10.7560/325421

For Alfred

The continuous drip polishes the stone.

CONTENTS

List of Illustrations *xi*

Preface *xiii*

1. Introduction: The Entablo Manuscript of San Pedro de Casta, Huarochirí *1*
2. The Entablo *93*
3. El Entablo *157*

   Acknowledgments *219*

   Glossary *221*

   References *225*

   Index *239*

ILLUSTRATIONS

MAP

Map 1.1. Canal system in San Pedro de Casta in the 1920s   *77*

FIGURES

Fig. 1.1. San Pedro de Casta   *3*
Fig. 1.2. The Entablo of San Pedro de Casta   *4*
Fig. 1.3. An *alguacil* reading out passages from the Entablo in 2018   *11*
Fig. 1.4. The traditional ceremonial site of Cuhuay during the 2019 *huayrona*   *14*
Fig. 1.5. A layer of masking tape once used to bind the book together that reads "ENTABLO"   *17*
Fig. 1.6. The *padrón de madera* (wooden register) that Tello observed in San Pedro de Casta   *19*
Fig. 1.7. A pencil entry at the top of the page reading "No estoy de acuerdo"   *20*
Fig. 1.8. Signatures (recorded in 1924?) signaling each individual's approval of the regulations of 1921   *20*
Fig. 1.9. Producing the records to account for the numbers of votes at the *huayrona*   *21*
Fig. 1.10. The image of the 1920s khipu-board *padrón*, placed inside the current *padrón* by the community authorities   *24*
Fig. 1.11. The community *padrón* in 2018   *25*
Fig. 1.12. Containers filled with *chicha* beer   *41*
Fig. 1.13. A *michco* for the Carhuayumac *parada* whipping the water to hurry it along the canal   *43*
Fig. 1.14. A *huallque (wallki, huallqui)*   *51*
Fig. 1.15. The *cura* (traditional healer and ritual specialist)   *64*
Fig. 1.16. Cumau waterfall   *65*

xi

xii LIST OF ILLUSTRATIONS

Fig. 1.17. Taquina (Singing Place)   66
Fig. 1.18. The Yacapar *huayrona* (group premises)   72
Fig. 1.19. The elders clean the road   79
Fig. 1.20. The functionaries of the 1979 *champería* chew coca leaves   80
Fig. 1.21. The well-thumbed pages of the manuscript after a century of use   82
Fig. 1.22. Nemesio Bautista's granddaughter, Doña Luzmila Salinas Bautista, demonstrating how a sacred stone inventoried in the Entablo is held   87
Fig. 1.23. Catalina's *puchka* and *shicra*: items used by women in the January rainmaking rituals.   88
Fig. 3.1. Folios 18v and 19r   196
Fig. 3.2. Folios 19v and 20r   198
Fig. 3.3. Folios 20v and 22r   199
Fig. 3.4. Folio 30r, which records maintenance work carried out on the Carhuayumac irrigation canal in 1947   215
Fig. 3.5. Folio 103r, an attached plain sheet of paper used to record grazing fees from livestock owners   218

PREFACE

Famed for its early colonial Quechua manuscript, the Huarochirí province of Lima enjoys a canonical standing among Andeanists and speakers of Quechua. Thanks to a renaissance of Huarochirí studies over the last two decades, as well as a growing interest in all things Huarochirí on social media in the last decade, today the province's reputation as an Andean holy land extends beyond the Peruvian Andes. I will never forget the disbelief of a Quechua-speaking Bolivian friend when I told her that Quechua is no longer spoken conversationally in Huarochirí (or at least not openly): "But it's the home of the first book! The Quechua bible!"

Nowhere else but Huarochirí can claim to have given rise to two of the only known detailed local accounts of ancestral Andean landscape rituals. Around seventy years into the colonial era, an Indigenous scribe penned a 31-chapter compendium of ancestor-focused customs in the Quechua language, containing descriptions of local rituals and origin myths, narrated in relation to regional ancestral law. This text (ca. 1608), which is widely regarded as unique, has come to be known among English speakers as the Huarochirí Manuscript (Salomon and Urioste 1991). It remains unique, as the only known detailed text on Andean customs of Indigenous Quechua authorship from the early colonial era. Now the emergence of a twentieth-century manuscript from Huarochirí in the academic realm urges us to consider the extent to which, and the means through which, communities in this province (and beyond) have recorded laws about their landscape rituals over time.

Three centuries after the Huarochirí Manuscript and less than a hundred years into the republican era, a team of community elders and a scribe from a Huarochirí village embarked on the endeavor of committing to script the regulations for their annual water customs, beginning with their ritualized canal-cleaning traditions. Written in a regional variety of Spanish in an unremarkable navy-blue leather-bound notebook, the Entablo manuscript of San Pedro de Casta (begun in 1921) echoes its Quechua language predecessor in various ways to a striking degree.

For example, both manuscripts devote attention to the naming of sites in the landscape and provide details about material goods given to the sacred ancestors as ritual offerings. Furthermore, both manuscripts constitute an effort by their respective producers to generate written accounts in a single target language. At times, the rich linguistic nature of the highly localized content appears to make this an impossible task in both cases. As the introductory chapter of this book explains, both Huarochirí texts are overwhelmingly concerned with the ritual management of water and irrigative infrastructure.

Perhaps not coincidentally, Huarochirí has a well-documented ethnographic record of persisting community use of khipus (quipus/kipus): knotted fiber records of pre-Hispanic origin. Salomon's in-depth ethnographic research (2004 and other works) on the patrimonial khipus of San Andrés de Tupicocha, Huarochirí, proposed that these devices were historically integral to the local kin groups' management of water.[1] The 1608 Huarochirí manuscript describes a lake-impounding ceremony carried out by the Concha kin group of San Damián, where a khipu account recorded the identities of those who failed to turn up for the work (Salomon and Urioste 1991: 142). This function bears a striking resemblance to the twentieth-century accountancy practices of San Pedro de Casta, located in the province's Santa Eulalia River valley.

San Pedro de Casta (also Casta) has a relatively recent tradition of hybrid khipu-alphabetic registers known as khipu boards. These registers were introduced in the colonial era and continued to be used in Casta as recently as the early twentieth century (Tello and Miranda 1923; Salomon and Niño-Murcia 2011) and probably even the mid-twentieth century (Bennison 2019, 2022; Hyland, Bennison, and Hyland 2021).

Khipu boards registered people's participation and performance in the October canal-cleaning ceremony in Casta—the *champería* (Tello and Miranda 1923). Tello and Miranda's study of Casta's *champería* mentions only one khipu board; the "padrón de madera," which corresponds to the Entablo's Padrón de Huallque (a *huallque* is a small pouch-like bag that the men must wear around their necks). This khipu board recorded whether workers had turned up for the canal-cleaning with the appropriate goods. Tello and Miranda (1923: 534) write that individuals were represented by cords hung from the wooden khipu board during a ceremony at the site of Huanca Acequia (a tract of canal close to the village nucleus):

---

1. The work of Sabine Hyland has further contributed to Huarochirí's reputation as a khipu hotspot. Her khipu research has explored two colonial examples from the Huarochirí village of Collata (Hyland 2017) as well as a republican-era example from Anchucaya (Hyland 2016).

Sobre una de sus caras aparecen los nombres de los obreros, y por medio de cordones de diferentes colores, que pasan a través de un agujero colocado al lado de cada nombre, y de nudos, se anota nemónicamente, no sólo la falta de asistencia, y la calidad del trabajo realizado, sino todo aquello que las autoridades exigen al obrero como accesorios indispensables para atender el trabajo: vestidos especiales, wallkis [hualquis; huallques].

On one of its faces the names of the workers are shown. It annotates mnemonically, by means of cords of different colors, which pass through a hole placed next to each name, and by means of knots, not only absences, and the quality of the work carried out, but everything that the authorities require of the worker, as essential accessories to attend to the work: special clothing, *wallkis* [*hualquis*; *huallques*].

The Entablo strongly suggests that multiple registers of this kind were used during Casta's water customs. Casta elder Doña Luzmila, who is in her eighties, explained to me in 2022 that she remembers multiple large wooden *entablos* being used during the *champería* in her childhood years. As I explain in chapter 1, the term *entablo*, used to refer to the 1921 manuscript, is also used in Casta to refer to khipu boards, whose functions the Entablo manuscript describes.

Doña Luzmila's memories of Casta's khipu boards are somewhat hazy. She could not remember precisely how many of them there were, but she was firm in her recollection that they were taken from the village at some point during her lifetime. Batting her hand toward the ground as she spoke disapprovingly about the village's *entablos* being removed, she wondered where they might be now: "¿Pero donde estarían? Alguien se ha llevado" (But wherever could they be now? Someone has taken them).[2]

Although the whereabouts of Casta's khipu boards today are unclear (if indeed they still exist), the Entablo manuscript provides further information about the aforementioned khipu board depicted and briefly described by Tello and Miranda (1923: 534) a century ago. It also provides information about other registers used during the *champería* that were almost certainly of the same type. In so doing, the Entablo gives us a rare insight into a khipu

---

2. Throughout this book, the Entablo and other Spanish-language primary sources such as fieldwork collaborators are cited in Spanish first, followed by the English translation in the main text. Secondary Spanish-language works such as scholarly literature and dictionary definitions are cited in English in the main text, with the original Spanish in a footnote. All translations are mine unless otherwise noted.

tradition that, at the time of writing in the 1920s, not only was alive but was an important element of community life. The Entablo is unique in being the only known source that provides instructions for the use of khipu boards by a group using them at the time of writing.

This book is the product of nearly four years' work conducted when I was employed as a research fellow on a research project based in the Department of Social Anthropology at the University of St. Andrews (Scotland). The project, funded by the Leverhulme Trust and entitled "Hidden Texts of the Andes: Deciphering the 'Khipus' (Cord Writing) of Peru," was led by Professor Sabine Hyland. My primary role in the project was to produce one of the principal outputs: a critical edition of the Entablo that would feature a transcription and a translation into English. Sabine Hyland and her husband, William Hyland, had been permitted to study and photograph the Entablo in 2015 during a khipu-focused research trip to Casta and other Huarochirí villages, funded by the National Geographic Society.

Working from the images of the Entablo generated by the Hylands' 2015 trip, in combination with my own photographs taken in 2018, I developed a diplomatic transcription of the Entablo.[3] Sabine Hyland also shared her own draft transcription as part of the materials she provided to support my own transcription of the manuscript.

Today the highest-ranking functionary in charge of organizing the October *champería*, the *principal*, must study the manuscript in order to be able to oversee this ceremony adequately throughout its week-long duration. As the Entablo is actively used and consulted by Casta's community authorities today, I wanted to bring these aspects of the manuscript to life by ensuring that my transcription included all its "layers" added over time: notes, markings, highlighted sections, and damage to the pages. Although I was not expected to conduct fieldwork as part of this research, I felt that my analysis of the Entablo—a text with nearly sixty pages full of idiosyncratic terminology and implicit local knowledge—would be richer for it.

I had designed the methodology for this research prior to the pandemic. As a single parent and carer at that time, I would need to structure fieldwork around school holidays and family commitments. I had planned to conduct two short field trips to Casta: one in 2018 and another in 2020. Although this second trip inevitably could not take place due to pandemic travel restrictions,

---

3. A page of the manuscript that had writing on both sides became lost at some point between 2015 (when Sabine Hyland and William Hyland photographed the text) and 2018 (when I photographed it). It is possible that their photographs of this lost folio could be the only remaining record.

I was able to incorporate some additional findings and observations from a research impact trip to Casta in 2022 into this book.

I could not travel to Casta during the *champería* in October until 2022. My ethnographic experience in Casta at that point consisted of a short trip while working on my master's degree in June 2009 and two weeks in late 2018 to early 2019 when I observed the *huayrona*, Casta's traditional accounts ceremony.

In 2012, when my child was a baby, he was portable. I was able to carry him on my back during the six months he accompanied me during my nine months of doctoral fieldwork in San Damián, Huarochirí. Furthermore, his father had taken leave from work to accompany me in the field.

Although I was unable to carry out long-term ethnography for this book due to workplace and family commitments, the knowledge I gained through my longer doctoral research on San Damián's water customs (Bennison 2016)—such as ways of speaking in Huarochirí and canal-cleaning ritual discourse—was helpful for transcribing, understanding, and contextualizing the Entablo. My analysis was further supported by my observations of Casta's *huayrona* in 2019 and parts of the *champería* in 2022. During both trips, I interviewed Casteños about the significance of the Entablo Manuscript and its contents and about the *champería*.

The methodology that informed the research for this book might therefore be characterized as patchwork ethnography, whereby "ethnographic processes and protocols [are] designed around short-term field visits, using fragmentary yet rigorous data" (Günel, Varma, and Watanabe 2020).[4]

This is an achievable model for marginalized scholars like myself who must negotiate family obligations, precarity, and other stigmatized factors that often make long-term, in-person fieldwork difficult or impossible (Günel, Varma, and Watanabe 2020).

As a scholar with multiple invisible disabilities that were diagnosed during the writing of this book, there were various moments when completing it and getting it to press felt like an insurmountable challenge. Each time I felt like I would not finish the book, I reminded myself of the beauty of the Entablo's opening pages and the generosity and kindness of Casta's people. Each moment spent working on the book—from the easier moments of laughter, singing, and dancing in Casta to the difficult long deskside nights and tears—has been a privilege and an honor.

---

4. I am grateful to Sonja Dobroski for bringing this publication to my attention.

THE ENTABLO MANUSCRIPT

1
INTRODUCTION

The Entablo Manuscript of San Pedro de Casta, Huarochirí

What if our assumptions about Andean customary law depending on oral transmission alone—without writing—are wrong? As elsewhere in the world, customary law or *costumbre* in the Andean region is generally considered to refer to unwritten law (Nuñez Palomino 1995: 12; Salomon 2018: 36). Central Andean community institutions are commonly thought to have persisted as unwritten law since colonial times. A significant clue that this has not always necessarily been the case, however, is the existence of the so-called Huarochirí Manuscript of 1608.[1] Produced in an early colonial context of intensive social, political, economic, and religious change, this Quechua-language text from the Huarochirí province of Lima describes the ritual laws—many concerned with water rights and irrigation—of a number of Huarochirí's ancestor-focused kin groups known as ayllus (for an English translation, see Salomon and Urioste 1991). This text is regarded as a unique source on early colonial Andean society because of its native authorship (Durston 2007).

Over three centuries later, in 1921, a group of ritual experts and authorities in the Huarochirí village of San Pedro de Casta wrote down their community's ritual laws in a book called "El Entablo." This set of ancestral laws, written in a regional variety of Spanish, sits at the heart of community life in Casta today, instructing how the community's annual canal-cleaning ritual must be organized. The Entablo demonstrates the intricacies of Andean community customary law, showing, just as the 1608 Huarochirí text did, that it may be passed down in written form. The constitutional community text, produced

---

1. Nuñez Palomino (1995: 12) acknowledges the importance of writing in the transmission of communal law in highland Peruvian communities in the late twentieth century. Nevertheless, he suggests that "communal law was created and transmitted in a predominantly oral way" historically.

after the Peruvian Constitution of 1920, forcefully challenges the notion that Andean customary law and national state-sanctioned law exist in two distinct and fundamentally separate domains: one oral, the other literate. A reading of the Entablo's rich content, which was continually updated and reformed in accordance with state law in the decades following the 1920s, compels us to consider the processes of change that brought about such a text in the first place and made reforms to ancestral law necessary. Furthermore, the manuscript raises questions about its relationship to the kinds of Andean inscriptive practices that its content evokes and describes.

The existing scholarship on Huarochirí already makes evident a degree of relationship between water management, customary law, and khipus (kipus, quipus) (Salomon 2004; Salomon and Niño-Murcia 2011). The Entablo's instructions on the use of hybrid khipu-text devices known as khipu boards allow us to appreciate the complexities of this relationship in greater depth. We can now seriously consider whether Andean fiber records called khipus encoded information that served to promote, or even oblige, compliance with customary law, to ensure that community members did all that was required to achieve water access. Indeed, it is the continued notion that water access requires piety toward the sacred ancestors, by carrying forward the laws of the past, that conceptually binds together the Huarochirí text of 1608 and the Entablo of 1921. In order to illuminate the textual bases of customary law in Casta and the genesis of the Entablo, we must therefore begin by exploring the centrality of water.

The Lifeblood of Casta

It is no exaggeration to state that water is everything in the highland Lima village of San Pedro de Casta. Water is at the heart of community life, which has attracted an increasingly steady stream of anthropologists to Casta (located 80 kilometers from Lima city) over the last century.[2] Community water management across the Andes is structured through rituals acknowledging the sacred status of the resource: water is considered to be owned and controlled by the founding (pre-Hispanic) ancestors of the respective communities (Sherbondy 1998).

---

2. Among others, Tello and Miranda (1923); Matos Mar (1958b); Ramírez Villacorta (1980); Ortiz Rescaniere (1980); Llanos and Osterling (1982); Gelles (1984b); Ráez Retamozo (1995); Ediciones Flora Tristán and CENDOC-Mujer (2002); Fernández (2003); and Apaza et al. (2006). Nestled in the high Santa Eulalia valley, Casta sits at 3,185 meters above sea level.

INTRODUCTION 3

FIGURE 1.1. *San Pedro de Casta*.

While some anthropologists have reported the "erosion" of ancestral water traditions in the last half century in Peruvian communities (Arguedas 2002; Gose 1994), Casta is well known for maintaining its traditions. The anthropologist Paul Gelles described Casta in the 1980s as a "small hydraulic society" (Gelles 1984b: 332).[3] This description is just as fitting today as it was in 1921, when the community authorities in Casta wrote about their faithful devotion to water in their own words, describing it as the lifeblood and fundamental basis of life in the village.

During the first week of October 1921, the village authorities in Casta oversaw the most important economic and social event in the ritual calendar: the annual canal-cleaning ritual known as the *champería* or *walla-walla* (CCSPC 1921: f. 19v).[4] After the *champería* ended following a week of toil and jubilant celebration, the authorities in Casta did not rest. Instead, they set about codifying the community's ancestral water laws dictating how the

---

3. "Una pequeña sociedad hidráulica" (Gelles 1984b: 332).
4. The *champería* in Casta is also known as the *warina* or *walina*. Today it is more commonly known as the Fiesta del Agua (Water Fiesta). The Quechua term "Yakuraymi" (Water Festival) was also used in Casta in the 1970s (Echeandia Valladares 1981: 171; Llanos and Osterling 1982: 115). The term *walla-walla* may be associated with the deity Wallallo (Tello and Miranda 1923: 540).

4 THE ENTABLO MANUSCRIPT

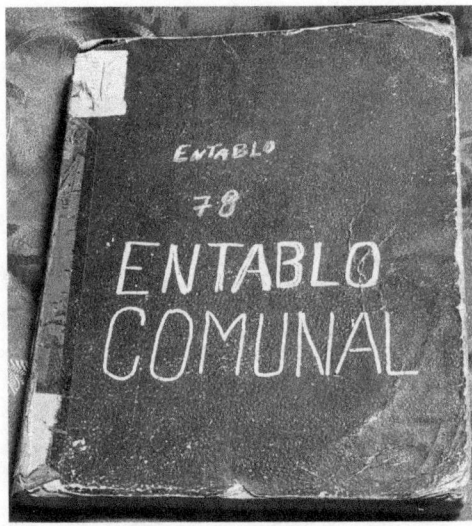

FIGURE 1.2. *The Entablo of San Pedro de Casta.*

champería must be carried out, which they did with exacting detail in a constitutional document they entitled "El Entablo."

Like many important community projects in Casta, producing the Entablo *champería* regulations was a collaborative effort. In a lined notebook apparently provided by the village notary,[5] the *síndico personero* (local state authority) Don Máximo Calistro took a feather quill into his hand and began to set down an agreed-upon definitive account of the regulations dictated by the top-ranking authorities and ritual experts.[6] Don Máximo appears to have quickly passed it over to another scribe—possibly the *gobernador* Nemesio Bautista[7]—though Don Máximo probably had the final say in the words that collaboratively made it onto the page.

A *síndico comunero* was formerly the highest-ranking authority in a village; in San Pedro de Huancaire, he was also the leading religious authority (Soler 1958: 248). The *síndico personero* acted in the interests of the state municipality and also in community interests. In the late nineteenth century the *personería* (municipal authorities) in Tupicocha became increasingly involved in functions of the *comunidad* (community) (Salomon and Niño-Murcia

---

5. A faint entry in pencil, signed "Notario SC," claims that he (whoever SC might be) provided and so owns the book in which the Entablo regulations were written (f. 53r).
6. According to Eloy Tomás Rojas Obispo, the president of the Comunidad Campesina de San Pedro de Casta in 2018, a condor feather quill was used to write the Entablo. The condor is a sacred bird in Andean society.
7. The handwriting in the early entries appears to correspond to his signature.

2011: 65).[8] This could very well have been the case in Casta too, which would explain the references to Casta's *ciudadanos* (citizens) in the opening page of the manuscript begun by Casta's *síndico personero* (CCSPC 1921: f. 3r). According to Echeandía (1981: 108), prior to the 1930s, both the síndico and the gobernador were in charge of distributing water in Casta. This may explain why these two authorities took charge of writing the Entablo's early entries.

The motivation for getting the ritual regulations down on paper appears to have come from Don Máximo Calistro, the *síndico personero* in 1921 and in subsequent years. An entry in the Entablo suggests that he spearheaded the Entablo project, explaining that the initiative was the "empeño de las autoridades precentes en primer lugar el Síndico Don Máximo Calistro" (the undertaking of the present authorities, first the Síndico Don Máximo Calistro) (CCSPC 1921: f. 18r). The motivations for the manuscript's production suggest that in Casta, just as in San Pedro de Huancaire, the *síndico personero* had authority over the village's religious customs.

In order to address an increasingly lax attitude toward traditional moral codes, the Entablo's constitution aimed to protect the integrity of ancestral water customs and to address the innovations and changes beginning to seep into local ways of life. The elders agreed to write the following:

> En vista de muchos controles y desacuerdos en las obligaciones comensando desde el teniente asta el ultimo que es el camachico no cumplen con sus obligaciones y deberes acordaron hacer constar popularmente bajo nuestras firmas afin de hacer cumplir y cumplan puntualmente y no aleguen motivo titulandose de no haber constancia y menos fuerza de ley.

> In light of the many interventions and disagreements concerning the obligations from the Teniente right down to the last functionary, which is the Camachico, the functionaries are not fulfilling their duties and obligations. They have agreed to collectively set down an official record, under [the jurisdiction of] our signatures so that they are obliged to fulfill their duties. They must fulfill them in a punctual manner and cannot give the excuse of taking on their roles without there being a written record and claiming diminished force of law. (CCSPC 1921: f. 3r)

---

8. In the late twentieth century a *personero* was a community member responsible for documents and land litigation (Isbell 1978: 254).

6 THE ENTABLO MANUSCRIPT

Ritual discourse in Casta's *champería* had broken with tradition, so in October 1921 the task of restoring proper ritual behavior needed to be regulated to ensure that all the ritual authorities or *funcionarios* (functionaries) fulfilled their duties sufficiently. The Entablo's instructions served as an official response to the claims of functionaries who had underperformed and claimed that the community had no codified laws detailing what was expected of them. Whether or not no antecedent records of the duties were indeed set out in the Entablo and whether the records were inaccessible or disagreeable to the functionaries is difficult to ascertain (this point is discussed later). One thing that quickly becomes clear when reading the Entablo is that the functionaries' work was under intense scrutiny. Because communities in the Peruvian Andes manage water at the community level (Guevara-Gil and Boelens 2010; Mayer 1989), any lack of cooperation during the *champería* posed a risk to community cohesion: the social and moral basis of community autonomy. As oral narratives told in the Huamalíes province attest, failure to uphold agreements about the distribution of workloads undermines community autonomy. Rebellion and failure to conform are said to inflict curses on communities (Howard-Malverde 1990: 69–70).

A reading of the Entablo strongly suggests that a key function of record-keeping in Andean communities historically has been to monitor and police social "input" so that moral and financial imbalances can be regulated or otherwise accounted for. As community infrastructure, record-keeping practices function to maximize the contributions of community members.[9] Most Andean communities have strict rules for organizing rituals, specifying the necessary goods and who must contribute what (Rösing 1995: 74). As we have seen in the case of the 1921 *champería*, obligations that are not clear (and set out in a consultable, formally agreed format) can result in conflict.

The Entablo Manuscript was intended to resolve intracommunity water conflicts in Casta within a framework of traditional Andean community justice, where precepts take into account the agency of the animate landscape. In Andean cosmology, ancestral beings known as huacas are deemed to own and control water.[10] Throughout the Andes, communities perform a series

---

9. "It would be no exaggeration to call coding of information on textile fiber a core infrastructure of Andean social organization" (Salomon 2013: 32). I have expanded on this point by arguing that the infrastructural functions of khipus and khipu boards support the maintenance of irrigative infrastructure through promoting cooperation and coherence within communities (Bennison 2022).

10. These beings tend to be known not as huacas but as *abuelos* (ancestors, literally "grandparents") in Huarochirí villages today (Bennison 2016). They are also referred to as *reynas* and *reyes* (queens and kings) in Casta.

of rituals each year in which they appeal to the local huacas to allow them to channel water through the canals to the fields. Because the ambivalent huaca ancestors are deemed to respond positively only to strictly traditional ritual discourse, community economies rely on irrigation rituals to be carried out fully and to the letter. Various ethnographers have described the disastrous impacts of failed rituals, where an absent or incomplete ritual is linked with a negative outcome, such as drought, excessive rain, and landslides or illness in people or animals (Gelles 2000b: 82; Gose 1994: 129; Gow and Condori 1976: 85; Isbell 1978: 59).

As shown in this chapter, a failed ritual is indicative of intracommunity conflict and represents an existential threat to the community as a legitimate productive unit. Just as in the 1920s, conflicts among community members in pre-Hispanic Huarochirí were deemed a barrier to irrigation, in that dissonance impeded communication with the ancestors who owned and controlled water (Spalding 1984: 66). Within this framework, social organization was likewise subject to strict regulation. During the 1979 *champería* in Casta, a ritual specialist (the *cura*) stated that new *comuneros* were not fulfilling their duties correctly, so the gods of the ancestors were punishing Casteños with a drought (Llanos and Osterling 1982: 123). Because malfunctioning rites indicate that the regulations governing the community hierarchy (with the apical ancestors situated at the top of the hierarchy) were not being observed, community elders oversaw compliance with ritual law, ensuring that ritual functionaries performed their duties correctly.

In this introduction I draw on ethnographic material gathered over a decade of research in Huarochirí villages, exploring ancestral water customs. Working on the 1921 Casta manuscript has allowed me retrospectively to read between the lines of many statements made by collaborators in the village of San Damián,[11] where I conducted doctoral fieldwork in 2012. Elderly collaborators explained the importance of carrying out rituals correctly and lamented that standards and "beliefs" have eroded during their lifetimes. When the late Don Eugenio Anchelia Llata, a former *curandero* (ritual expert and healer), told me that bad ritual behavior "se registra" (gets registered) because it harms the sacred ancestors, I did not fully understand what he meant until I read the Entablo.

My aim in the following discussion is to contextualize this ritual manuscript for the reader. To do so, I draw on the insights and expertise of my collaborators in San Damián and in Casta who generously shared their time with me, explaining how things work in their respective villages. Although

---

11. San Damián sits at the headwaters of the Lurín River valley.

the impact of twentieth-century social change on ritual discourse in these two villages differs, the degree of importance placed on upholding ideals and standards does not. In the Andes, the fulfillment of ritual obligations constitutes an ancient law, upheld by the jurisdiction of the community authorities, who ensure that people fulfill their ritual duties (Fernández Osco 2000: 95). As the work of Salomon (1998, 2002a, 2004, 2018) shows, customary law guides schedules and standards for community work and ritual practices in different communities within Huarochirí and beyond.

Various ethnographies of Andean communities have illuminated how burdensome it is to fulfill functionary roles (*pasar cargo*). *Cargo* duties place considerable pressure on individuals and their spouses and kin during the period of office (Allen 2002: 92; Gelles 2000b: 101; Isbell 1978: 168; Mayer 2002: 127). This is also the case for the functionaries of Casta, particularly prior to the 1930s, after which the number of *comuneros* increased and individual labor contributions consequently decreased (Gelles 1984b). The Entablo details the respective labor duties of each of the functionaries, giving exacting instructions for the quantities of material obligations (*obligaciones*)—such as food, alcohol, and coca leaf—and other items that they were obliged to submit during the *champería*. For this reason, I reflect on individual functionary roles only briefly in this introduction.

While an analysis of the *champería* as it is celebrated today in Casta is beyond the scope of this work, existing ethnographies carried out over the last forty years give detailed insights into the ceremony as it was conducted in the late twentieth century. Among these are an article by Llanos and Osterling (1982), which provides an insightful and in-depth description of the event. Their research describes some of the Entablo's "secret" ceremonies as they observed them over half a century later in 1979, including some ceremonies not discussed in the close-grained description of the 1922 *champería* by Tello and Miranda (1923).

The noteworthy article on Casta's *champería* by Paul Gelles (1984b) analyzes the traditional forms of cooperation and reciprocity through which the canal-cleaning labor is organized. The article explores the logics of the *faena* (communal work), demonstrating the centrality of *faena* labor in Casta's economy and in the maintenance of irrigative infrastructure. The Entablo has received little scholarly attention since anthropologist Paul Gelles consulted and briefly referenced it in the 1980s for his master's degree research on Casta's irrigation customs (Gelles 1984a). When I visited Casta in 2009 for my own master's degree at the University of Stirling and mentioned the Entablo in passing, the community president was gobsmacked that I had heard of it.

During the years I worked on this book, another publication that discusses the Entablo came to light. Elías Rengifo de la Cruz's study of the Entablo is based on a Casteño's transcription of the first section of the manuscript and cites only short sections (Rengifo de la Cruz 2018: 8). His study differs from mine considerably in that he characterizes the Entablo as a sacred text produced in a context detached from village politics (Rengifo de la Cruz 2018: 34–35). As such, our respective analyses of the manuscript diverge in terms of both its contextualization and the related themes explored. Despite summarizing the Entablo as a "libro de contabilidad" (book of accountancy) with an intertextual character, Rengifo de la Cruz (2018: 33–36) places this intertextuality firmly in the context of poetry, testimony, and the oral domain. This study does not appear to identify the manuscript's descriptions of and broader association with khipu accountancy; for Rengifo de la Cruz (2018: 39), the manuscript is only fulfilled completely when expressed in the oral domain.

This book makes an original contribution to the literature on Casta's *champería*, presenting the first published transcription of the Casta's internal regulations for the ceremony. Since the Entablo provides a new perspective on the ritual, free from the mediated lens of anthropologists, one aim of this book is to privilege the voices of local people throughout. The analyses of the Entablo presented here respond to new questions generated by the text's rich content. For example, this introductory essay explores why the Entablo was written when it was and how it fits into the cultural and political context of the Lima highlands in the 1920s.

The book includes two further chapters: an English translation of the Entablo (chapter 2) and a diplomatic transcription of it retaining the original spellings in the Spanish (chapter 3).

The Codification of Cooperation in Andean Customary Law

As Escalante (2010: 251) notes, traditional Andean systems of community organization place emphasis on adherence to traditional ritual law (*costumbre*), promoting water as a valuable resource. Community organization stimulates maintenance work and reduces conflicts (Escalante 2010: 251). Irrigation rituals are especially important in Andean communities. Through the performance of elaborate customs in and along canals and reservoirs, individual groups legitimize and (re)define their water rights and (re)produce their identity in relation to other groups. Furthermore, these customs mobilize group memory and confraternity: irrigators repay a moral debt to the founding ancestors who constructed the irrigation systems, so that they may be entitled to use the canals and the waters they channel through them every year during the long dry season. As Sherbondy (1998: 213) explains:

> Community after community recounts their mytho-histories of how their original ancestors established claims to the lands and waters of that geographical site for the use of their descendants and heirs. Rights to specific canals were based on this original principle and on the claim that they, the community, built the canals, maintain them, and perform the rituals for their care. This fundamental concept continues to define water rights throughout the Andes.

This ideology constitutes the basis of the ritual descriptions and origin myths in the Huarochirí Manuscript of 1608. Its anonymous Indigenous author described the deeds of the mountain-ancestor Pariacaca, who laid down regulations for his worship in ancient times, specifying the manner in which his descendants should honor him under the guidance of specific authorities overseeing the rituals (chapter 9 in Salomon and Urioste 1991: 71). The 1608 manuscript is concerned with mapping the water customs (tutelary rights) of the province's ayllus (extended kin groups) within a context of early colonial social change and a perceived risk to the vitality of these customs. In this sense, the ideology behind the Spanish-language Entablo resembles that of the earlier Quechua-language text, which was also penned during a time of intensive social, political, and legal change.

When the 1921 authorities in Casta wrote down the regulations for the *champería*, instructing that they be consulted by the ritual authorities each year, it is possible that they deemed the traditional concept of ancestor-endowed water rights to be under threat. Did the sudden interest of the Peruvian state in inserting the Indigenous population into the national economy in the early twentieth century threaten to undermine community autonomy? While Andean community law or "ayllu law" (Fernández Osco 2000) resolved conflicts based on collectively agreed regulations for the application of justice and for community production (see also Mayer 1989: 41), national state law based on capitalist economics posed a risk to community cohesion. As Rösing (1995: 85) points out, the introduction of "modernization" and individual profit maximization undermined the ethics of reciprocity and posed a risk to the persistence of Andean ritual and religion.

In his work on the application of *justicia de acuerdos* (agreement justice) in Aymara-speaking Bolivian communities, Fernández Osco (2001: 18) points out that an important aspect of Andean community justice is the fundamental

FIGURE 1.3. *An* alguacil *reading out passages from the Entablo in 2018.*

idea that it is agreed on by all and for all. In this respect, local regulations are likely to show a degree of variability across different communities, although some aspects of legal infrastructure rooted in the Inca state and the colonial era may feature pan-Andean universalisms. Individual labor obligations are calculated in relation to local factors, such as the size and characteristics of the local irrigative infrastructure and the size of the labor force. For this reason, while there may be shared traditions among Andean communities, ethnographies of twentieth-century Andean communities show a great deal of diversity in terms of the distribution of resources and labor (Mayer 1989: 42). When reading the Entablo, we can observe that the category-based regulations it sets down in the delegation of work are transparent, measured, and meticulously defined. Gose (1994: 95) notes the calculated egalitarianism that characterizes the division of labor in the canal-cleaning rituals of Huaquirca, Peru. This characteristic of Andean ritual makes ritual accountancy an important tool in the prevention of conflict in that the parameters for individual responsibilities and contributions in labor and in kind are agreed on and recorded in the public domain.

In the Andean string recording devices known as khipus, the standards for ritual performance were laid bare. According to a 1950 article in the Bolivian newspaper *El Diario*, chronicles produced by sixteenth-century friars analyzed by "Arias" mentioned the Inca practice of attributing numerical values to categories of immoral and moral behaviors in the application of justice. "Reminders" or "warnings" (*recordatorios*) of these codes of law, which also showed the respective sanctions corresponding to different categories of offenses, were known as *unañcha* (Fernández Osco 2001: 12).[12] The highly visible nature of the legal procedure surely made these "reminders" a key resource in conflict avoidance. The Quechua term *unancha* (*uñancha* or *unanchay*) appears to denote a clearly defined justice system and, more generally, something indicated visually through signs or indication marks (Gonçalez Holguín [1608] 1952: 355): "that which is stamped, branded, or marked" (668).[13] This definition demonstrates how marking formed part of record-keeping to account for (and recall progress made in) the completion of tasks.[14] As Mackey (2002: 336) points out, khipu records offer tangible evidence of data relating to a person's fulfillment of obligations, "providing an enduring record of a task's performance."

Andean justice is founded on proportionality (Bennison 2022; Fernández Osco 2001; Gose 1994: 95; Trawick 2002). As a "basic moral principle that clearly defines everyone's rights" (Trawick 2002: 42), proportionality defines the logics of reciprocity managed through ritual, where expectations for individuals are clear. Before attending a canal-cleaning ritual, all participants must know their individual obligations in order to fulfill them. People incur a "sacrificial debt" if they do not give a landscape being the expected sacrificial "payment" or if disagreements are left unresolved (Rösing 1995: 76).

According to Rösing (1995: 76), unmitigated "sacrificial debts" prevent the ancestors from providing water access. Since insufficient ritual "payment" by individuals can affect the entire community, punishment must be proportional to the crime. The responses of the sacred ancestors are understood to be proportionate (Bennison 2016: 166), so proportionality is closely regulated. The overseeing of proportional justice through the public rendering of accounts prevents dissonance in that regulations for individual responsibilities and contributions in labor and in kind are agreed on and recorded in the public sphere (Bennison 2022). As Trawick (2001: 14) explains, an absence of proportionality in the determining of duties, resources, and rights leads to conflict and is a root cause of the breakdown of communal life. Conflicts in a group prevent good communication with the water-owning ancestors, so conflict management is important for securing access to water. In

---

12. No further information about "Arias" is provided in the referenced work.
13. "Vnancha. Lo sellado, o herrado, o señalado" (Gonçalez Holguín [1608] 1952: 355).
14. I wish to thank the anonymous reviewer who suggested that I expand on my discussion of *unañcha* by referring to this specific entry.

pre-Hispanic Huarochirí, priests known as *yancas* monitored the irrigation systems. This work entailed making sure that there were no conflicts among ayllu members, which could threaten community coherence and impede communication with the ancestors (Spalding 1984: 66).

The Entablo tells us that the weighing of coca leaf submissions was carried out publicly and was subject to strict controls: the functionaries were obliged to "show their obligations to the workers in legal weights and satisfactory measurements" (f. 4v). Having clearly defined regulations for the submissions aided in conflict avoidance, as did the public use of a balance scale. The Saturday carnival regulations stipulate the use of a device call a *huipi* (f. 24r). This is a traditional (possibly pre-Hispanic) balance scale, whose use in the *champería* was observed by Tello and Miranda (1923: 532) in the 1920s and by Echeandia Valladares (1981: 157) in the 1970s. The process of weighing coca using the *huipi* was participatory; all *champería* attendees in the 1970s were involved in agreeing or disagreeing on whether the weighed goods fulfilled the necessary weight obligations (Echeandia Valladares 1981: 157). This was still the case in 2022; each bag of coca is lifted up for all to see while suspended from the *huipi*.

Tello and Miranda (1923) describe the Saturday *champería* proceedings in Casta, where the *tribunal de los ancianos* (jury of the elders) or *gran audiencia* (high court) saw the elders decide the punishments for those who failed to uphold the ritual laws imposed by the ancestors. During the Wari Runa, anyone present—man, woman, or child—can voice accusations against others and demand the corresponding punishment (Tello and Miranda 1923: 548). In this respect, the *champería* is not complete until all social tensions and ritual or labor debts are resolved. As the Entablo tells us, the Friday and Saturday afternoon performance scores for the *originario* (native) men and women were approved using a device called a *planilla* (report list), which resulted in a set of different punishment numbers being issued for the men and women (see f. 14v and f. 16r). Different number sequences corresponded to those who had fulfilled or surpassed their *champería* obligations: those who had not fulfilled them were given a score categorizing them as rebels and assigning a degree of debt to them (likewise indicated by a numerical sequence).[15]

The *planilla* is later "washed" by the *camachico* (f. 15v), suggesting that the device is either a khipu or khipu board whose cords are unknotted ("washed" clean of knots). Once the numbers indicating a degree of debt were approved

---

15. Hyland (2016: 493) describes the recording of labor contributions in neighboring Anchucaya, where authorities called *kuimeres* calculated each ayllu's debts for work not completed during the annual Watancha reckoning of accounts. Beyond the immediate risk posed by incurring debts during the *champería*, it was in the interest of labor groups to discourage the accumulation of labor debts.

14 THE ENTABLO MANUSCRIPT

FIGURE 1.4. *The traditional ceremonial site of Cuhuay during the 2019* huayrona.

and the *planilla* was "washed," the khipu board "Padrón General de los Hombres y Mujeres" (General Padrón of the Men and Women) was carried out at the traditional ceremonial site, Cuhuay, where the corrective punishments were carried out (ff. 15v–16r). This practice resembles the one recently observed by Hall (2014). The issuing of *faena* labor "scores" by authorities on paper *padrones* in Llanchu, Cusco, is taken seriously by participants: their number scores have important social repercussions. The value categories "rebel" and "surpassed" entered onto the Casta *planilla* were not technically numerical (despite being hierarchical in scale). But corresponding numerical values were entered onto the cords, which encourages us to consider the ways in which numbers would have represented nonnumerical values on the other recording devices used at the *champería* and in khipus more generally. In a hierarchical society, could classification categories have been organized along a spectrum ranging between positive and negative values? The aforementioned description of Inca-era khipu-like *uñancha* "reminders" entails the structuring of positive and negative values on each hand, with each finger signifying a category (Fernández Osco 2001: 12). The *champería* punishments appear to be part of such a framework of codified ayllu law (Bennison 2022).

The *justicia de acuerdos* system requires that punishments be commensurate with offenses; otherwise the *pena* (penalty, shame) remains in the community (Fernández Osco 2001: 12). Within such a framework, the "washing" of the *planilla* likely signaled that ritual punishments directed at nullifying the debt had been either formally agreed on or already carried out.

Although the use of fully corded records is not explicit in the Entablo, Tello and Miranda (1923) describe the use of braided cords during the judicial procedures at Cuhuay. The *mayoralas* (women stewards) newly elected in 1922 for the coming year were obliged to wear "ancient style" clothing and kneel down before the tribunal with their heads bowed (Tello and Miranda 1923: 547).[16] While the *mayoralas* received advice and instructions from the principal elder, the *alfereces* (standard-bearers) placed "a long thick cord, exquisitely braided and of different colors" on their necks (Tello and Miranda 1923: 547).[17] Following this, the *músicos* (musicians) likewise would "kneel below the cord held [up] by the *alfereces* and receive the exhortations and advice of the elders" (547).[18] Given that two functionaries held the "braided cords," we could venture that these were khipus of some kind: as Salomon (2016: 180) explains, ritual khipu handling in Tupicocha "is always done using vertical or hanging deployment, and always between at least two people close together."[19]

In the same way that traditional Andean justice was a process of arbitration conducted in sacred sites in the presence of ancestral beings or mummies (Fernández Osco 2001: 12), entries in the Entablo specify that punishments be carried out at sacred sites, in public view before the adjudicating community elders. On the Thursday, the functionaries known as *michcos* should be whipped at Cuhuay (CCSPC 1921: f. 12r). The role of the elders in important community matters such as the application of justice ensures continuity,

---

16. As Doña Luzmila Salinas Bautista explained, women had to wear leather moccasins (*llanquis*) to the *champería* in the past and risked being punished by the functionaries for wearing footwear "from the coast" like sneakers. Doña Anselma Bautista Pérez explained that women today are expected to dress appropriately, wearing their aprons over their skirts. According to Tello and Miranda (1923: 534), workers in the *champería* were attributed data on a khipu board based on their fulfillment of the regulations for "special clothing," among other criteria.
17. "Un largo cordón grueso, primorosamente trenzado y de diversos colores" (Tello and Miranda 1923: 547).
18. "Se arrodillan bajo el cordón sostenido por los alférez, y reciben las exhortaciones y consejos de los ancianos" (Tello and Miranda 1923: 547).
19. The Entablo tells us that before this procedure the *alfereces* must prepare two *timbladeras* (ritual drinking vessels with handles on either side) by conjoining pairs of cups using strips of ribbon (f. 15v). The general work of the *alfereces* here appears to include the ceremonial conjoining of entities using cords.

consistency, and clarity in terms of agreeing to the appropriate sanctions for any conduct contravening tradition, which could offend the water-owning ancestors. The elders are temporally and ideologically closest to the ancestors and represent their power and authority.

What Is an *Entablo*?

The word *entablo* is dynamic. It refers to a text produced through a process of collective agreement, whereby a memory or event is established or immortalized as an official narrative or fact. It refers to a set of codified ordinances deemed conducive to achieving a moral or social goal. Furthermore, an *entablo* is a form of legalistic accountancy: the use of this term in Casta in the early twentieth century and today is rooted in record-keeping traditions from the colonial era (1532–1821). A Casta elder named Don Porfirio explained that an *entablo* is "lo que queda en escrito" (that which gets set down in written form; a looser translation might be "the version of events that ends up in the books"). In this respect, an *entablo* is a "definitive, official account of events." Eloy Rojas Obispo, the president of the Comunidad Campesina de San Pedro de Casta, described the Casta Entablo as a *reglamento* (set of regulations). When I asked elder Don Eufronio Obispo Rojas what *entablo* means, he summed it up as "una norma o ley" (a code of conduct or law).

The Entablo's status as a book of ordinances dictating the agreed-on ritual submissions for the *champería* tracks with the colonial usage of the term; the Spanish verb *entablar* is related to religious judiciary accountancy. The Real Academia Española *Diccionario de autoridades* defines *entablar* thus:

> Also to register, note down, and write in the church tablets, where the sacred records of pious memories and chaplaincies are set down, any other new memory or chaplaincy so that its foundation is recorded. It is a term used in legal matters and principally in the Ecclesiastical Tribunals. (Real Academia Española [1726–1732] 2014, s.v. "entablar")[20]

---

20. "Vale tambien registrar, notar y escribir en las tablas de las Iglesias, donde se sientan las fundaciones de Memórias pias y Capellanias que en ellas estàn situadas y fundadas, alguna otra nueva Memória o Capellanía, para que conste de su fundación. Es término usado en lo jurídico, y principalmente en los Tribunales Eclesiásticos" (Real Academia Española [1726–1732] 2014, s.v. "entablar"). In various colonial-era Latin American contexts, pious memories (*memorías pías*) and chaplaincies (*capellanías*) were forms of church revenue that covered costs such as providing a living for clerics, expenses for funeral masses, and candles and other goods associated with saint worship (Bauer 1983).

FIGURE 1.5. *A layer of masking tape once used to bind the book together in the absence of a spine (due to regular use) that reads "ENTABLO." Subsequent superimposed layers of sticky tape have distorted the writing beneath.*

In colonial usage, the term therefore refers to the recording of payments to the church. The use of *entablos* (also *entables*) for recording tithes is documented in eighteenth-century pastoral visitation reports. In some Andean communities, these *entablos* took the format of khipu boards (Hyland, Bennison, and Hyland 2021). The khipu boards are referred to in the Entablo manuscript as *padrones* (registers or census accounts), yet locals in Casta explained that the *padrones* are also *entablos*. The *entablos* in Casta were concerned with the submission of ritual payments and labor within the context of ancestral irrigation ritual as well as with the tribute payments submitted to the church. In this sense, these khipu-board *entablos* of Casta were syncretic in principle, combining the sacred inscriptive traditions of the pre-Hispanic Andes with those of the church. Likewise, *entablos* were encoded with both Christian and Andean principles of law, obligation, and religious piety.

Colonial usage of the verb *entablar* signified a set of orders through which any desired outcome or goal can be more easily achieved by setting out the means through which it should be completed and the orders for its fulfillment.[21] In this sense, to a colonial-era Quechua speaker, the verb *entablar*

---

21. Another entry in the *Diccionario de autoridades* defines *entablar* in the following way: "Metaphoricamente significa disponer, prevenir y preparar lo necessario para que se consiga y pueda más fácilmente lograrse: como una pretensión, un negociado, una

may not have seemed worlds apart from the Quechua concept of *camay*, which is associated with ideas of justice, law, fulfillment of work, obligation, and notions of totality (Gonçalez Holguín [1608] 1952: 45–48).[22]

In his study of the Huarochirí Manuscript of 1608, Urioste (1983: xxiii) identifies both "superficial conversion to Christianity" and "deception of clerics in order to maintain the ethnic religion" as themes of the manuscript. Paulson (1990: 52) characterizes the superficial conversion of the native population described in the Huarochirí Manuscript as ambiguous "double talk." A notable instance of superficial conversion is the canal-cleaning ritual described in chapter 6 of the Huarochirí Manuscript, where the narrator gives a detailed eyewitness account of the ritual dedicated to the beautiful huaca Chuqui Suso. The Huarochirí Manuscript explains that the Cupara ayllu celebrated the culmination of the annual canal cleaning by dancing and drinking in honor of Chuqui Suso, yet they trick their padre into thinking that these acts are solely to celebrate the completed work (Salomon and Urioste 1991: 64–65). Given the context of subversive resistance among the early colonial Andean population, it is fitting that the verb *entablar* came to be used in relation to the "idolatrous" khipu laws of the Inca and his government during this time. As I have explained elsewhere, Felipe Guaman Poma de Ayala used the verb *entablar* in his early seventeenth-century *Nueva Corónica*. When explaining that the Inca laws relating to huaca worship were recorded throughout the empire,[23] he wrote: "tenía muy entablado esta ley de la ydúlatras y serimonias de los demonios en este rreyno" (he had this law about the idolatries and ceremonial worship of the devils set down in legal records throughout this kingdom: Guaman Poma de Ayala 1615/1616: 183 [185]; see also Bennison 2019). We do not know if Inca-style khipus were ever referred to as *entablos* in the same way that khipu boards eventually were. However, it is clear from Guaman Poma's account that the early colonial ecclesiastical connotations of *entablar* reflected the medium through which moral codes of law were transmitted throughout the Inca Empire.

As explained earlier, the word *entablo* is used in Casta today to refer to

---

dependéncia, dando los medios y órdenes conducentes para su logro" (Metaphorically, it means arranging, making provisions, and preparing what is necessary so that something can be accomplished more easily, such as an aim, a negotiation, a responsibility, giving the means and instructions conducive to its achievement: Real Academia Española [1726–1732] 2014, s.v. "entablar").

22. For an in-depth study of *camay* and related Quechua terms in the Huarochirí Manuscript, see Taylor 1974.

23. Both the Entablo and Guaman Poma's account feature ritual laments designed to bring on rain (*waqachiku* in Quechua), suggesting a degree of continuity in these accounts of Inca ritual law despite having been written three centuries apart (Bennison 2019).

FIGURE 1.6. *The* padrón de madera *(wooden register) that Tello observed in San Pedro de Casta corresponds with the* padrón de huallque *of the Entablo (drawing from Tello and Miranda 1923).*

the khipu boards that were used to record and grade the performance of participants in the *champería* (Hyland, Bennison, and Hyland 2021). It is worth reflecting on the semantic associations of the noun *padrón*, which can be translated into English as "master" or make reference to a paternal ancestor or "protector." In the eighteenth century, *padrón* referred to a public notice of disgrace announcing bad deeds that remain in the public memory.[24] This sense was likely to have applied to the khipu-board *padrones* introduced during the colonial era (Hyland, Bennison, and Hyland 2021) which formed the basis for public punishments in early- to mid-twentieth century Casta. While the khipu-board *padrones* functioned to legitimize resource rights for community members, they may also have come to be seen as icons of oppression, which could have contributed to their abandonment. Nevertheless, the Entablo manuscript still in use today evokes their general logic.

A Community's Binding Agreement: Why the Entablo Is Like a Khipu

As a set of regulations based on the *justicia de acuerdos* system, the Entablo would not be binding until all the (male) community members signed in agreement with its terms. This is made explicit at various points in the text when reforms to the regulations are followed by signatures of the community members, complete with elaborate flourishes.[25] The authorities may have faced

---

24. The *Diccionario de autoridades* includes the following definition of *padrón*: "Metaphoricamente se llama la nota pública de infamia o desdoro, que queda en la memoria, por alguna acción mal hecha" (Real Academia Española [1726–1732] 2014, s.v. "padrón").
25. As the work of Burns (2010) demonstrates, the practice of accompanying signatures with fancy flourishes has a long history in Peru, as far back as the sixteenth century.

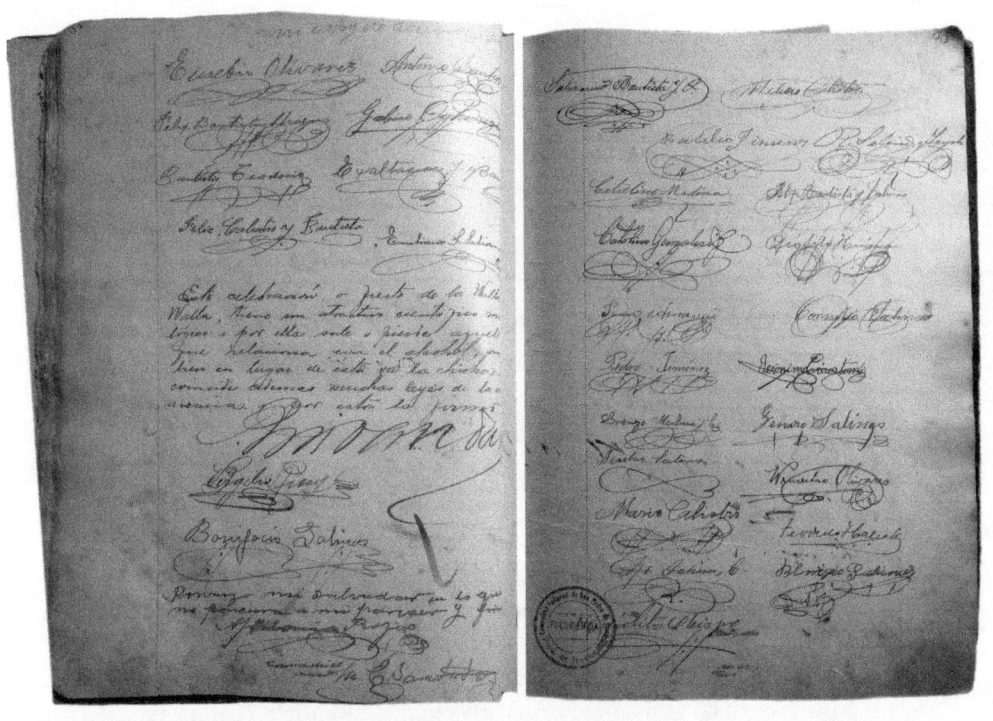

LEFT: FIGURE 1.7. *A pencil entry at the top of the page reading "No estoy de acuerdo." The bottom of the page features the signature of a* camachico menor.

RIGHT: FIGURE 1.8. *Signatures (recorded in 1924?) signaling each individual's approval of the regulations of 1921. The stamp reads "Presidencia: Comunidad Indígena de San Pedro de Casta, Prov. de Huarochirí" (President's Office: Indigenous Community of San Pedro de Casta, Province of Huarochirí).*

challenges in getting their original agreement set out in 1921 approved if all the necessary signatures did not feature in the book. An entry in pencil by the notary signed "Notario SC" reads: "Hago saber que no estoy de acuerdo en este entablo porque es de pocos todavía" (I hereby make it known within this *entablo* that I do not agree, because it is [representative] of so few at this point) (CCSPC 1921: f. 1r). This entry mirrors another in the same hand: "No estoy de acuerdo" (I do not agree) (CCSPC 1921: f. 19v).[26]

This evidence suggests that the notary had the power to determine what

---

Salomon (2004: 165) proposes that unusual knot formations on the Tupicocha khipus may be influenced by rubric flourishes in cursive script, which also feature prominently in the Tupicocha paper archive.

26. Or, alternatively, "I do not approve."

FIGURE 1.9. *Producing the records to account for the numbers of votes at the* huayrona.

constituted an *entablo* or not as well as what constituted a *constancia* (official record). Although the three elders were elected by the community to dictate the Entablo, it took three years to be granted *constancia* status. Consequently, the signatures of the authorities and community members may not have been added until 1924, when the Entablo regulations were ratified. The signatures are not dated, but the pencil entry objection (presumably by "Notario SC") suggests that the ratification of the Entablo would have required the agreement of the entire community. Without collective approval, the document categorically would not have fulfilled the criteria for an *entablo* or agreement.

As Guevara-Gil and Boelens (2010: 40) point out, peasant communities and irrigation committees in the Peruvian Andes resolve water conflicts internally, through discussing matters in the open; any suggested solutions are implemented only when the assembly approves them. In this respect, the Entablo illuminates the effort required to establish a collective agreement approved by all members of the community. Khipu accounts also had to be collectively approved, as discussed later.

The Entablo is like a khipu in many ways. Villagers in Casta talk about their century-old treasured manuscript in ways that closely resemble the way locals in central Peruvian Andean villages talk about their khipu patrimony. In both Tupicocha (Huarochirí, Lima) and Rapaz (Oyón province, Lima) they describe their khipus as their Magna Carta (Salomon 2013: 27, 2018). Tupicochanos also described their khipus as the community's constitution (Salomon 2016: 182). The Entablo paper manuscript is described in a similarly constitutional light. I was urged to consult it by Casta's ritual specialist, or *yachak*, Doña Catalina Olivares, who told me: "Allí te cuenta como empezó el pueblo" (There it tells you how the village began).

In the sense that khipus delineated customary obligations deemed foundational to the smooth running of social and economic life in Andean communities (Hyland 2016), the Entablo may also be likened to a Magna Carta. When the elder Don Eufronio Obispo Rojas explained why the Entablo was produced, he described the evolution of the community archives, based on what he had been told about antecedents to the 1921 manuscript. He explained that a wooden *padrón* had been used in the past during the *champería*. It was now either in the church (the church caretaker generously searched for it but could not find it), or in the possession of an elder. Aside from the wooden *padrón*, Don Eufronio mentioned an account called the *padroncillo*, which he explained either was a khipu or was "like a khipu" and was used to record obligations and mistakes. According to Pearce (2001: 72), early eighteenth-century tribute rolls ordered by the viceregal administration in Peruvian villages and *repartimientos* were known as both *padrones* and *padroncillos*. It is therefore possible that the words *padrón* and *padroncillo* were synonymous in Casta. While the *padroncillo* in the Entablo may refer to a khipu-board *padrón*, we should not discount the possibility that the *padroncillo* was an older-style khipu suspended from a primary cord, rather than from a (colonially introduced) board.

Early twentieth-century ethnographic evidence suggests that older Inca-style khipus were used in neighboring Anchucaya until 1910, when the younger community members insisted on switching to paper documents (Hyland 2016: 496). Although it is possible that the Entablo, khipu boards, and older-style Inca khipus were all used in Casta in the 1920s or earlier, it would be difficult to confirm this in the absence of living firsthand witnesses. Nevertheless, ethnographic evidence suggests that Casteños kept an Inca-style "old" khipu. A collaborator in her eighties remembers seeing a khipu from Casta in her childhood. Doña Catalina Olivares, known today as the *yachak* (knower), in describing the moment a local woman brought an *equipo* from their village to show her school class for a "show and tell," explained that she and her young classmates did not pay much attention to the *equipo* (khipu; a pun: *equipo* also denotes "team" in Spanish). She said, laughing, "¡¿Pa que vamos a estar interesados si estamos jovenes, pues?!" (What would we be interested in that for if we're young?!). Nevertheless, she does recall some aspects of its appearance:

nudito, nudito tenía el quipu así. Era de colores la raspita. Los equipos eran así como mis trenzas, las pitas eran de colores, había un nudo por aca, otro nudo por aca... ¡eso era las letras pues, que hablan! Cada nudo tenía una palabra, el otro otra palabra. Para contestar pues, es que lo dice. Era de color marrón, negro, blanco, y según de tamano era el nudo.

The quipu had a little knot, a little knot, like this. The branch [primary cord?] had colors. The *equipos* were like this, like my braids. The string had colors, there was one knot here, another knot here... that was the letters, which speak! Each knot had a word, the other another word. For confirming [things], seeing what it says. It was colored brown, black, white and the knot was according to size.

Unfortunately, Julio C. Tello's work on Casta does not provide any further information about the village's khipu(s). Although his unpublished field notes on Casta (Tello [1922] n.d.) also contain numerical data from khipus, the khipu notes appear to be entirely unrelated to the notes on Casta.[27] Catalina Olivares reckoned the presentation on the Casta khipu must have been around seventy-seven years ago, which would suggest that the khipu was no longer being actively used as a register at that point (in the 1950s).

Regardless of when khipus fell out of active use in Casta, Don Eufronio's understanding of the importance of the device known as the *padroncillo* suggests that its function was similar to that of the Entablo: "Antes del 1920, el padroncillo era la ley" (Before 1920, the *padroncillo* was the law).

When the community authorities in Casta granted me permission to consult the Entablo in December 2018, following the advice of Hyland, I brought with me a copy of Tello and Miranda's 1923 image depicting a khipu-board *padrón* (census) from Casta that they had observed being used in the *champería*. After our brief discussion of the image, the *secretario* (secretary) quite naturally placed the sheet of paper within the pages of the current *padrón comunal* (community census), explaining that the *padrón* in the image and the *padrón comunal* that he had placed on his desk were both *entablos*. Thus, placing an *entablo* or *padrón* within another *entablo* or *padrón* is logical, in the same way that the Entablo manuscript, itself a *padrón*, describes the use of the khipu-board *padrones* during the *champería*. According to Mannheim (2015b: 227), narratives in which an embedded part provides an iconic key to

---

27. In between the Casta narratives and the raw khipu data are notes on photography and other Peruvian archaeological sites. Given that the khipu data are completely uncontextualized, not attributed to Casta, and written upside down, starting from the opposite end of the notebook, it seems unlikely that these notes correspond to Casta.

FIGURE 1.10. *The image of the 1920s khipu-board* padrón, *placed inside the current* padrón *by the community authorities. On the left page, personal information has been concealed.*

understanding the whole are a common interpretive strategy in Inca semiotic practices, found in visual art, textiles, khipus, and landscapes. Similarly, might interrelated khipus have been used to encode subset data at different scales in this way in the colonial or pre-Hispanic era(s)?[28]

Casta's intertextual community accounts also include a more recent set of regulations by which all the *comuneros* listed in the *padrón comunal* must abide. The *alguacil* (constable) stated that the Entablo is inseparable from this text, explaining that the current *estatuto comunal* (community statute)

---

28. Hamilton (2018) illuminates the importance of scale as a mode of expression in Inca material culture. I am grateful to Sabine Hyland for recommending this source.

FIGURE 1.11. *The community padrón in 2018.*

"va con el Entablo" (goes with the Entablo). The *estatuto comunal* is a recent word-processed document of unclear date, which explains the history of the village and sets out (in 148 article entries) everything that is expected of members of the peasant community and punishments for noncompliance. Huarochirí communities started producing community statutes as early as 1905, repeatedly updating or replacing them to conform with the impact of national institutions on community life (Salomon and Niño-Murcia 2011: 161).

It is likely that Casta's internal statute was reformed at some point following the Ley General de Comunidades Campesinas of 1987, which specified the kinds of information to be included in community statutes. Nuñez Palomino (1995: 12) states that almost all peasant communities in Peru have an internal statute that regulates communal authorities' duties, election procedures, communal work, and fines. Both the *estatuto comunal* and the Entablo in Casta contain all the regulations that community membership is subject to: both texts set out membership agreements within the community.

The Entablo was written by the authorities in consultation with three *notables* (notables: individuals who had fulfilled their community obligations in their lifetimes). They would have been considered experts in water management and the kinds of ancestral knowledge required for water access. As de la Cadena (1989: 98–99) points out, ritual experts such as *curanderos* are consulted in decisions affecting the community. At the end of the instructions in the Entablo for the final Monday, the ritual experts are named, with an explanation that the community authorities elected these three notables, whose knowledge or "memories" formed the basis for the Entablo:

> con lo que se dió término la presente memoria de nuestras costumbres [a large period in blue ballpoint] desde los tiempos de su fundasión que fue formado por los indigenas y a la que hoy llevamos un recuerdo la constancia del ante pasado y queda para lo susecivo escrita lo que nos recordamos nosotros los dictadores que hemos alcanzado algunas partes lo que han sido exacto siendo así esta memoria dictado o dirigida por los señores mayores [in the margin in red ballpoint: X] elegidos por el pueblo en primer lugar Don Vicente A. Reyes, Don Jacinto Bautista y Félix B. Chagua con lo que se terminó el precente recuerdo.

> This brings an end to this memory of our *costumbres* [a large period in blue ballpoint] since the times when it [the memory] was founded by the Indigenous [people] who began it, and to the one for which today we carry forward a memory [of] the official record of the ancestors. What is written remains for what is yet to come, based on what we, the dictators [the elders dictating the regulations], remember. We have managed to make some parts be exact. Such is this memory that was dictated or directed by the elders [in the margin in red ballpoint: X] chosen to do so by the village: first, Don Vicente A. Reyes, Don Jacinto Bautista, and Félix B. Chagua, and with this we bring an end to this memory. (CCSPC 1921: f. 17v)

We can appreciate the effort made throughout the Entablo to emphasize the importance of honoring the past. Specifically, its creators were concerned with promoting pre-Hispanic traditions and expressed their desire to have ritual discourse correspond as much as possible with "muchas leyes de la era arcaica" (many laws of the archaic era; CCSPC 1921: f. 19v).[29]

The inclusion of the elders in the production of the Entablo resembles the role of experts in khipu practices. In his analysis of an accountancy custom analogous to khipu accountancy (which features in the Entablo), Mayer (2002: 129) mentions that two *varayoq* (*varayuq*: staff-holders, traditional community authorities) overseeing the pebble-based division of labor enumerations in Tangor in 1969 were "not only counting, they were memorizing the names

---

29. This reference echoes the 1608 Huarochirí Manuscript, where many of the laws and customs detailed are described as being from "ancient times" (*ñawpa pacha*) or "very ancient times" (*ancha ñawpa pacha*) (Salomon and Urioste 1991).

and the services rendered. Their memories constituted the record, and they remained available as expert witnesses in case of disagreements." If disagreements concerning the *champería* obligations threatened community cohesion in Casta, it would be logical for individuals learned in khipu accountancy to be consulted, because they would have memorized sets of data held in their records (see Platt 2002). In the same way that the memories of the *varayuq* constituted the record of the accounts, the record of regulations is referred to throughout the Entablo as a *memoria* (memory). A colonial era manuscript kept in Casta's community archive, "Auto redondo" (CCSPC 1711–1808), reports that three elders should be recruited to help the priest "tratar de la materia" (deal with the matter) when obliged by decree to produce a register of the doctrine based on the registers of the "ayllo, o parcialidad" (sector) (CCSPC 1711–1808: f. 54v).[30] It is unclear whether Casta's ayllu records would have been "old" Inca-style khipus or khipu boards in the early nineteenth century. A Roman Catholic religious order, the Mercedarians, introduced khipu boards in the sixteenth century (Hyland, Bennison, and Hyland 2021: 403). In any event, it seems clear that the three elders to be recruited by the priest would be nominated based on their memories and/or their ability to interpret the (re)cords.

In her analysis of Inca Garcilaso de la Vega's seventeenth-century chronicle, Beyersdorff (2005: 299–300) argues for high levels of similarity between *hamawt'a* (philosophers) who publicly disseminated khipu records (these experts were *khipukamayuq*) and *harawikuq* (poets), because both roles relied on memory. In the Inca era, *arawi* (*harawi*) narratives instructed on general ritual logic. An early colonial narrative written in Quechua by Guaman Poma (the Warikza Arawi) is a highly structured normative guide to performing Inca state ritual (Mannheim 2015b: 227).

The expression of disagreement in the Entablo by "Notario SC" resembles the way agreements and disagreements could be noted in khipu cords (Pimentel 2014) and negotiated in them (Curatola and de la Puente Luna 2013). Pimentel (2014) suggests that khipus were central in the organization of community events. His work draws on research in the 1990s with collaborator Don Mario Crispín, a Bolivian Aymara speaker who learned about khipus from two elderly *khipukamayuq* (Pimentel 2014). According to Pimentel (2014: 193), Don Mario's description of a harvest khipu (*khipu cosecha*) determined a reading of one such khipu as "come to an agreement

---

30. In Casta this term refers to the two groups Yañac and Yacapar, which are discussed later in this chapter.

about organizing a community fiesta."[31] His interpretation of a suggestion to "reach an agreement" corresponded to the linking of separate khipu cords suspended from the primary cord. Furthermore, he explained that a suggestion can be attributed a negative "response," indicated through knotting (Pimentel 2014: 193). Salomon (2004) in his work on the Tupicocha khipus explains that cords were reknotted to reflect community decisions, suggesting that khipus may have provided a framework for agreeing on the specifics of community events.

If this was the case, a khipu geared at dividing the labor for the canal-cleaning ritual in colonial Casta, translated into Spanish, could have recorded sets of information about the obligations of the respective functionaries, like the Entablo. The Entablo mentions the use of eight *nómina* (roster) accounts in the instructions for the final Sunday of the *champería*, when the names of all members (men and women) of each *parada* (work party) were recorded in one of two *nóminas*: one for those who turned up and fulfilled their assigned duties, and one for those who did not (CCSPC 1921: f. 17r). These accounts are taken at Cuhuay, where individuals are expected to explain to the authorities if they have been absent, so further data relating to individual performance may have been recorded in (or on the basis of) these nomenclature accounts.

In contrast to the traditional community-based system, state law was relatively out of sight, out of the community authorities' hands, and removed from the traditional justice system. Shifts in law could have threatened the local economy and ways of life. Bolivian state law in the late nineteenth and early twentieth century had a paternalistic approach toward community law: Indigenous groups were not deemed capable of resolving their own conflicts (Fernández Osco 2001). This resembles the situation in Peru, where records kept by Indigenous communities from 1920 on were subject to state scrutiny (Hall 2014: 15). It is surely for this reason that the Entablo, like other early twentieth-century manuscripts from Huarochirí, was largely written in the "privileged language of the law" (Salomon and Niño-Murcia 2011: 87). Did specific changes in Peruvian state law pose a risk to Andean approaches to justice and resource rights?

Interlegality and the National Constitution of 1920

In 1920, a year before the Entablo was penned, the Peruvian Constitution formally recognized the country's Indigenous communities, which would be

---

31. "Ponerse de acuerdo para una fiesta en comunidad" (Pimentel 2014: 193).

subject to a "special set of laws for their development and culture in harmony with their needs" (article 58).³² When the authorities in Casta decided to organize the community's internal legal codes on paper, their response to the prospect of achieving legal recognition as an institution was to stress the need for continued community autonomy. The Entablo therefore represents an ideological response to the economic, political, and spiritual threat of modernity and development associated with increased state intervention in Indigenous community affairs and codes of justice, interpreted as an existential threat to community autonomy.³³ As Guevara-Gil (2006: 138) points out, "Local expressions of the state are a far cry from the theoretical self-portrayal (i.e., the Constitution) which emphasizes the normative hierarchy, bureaucratic specialization of functions and neatly established lines of command."

---

32. Articles 58 and 41 of the 1920 Constitution were concerned with Peru's Indigenous communities:

> Art. 58.—El Estado protegerá a la raza indígena y dictará leyes especiales para su desarrollo y cultura en armonía con sus necesidades. La Nación reconoce la existencia legal de las comunidades de indígenas y la ley declarará los derechos que les correspondan.
>
> Art. 41.—Los bienes de propiedad del Estado, de instituciones públicas y de comunidades de indígenas son imprescriptibles y sólo podrán transferirse mediante título público, en los casos y en la forma que establezca la ley.
>
> Art. 58.—The State shall protect the Indigenous communities and shall dictate special laws for their development and culture in harmony with their needs. The nation recognizes the legal existence of Indigenous communities and the law shall declare the rights that correspond to them.
>
> Art. 41.—The assets owned by the State, public institutions and Indigenous communities are imprescriptible and may only be transferred by public title in the manner established by law and in cases established through law.

33. Although people in Huarochirí tend to self-identify as mestizo today (Salomon 2002b, Bennison 2016), any changes to ritual discourse continue to be deemed an affront to the sacred ancestors, to community values and to group legitimacy. Elsewhere, I have described the relational expression of identity in Huarochirí communities, where a conviction that the landscape is animate and worthy of ritual veneration is a central and common reference in the expression of group belonging and ethnic identity. Marisol de la Cadena has proposed the term 'Indigenous cosmopolitics' to refer to the political significance of manifestations of animate landscape in the worldview or "cosmopolitics" of Indigenous Peruvians (de la Cadena 2010). Building on de la Cadena's work, I have used the term 'mestizo cosmopolitics' for predominantly Spanish-speaking regions such as Huarochirí and Northern Peru, where people tend to avoid self-defining as Indigenous (Bennison 2016). Ana Mariella Bacigalupo likewise uses the term "mestizo cosmopolitics" in relation to Northern Peru (Bacigalupo 2022).

The Casta authorities sought to utilize the formalization process impelled by the national constitution to address community-based needs in a way that is characteristic of Indigenous approaches to water management: Guevara-Gil (2006: 138) points out that legal norms "acquire meaning as they are interpreted, enforced and manipulated in social settings." As Salomon et al. (2011) explain, the ayllu groups in Tupicocha, Huarochirí, replaced their khipus with modernist constitutions in the 1920s. This appears to describe the evolution of community record-keeping in Casta; as mentioned earlier, a collaborator explained that the Entablo replaced an older khipu (or khipu-board) device.

Andean communities' replacement of their ancestor-pleasing khipus with modern constitutions following the national constitution of 1920 is worthy of note. Drawing on the work of Bruno Latour, de la Cadena (2015: 92–93) points out that the ontological distinction between humanity and nature was foundational to modern constitutions and thereby to the emergence of modern politics.

Although decolonial politics in Andean nations has seen the inclusion of landscape beings in national constitutions (namely Ecuador and Bolivia), the Entablo tells us that, at the community level, Andean groups have included—and even privileged—the needs of ancestral landscape beings in their own "modernist" constitutions for at least a century. Although the coloniality of politics is founded on the agreement that humanity and nature are separate (de la Cadena 2015: 93), Casta's constitutional agreement holds that human life relies on accessing water through ancestral ritual.

By adopting a Spanish-language constitutional written model to legitimize the "Inca laws" dictating the obligations for the *champería*, the makers of the Entablo used a strategy similar to one adopted several centuries earlier: the early colonial account of Inca laws by the native chronicler Guaman Poma de Ayala, who enacted Spanish law for Andean purposes (Harrison 2015: 141). Like the makers of the Entablo centuries later, Guaman Poma appealed to different legal institutions; divine (Christian) law, the dominant (Royal Castilian) codified law, and Andean customary law. Moreover, his lists of Inca codes of law "are supplemented with extensive explications of the administrative structure, including Quechua nomenclature to pinpoint the duties of Inca officials to enforce these laws" (Harrison 2015: 144). As explained earlier, Guaman Poma used the verb *entablar* when describing the Inca's dissemination of law. The Entablo resembles Guaman Poma's *Nueva Corónica* in these respects.

The 1921 community authorities were hopeful that state representatives would formally acknowledge their own legal codes based on ancestral water customs and thereby help to prevent their erosion. Prior to the Agrarian Reform of 1969, Peruvian water legislation was based on the 1902 Código de Aguas, which permitted the decentralized management of water, where local authorities were to resolve any conflicts (Escalante 2010: 250).[34] As such, it is unclear whether Huarochirí communities were affected by changes in water legislation, because the legislation in place does not appear to have directly undermined local traditional models of water management. It appears more likely that Casta's shifting legal landscape was a result of the 1920 constitution, which was geared at modernizing and promoting national integration (Harvey and Knox 2015: 28). The constitution laid the social, political, and legal foundations for intensive social change in rural Andean communities, where local models of justice were based on earlier traditions and on the authority of the people and places representing the ancestral past.

The resolution of conflicts within the *justicia de acuerdos* system in Casta is traditionally managed by community elders granted the title "notables" after fulfilling their *cargo* duties during their lifetimes (Ramírez Villacorta 1980). In this sense, the centralizing effects of the national constitution may have been interpreted by elders as a threat to their power within the community, where they had high status in matters of justice.

As explained earlier, scholars generally conceive of the transmission of the principles of Andean customary law and traditional justice as an oral phenomenon (Drzewieniecki 1995; Howard, Andrade Ciudad, and Pedro Ricoy 2018: 221). This view reflects a wider understanding of Andean rural communities as being predominantly oral; however, this premise has been challenged in the last decade, based on archival research in Andean communities (de la Puente Luna and Honores 2016; Platt 2018; Salomon and Niño-Murcia 2011; see also Burns 2010). The Andean people's enthusiasm and dedication to record-keeping is undeniable if we consider the role of written records in policing and adjudicating water rights in Andean communities (Bennison 2019; de la Puente Luna and Honores 2016; Hyland, Bennison, and Hyland 2021; Salomon 1998, 2004: 49–50).

Likewise, khipu research represents one of the most iconic examples of the fact that Andean communities embraced the economic and political advantages of competency in a range of inscriptive media, including for litigation purposes and, in the case of khipu literacy, for organizing native

---

34. It is unclear whether a state reform to the 1902 Código de Aguas—which created Comisiones Técnicas (Technical Commissions) tasked with overseeing water distribution in coastal valleys, including Lima in 1918 (Guevara Pérez 2015: 327)—had any impact in Casta.

rebellions (for the use of khipu missives in native uprisings, see Hyland 2017 and Spalding 2012). We also know that khipus were used by authorities who facilitated the colonial projects of conversion (de la Puente Luna 2019) and tribute collection (Medrano and Urton 2018).

As explained earlier, the Entablo's precepts illuminate the role of colonial-era accounting practices, such as khipu-board *padrones* for recording individuals' compliance with their ritual obligations, which included both Andean legal codes and colonial tribute obligations. In this respect, the content of the Entablo suggests that Andean laws relating to irrigation rituals came to be codified in colonial records designed to assist Christianization.[35] Similarly, the Huarochirí Manuscript constitutes an example of the packaging of ritual discourse and associated group resource rights into a "legitimized" paper format during the Christianization campaigns in the early colonial era (Bennison 2016: 10).

Since *khipukamayuq* authorities were tasked with recording various data-sets central to the promotion of Christian moral codes (de la Puente Luna 2019; Hyland 2021), we can appreciate that early colonial scribes must have been powerful individuals, owing to their transliteracy skills and the access to information and privilege that such a mediative status must have brought.[36] As Martínez-Céspedes (2016: 49) points out, the success of priests depended heavily on these cultural intermediaries. Burns (2010) illuminates the powerful role that notaries played in colonial Peru, where they bridged complex webs of social relationships. Water management in the Peruvian Andes continues to require local stakeholders to "bridge" and negotiate multiple ideological domains, including their own traditional model informed by local customs and the model of the state (Gelles 2000a; Vera Delgado and Zwartzeveen 2008). The need to acquire legitimacy within hegemonic power structures, while simultaneously expressing identity-based water rights, has persisted beyond the colonial era until the present. As Vera and Zwarteveen (2008: 119) assert, Indigenous peasants in Peru "pursue a dual strategy to obtain legitimacy as citizens and water-right holders. On the one hand, they

---

35. As Martínez Céspedes (2016) explains, *padrones* were designed to provide priests with up-to-date information about their parishioner base, including names and gender, all categorized by *parcialidad*. Although such records would have facilitated the administration of tribute payment, many *padrones* featured khipu cords and were used to record the submission of goods that were likely to have had little value to church authorities, such as stitched *huallque* bags worn by ritual participants (Hyland, Bennison, and Hyland 2021; Tello and Miranda 1923).
36. The respective works of Martínez Céspedes (2016) and de la Puente and Honores (2016) emphasize the role that Indigenous authorities played in upholding the colonial legal administrative system in rural villages, where these native elites wielded considerable power as experts in the workings of the royal judicial system.

actively affirm their own culture, language and traditions to demonstrate their own 'otherness'. On the other, they pragmatically and strategically appropriate and borrow elements of these same hegemonic discourses and insert those into their own modes of thinking and doing to construct a dynamic alternative to modernity and development."

The Entablo is a highly localized and idiosyncratic product of legal and economic pluralism and syncretism.[37] With its focus on preserving "muchas leyes de la era arcaica" (many laws of the archaic era; f. 19v), its instructions for the ecclesiastical magistrates (f. 27r), and two constitutional reforms in 1939 and 1947, the manuscript combines elements of pre-Hispanic, colonial-era ecclesiastic, and Peruvian state moral codes with infrastructural norms. Thus, the Entablo reflects centuries of "interlegality": "the use, the coexistence, and the transformation of diverse legal systems in one specific social setting, which create a situation of legal porosity" (de la Puente Luna and Honores 2016: 14).[38] De la Puente Luna and Honores (2016) show the ways in which native alcaldes (magistrates) in early seventeenth-century Huarochirí used both Andean and Spanish legal norms in their early colonial construction of law.

The Spanish Crown was not interested in radically altering the basis of the pre-Hispanic Andean economy, since it sought to claim tribute from surplus production that the existing basis of production generated (Spalding 1984). Nevertheless, the colonial era saw the development of a fragmented judicial hierarchy. Throughout the Peruvian provinces, this legal system included *curacas*, elite native lords responsible for ensuring that the Indigenous peoples under their jurisdiction complied with tribute and labor obligation regulations and abandoned pre-Hispanic customs in favor of Catholic religious practice (Spalding 2012: 38). The legal system also included their superiors, *corregidores de indios* (provincial magistrates in charge of exercising royal jurisdiction and collecting tribute from the "Indian" population) appointed by the king or by the viceroy to exercise royal law and oversee the fulfillment of tribute and labor obligation of the native population (Spalding 2012: 406). Within this environment of legal and religious pluralism, a syncretistic form of ritual accountancy developed in line with the power structures of colonial and local-level agents and in response to the ways in which they strategically interpreted and applied the respective legal systems.

---

37. On the ways in which religion in Latin America (including Andean Catholicism) may be defined as both syncretistic and pluralistic, see Spica 2018.
38. "Por 'interlegalidad' entendemos el uso, la coexistencia y la transformación de diversos ordenamientos jurídicos en un espacio social específico, los mismos que configuran una situación de porosidad normativa" (de la Puente Luna and Honores 2016: 14).

As Guevara-Gil (2006: 138) points out, legal norms "acquire meaning as they are interpreted, enforced and manipulated in social settings." This statement is just as true for comprehending the production of the Entablo, which represented the "officialization" of a highly localized manifestation of Andean customary law during a key moment in Peruvian state constitutional history, as it is for comprehending its colonially rooted intertextual links to the khipu-board *padrones* mentioned within it, which were themselves a hybridized fusion of pre-Hispanic and Christian legal inscriptive traditions. Readers should therefore be mindful that the kind of pre-Hispanic jurisdiction that the Entablo seeks to preserve was adapted and reformulated significantly during the early colonial era, when Indigenous authorities drew on both pre-Hispanic Andean and Castilian legal traditions, resulting in intermingling between the two legal dimensions (de la Puente Luna and Honores 2016).

Recourse to innovative legal methods, in order to preserve the traditional practices linked to irrigation canals, has a long history in Huarochirí: as de la Puente Luna and Honores (2016) mention, a 1596 lawsuit concerning the use of the Marhuaca canal in Huarochirí refers to the activities of some of the water experts, *curacas*, alcaldes, and lesser officials who oversaw the inspection, maintenance, and repair of the canals and river intakes (considered to be community property). These authorities also oversaw the distribution of the resource through turns and dividing up the canal trajectory (between the members of a *parcialidad* and among *parcialidades*) and the resolution of conflicts; this ensured that the *costumbre* instructions on its use were upheld.

For the purposes of identifying the origins of the traditional authority system described in the 1921 manuscript, we might look to the late colonial era. Pérez Galán (2004: 59) argues that the traditional authority system in Pisac, Peru, as it can be observed today, originated at the end of the eighteenth century, when the colonial Bourbon administration, via the colonial government, reduced the powers of the elite native *curacas*. Their influence over the Indigenous population was deemed a risk to the Crown, given numerous incidences of Indigenous uprisings throughout the eighteenth century. Nevertheless, the khipu-based inscriptive traditions predating the Entablo and the hybrid khipu-boards used during the *champería* until the first half of the twentieth century probably began to record church-based obligations and festivities during the early colonial era, when *curacas* assisted with the colonial project of Christianization. In one account, an early colonial *curaca* from a parish at Lake Titicaca had the Catholic calendar recorded on a khipu for such purposes (de la Puente 2019: 443).

We cannot know all the ways in which the Inca-mandated regulations for the *champería* changed over time. Nonetheless, it is clear that over the course of three centuries from the early seventeenth century to the early twentieth century the authorities in Casta controlled the ritual discourse to a high degree, aided by khipus and khipu boards.

The Entablo manuscript was written at a significant moment in Peruvian political history, at the beginning of the Augusto Leguía presidency, which was highly focused on the project of nation-building, modernizing, and associated infrastructural development such as roadbuilding (Bennison 2022; Harvey and Knox 2015). Within the context of early twentieth-century nation-building, "Indians were governmentalized in order to reduce or eliminate the obstacle that they represented to the industrial nation" (Drinot 2011: 14). The 1920 constitution gave legal form to the broader project of social and ethnic change in the name of "progress." The Entablo of 1921 was modeled on the state constitution that was designed to align Indigenous groups with national labor priorities. Nevertheless, the Entablo represents the legal system of Indigenous communities in Huarochirí in the early to mid-twentieth century, which rejected outside influences and maintained autonomous institutions and moral codes of law (Matos Mar 1958a: 16).

It is possible that the codification of these regulations in a Spanish-language paper format may have been deemed a legal necessity because of the 1920 constitution. In her research on community census records (*padrones*, the plural form of *padrón*), Hall (2014) highlights the ways in which national-level legislation influenced community record-keeping from the year 1920, when the requirement for the newly promulgated *comunidades indígenas* (Indigenous communities) to maintain lists of their populations for state scrutiny was enshrined in law. Often the community documents associated with this period contained data exceeding these legal requirements. Because these community records were subject to state scrutiny, community archives were written in Spanish (Hall 2014: 15). In this sense, highly localized ritual discourse (that may have been communicated to some extent in Indigenous languages in early twentieth-century Casta) needed to be made intelligible to government officials from beyond Casta.

Various representatives of state authority in Casta approved the 1921 internal community regulations, including the *gobernador* (governor), Don Nemesio Bautista, as well as the municipal mayor, Pascual Calistro, and his council team (f. 22v).

Idiosyncratic terms and Indigenous-language words corresponding to water sources and functionary roles are "glossed" into Spanish at various points throughout the text, suggesting an intended urban readership. In his study of twentieth-century archives written by *curacas* and other provincial authorities in Bolivia, Platt (2018: 44–45) notes that speakers of Quechua and Aymara faced technical challenges in reproducing the Spanish language in a written format, writing in the way multilingual Quechua and Aymara speakers pronounce the Spanish language.

Sacred Water Sources of Huarochirí: The Quechua Manuscript of 1608

Huarochirí is famous for its textual history. Its high-altitude villages have a remarkably rich tradition of community record-keeping, including not only manuscripts but also khipus and hybrid khipu boards (Hyland 2016; Hyland, Bennison, and Hyland 2021; Salomon 2004; Salomon and Niño-Murcia 2011; Tello and Miranda 1923). The continued adoration of the sacred water-owning ancestors represents a common thread in all these inscriptive records.

Scholars have noted that the Huarochirí Manuscript of 1608 is biblical in its nature (Salomon 1991: 2–3). The Entablo is described in similar terms: an *alguacil* in office in December 2018 explained, "Es una biblia para nosotros" (For us, it's a bible). An elder in Casta explained that khipus were like the Old Testament and the khipu-board *padrones* were like the New Testament. This analogy highlights the sacred status of these texts and suggests a diachronic relationship between khipus and khipu boards.

The preface to the Huarochirí Manuscript reads:

If the ancestors of the people called Indians had known writing in earlier times, then the lives they lived would not have faded from view until now.

As the mighty past of the Spanish Vira Cochas is visible until now, so, too, would theirs be.

But since things are as they are, and since nothing has been written until now,

I set forth here the lives of the ancestors of the Huaro Cheri people, who all descend from one forefather:

What faith they held, how they live up until now, those things and more;

Village by village it will be written down: how they lived from their dawning age onward. (Salomon and Urioste 1991: 41)

The producers of both the Huarochirí Manuscript and the Entablo had a concern for capturing ancestral traditions in writing to preserve the memory of the past from remote times. These producers, or sets of producers, deemed writing a suitable medium for this aim. The producers of the 1608 text were preoccupied with questions of visibility, which appears to be a common theme in Peruvian manuscripts dealing with ancestral connections to the landscape.

The research of Pérez Galán (2004: 189) is helpful in understanding the relationship between the past and visibility in Andean society. She suggests that there is an etymological link between the Quechua noun *ñawi* (eye) and the adverb *ñawpa* (in front), which refers to past events. People in Pisac who know a lot about the past are referred to with the term *ñawpawiñay* (Pérez Galán 2004: 189), which indicates that they preserve the past by carrying it forward, giving it continued vitality. As such, the past is conceived as being in front of ourselves and as such within our scope of vision. Within this framework underpinning the relationship between time and space, we can appreciate that the project of preserving the past in Andean society places high value on visible media for representing and (as above) consolidating legitimacy in relation to the past.

At the beginning of both the Huarochirí Manuscript and the Entablo, concerns about visibility are voiced as a key motivating aim, followed by in-depth accounts of ancestral customs. Both texts were produced during periods of intensive legal change, when it would have been important to ensure the continued legitimacy of group access to resources. Various scholars have pointed out that traditional Andean approaches to water management are not always compatible with state approaches: the state perspective tends to view water exclusively as a resource (Gelles 2000).

The Entablo, as a set of regulations with local legal status, illuminates the importance of state legal affairs and policy for influencing accountancy practices relating to water management in rural Andean communities. Although the changing political-legal environment in the early 1920s led Casteños to adopt a paper-pen format for their ritual regulations, the content of the Entablo makes it clear that they saw the creation of this manuscript as an opportunity to resist outside influences and to safeguard ancestral politics and ways of life. The book was aligned with the khipu-board *padrones* and given the same generic name for such devices (*entablo*). This is testimony to the resistance and wit of the local authorities and elders who sought to protect and officialize local ancestral laws in a format that was both understandable and acceptable to state authorities in Lima.

The format and presentation of the Entablo are hegemonic in some respects, but as a theoretical and political project it is decidedly counter-hegemonic in that it resists discourses that place national state law above

Indigenous customary law. Furthermore, its regulations made the use of the khipu-board *padrones* obligatory: this modern-style local constitution aimed to ensure the vitality of pre-Hispanic economic practices in the face of changing times. Although the khipu-board *entablos* developed in a colonial context, having been introduced in Central Andean communities by the Mercederians (Hyland, Ware, and Clark 2014; Hyland, Bennison, and Hyland 2021), the introduction of these devices attests to the fact that khipu accountancy was deeply tied to and inseparable from ancestral Andean ways of managing water and mobilizing labor. The Entablo Manuscript is part of this history.

Huarochirí, Land of the Channel-Makers

Early colonial sources attest to the presence of two ethnic groups in highland villages: the *llacuazes*, associated with the high puna lands, and the *huaris*, associated with the relatively lower irrigated lands (Duviols 1973). While the *llacuazes* worshipped lightning deities, *huaris* worshipped the ocean deity Wari (Huari), whom they credited with creating their irrigation canals and marking out the boundaries of their fields (Duviols 1973; Tello 1923).[39] The lexica of irrigation traditions in Casta suggest that the *champería* has *huari* origins: an alternative name for the ritual is the *warina* or *walina* (Tello and Miranda 1923). Today this word signifying a Wari domain refers more commonly to the *hualina* water songs sung throughout the *champería*.

The meeting places of ayllus or *parcialidades* in Casta and other Huarochirí villages are known as *huayronas*. This may be a contraction of *wari runa* (Tello and Miranda 1923: 546), Quechua for "Wari people" or "Wari civilization." Casteños used to refer to *huayronas* as *huayrunas* (Soler 1958: 172), while the ancestor-focused traditions carried out between the Friday and Sunday were called "Wari Runa" (Tello and Miranda 1923: 546). Evidently, the origins of the canals have been central to notions of group identity through time.

The toponym Huarochirí is of Aymara etymology. Its elements (*huat-ru-ch-ri*) mean "he who makes furrows for irrigation" or "he who makes terraces" (Bennison 2016; Rodolfo Cerrón Palomino, personal communication, 2014). The toponym appears to indicate that the province was known for its irrigative infrastructure in the pre-Hispanic era. The Aymara noun *huatru* (*wachu*) in the toponym Huarochirí means "furrow," "groove," or "rank file,"

---

39. As the Entablo shows, irrigation traditions and community boundary customs were still related in the 1920s, as they are today.

denoting a hierarchical ordering system as well as a furrow for irrigation.[40] This semantic association demonstrates that the irrigation system is deeply linked to the social order (Pérez Galán 2008; Bennison 2022). Andean accountancy practices structure social order in a linear format, allowing individuals to move through the hierarchy (Abercrombie 1998). In Llanchu, Peru, individuals are graded on *padrones* and ranked hierarchically according to the labor they invest (Hall 2014: 9–11). Hall's hypothesis that the *padrón* system incorporates khipu logic is supported by the fact that the Entablo reveals the role of hybrid khipu-board *padrones* in grading community members.

The organizing system through which the community authorities in some Andean areas progress is known as *wachu* (*huacho*) (Pérez Galán 2004; Rösing 2003). The term was used in Huarochirí communities in the early twentieth century in the ordering of work categories; archival evidence suggests that *wachu* obligations were encoded in khipus in Anchucaya, not far from Casta (Bennison 2022; Hyland 2016: 495). The term *wachu* is equivalent to *cargo* in Pisac today (Pérez Galán 2004: 15): the series of obligations through which authorities progress in a ladder-like "prestige hierarchy" (Isbell 1978: 86).

This structure is evident throughout the Entablo, where the status of functionaries is repeatedly presented in rank order, from the highest-ranking "down to the last functionary" ("hasta el último alguacil"). The hierarchy is performed and legitimized throughout the *champería* when the functionaries file out in order and through the proportionate material obligations to be submitted by the respective functionaries.

Community Organization

Like many other Andean communities in Peru today, Casta has a traditional authority system as well as a system of (eight) community authorities who form the *junta directiva* (board of directors) of the Comunidad Campesina. The hierarchichal order of Casta's *champería* functionaries or traditional authorities is as follows:

- The *mayores* or *notables* (elders or notables): the high-status individuals who have fulfilled all their cargos and collectively form the Consejo de Notables (Council of Notables), otherwise known as the Tribunal de Honor (Court of Honor). The *mayores* supervise community life, give guidance and advice to the authorities

---

40. The Quechua noun *wachu* has related connotations.

and community members, and propose solutions for conflicts that arise.

- The *principal*: the maximal authority in charge of overseeing traditional community events. The *principal* oversees the work of all the staff-holding authorities and advises them.

- The *alcalde campo* (rural mayor): the authority directly in charge of organizing and executing the *champería*. He must also monitor the community boundaries and their demarcation points as well as the good conservation of the canal from Carhuayumac to Santil. The *alcalde campo* is also referred to in the Entablo as "el Campo" ("the Campo").

- The *regidor mayor* (village regulator): the authority in charge of delegating tasks to his subordinate functionaries and ensuring that labor obligations are fulfilled. The *regidor mayor* not only represents the village but literally "is the village" (Llanos and Osterling 1982: 120). Not only is the *regidor mayor* consubstantial with the village, but a sacred stone referred to as *el pueblo* (the village) likewise "es él" (is him). He directs the work of the single women in communal labor events, ordering them to fulfill their obligations.

- The *regidor campo* (rural regulator): the authority in charge of inspecting the community territory boundaries and organizing the road-cleaning *faena* in December.

- The *alguacil mayor* (chief constable):[41] the community authority responsible for maintaining public order. His duties in the *champería* are varied and include working with the *teniente gobernador* (lieutenant governor) and the governor to maintain public order.

- The *alguacil menor* (assistant constable): a bottom-ranking functionary whose duties are to support the work of superiors, including state authorities, by carrying out their orders.

- The *camachicos* (law enforcers): the two functionaries in charge of ensuring the application of individuals' skills, knowledge, and effort, in addition to collecting and distributing the chicha beer.

---

41. See Spalding 1984: 217.

FIGURE 1.12. *Containers filled with* chicha *beer were brought to the ceremonial site of Cuhuay by the kinswomen of the* camachicos *in 2022.*

In addition to these functionaries, the Entablo also details the duties of the *mayordomos* (auxiliaries) who assist the functionaries on Monday and Tuesday by overseeing the work on the irrigation system. The individuals who are elected to become staff-holding functionaries the following year (the *alcalde* [*campo*], *regidor mayor*, *regidor campo*, and *alguacil mayor*) serve on the Wednesday as a special kind of *mayordomo* called a *michco*.

In Casta today, the *michco* authorities are also called *michicos*, a hispanicized form of the Quechua word *michikuy*, which is composed of the verb *michiy* and the suffix *-ku*. The Quechua verb *michiy* means *pastorear* (Lara 1971: 173), which can be translated "to herd" or "to keep watch over." In Jaqaru, *michiku* means *policía de seguridad* (security officer) (Belleza Castro 1995: 112). The *michcos* are in charge of getting their *parada* work parties to the right place when instructed to do so and are also responsible for maintaining the energy of the workers by doling out rations of coca. When they guide the *parada* processions from site to site, they lead the cheer.

The *michcos* don distinctive garb: a *ch'ullu* (knitted hat with earflaps) beneath a sombrero, sunglasses, and a *carishmanta* (*kalashmanta*, a brightly colored rectangular carry cloth) worn around the shoulders. Their outfit today also typically includes Wellington boots, and they carry a staff in one hand and a whip in the other. The *michcos* appear to embody abundance; today they are affectionately referred to using the term *panzón tayta* (papa potbelly; *panzón* in Spanish means "potbelly" and the Quechua term *tayta* refers to a male relative or ancestor). The *michcos* bring energy to the *champería* with a distinctive hippity-hopping dance, twirling their whips beside them as they go. While dancing, each *michco* uses his whip to "hurry" the water as it comes through the canal, striking it with force so that it reaches the next *michco* and his corresponding section of canal faster. Meanwhile, the *michcos* stationed further along the canal each impatiently await their turn in this dramatic relay, shouting "¡Quiero agua!" (I want water!).

Collectively, the job of all these functionaries is to enforce compliance with proper ritual conduct. The functionaries in Casta are also known as *autoridades de vara* (staff-bearing authorities) (Llanos and Osterling 1982: 119). Like the traditional staff-holding authorities (*varayuq* in Quechua) in other Andean communities, they are responsible for upholding ancestral community laws. As in Casta, traditional authorities in other Andean communities associate their social organization and irrigation governance with the Incas (Pérez Galán 2004; Trawick 2002: 39). The Inca era is idealized in Huarochirí today: collaborators in San Damián explained that the Incas were the "perfect campesinos" because they are remembered as having strictly policed ritual laws.

Ráez Retamozo (2001a: 335) describes the duties of the *varayos* of the canal-cleaning ritual in Lachaqui in Canta, Lima, who are known as *policías* (police officers). Likewise, Mayer (2002: 125–126) describes the *varayoq/varayuq* ritual authorities in Tangor, Peru, as a "moral force," who "were allowed to have whips and used them occasionally to punish petty crimes ... and oversaw the proper performance of fiestas, ceremonies, and processions." In a similar vein, Salomon (2004: 83) has explained that *varayo* staff-holders in Tupicocha, Huarochirí, "notify and remind people about policies, they detect infractions, and they bring noncooperators to justice." The functionaries of Casta maintain the order necessary for maintaining the canals. They embody and police the moral-political regime of "Inca" water laws that the makers of the Entablo deemed to be at risk.

Regulating Rituals and the Cosmological Importance of Specificity

De la Cadena (1989: 98–99) points out that a common source of conflict in Andean communities is the tensions that can emerge when traditional and modern forms of knowledge clash among *comuneros* with a high-school

FIGURE 1.13. *A* michco *for the Carhuayumac* parada *whipping the water to hurry it along the canal. Photo: Luis Miguel Silva-Novoa Sánchez.*

education and ritual authorities such as diviners and *curanderos*. In neighboring villages, social change before and during the mid-twentieth century had a considerable impact on community cohesion. For example, community elders in the 1950s in San Pedro de Huancaire considered the effects of modernity on the morals of the young to be the cause of a ruined potato harvest (Soler 1958: 221). Similarly, community elders in Pinchimuro, Cusco, in the 1970s despaired at the disorderly conduct of the youth in fiestas associated with Pachamama, the earth deity who controls the prosperity of the crops. The elders blamed the youths for increasingly inferior potato harvests (Gow and Condori 1976: 85).

As ethnographic research in Puquio in 1956 showed, communities are bound by agreements with the deities. A ritual authority in charge of representing the community to its powerful mountain being (Wamani) and vice versa told Arguedas (2002: 169): "The Wamani became angry if the *naturales* did not give him what had been agreed upon," explaining: "You end up giving it to him. He gets mad if you don't pay."

During a ritual conducted at the site of a newly constructed dam, each of the communities in Puquio sings hymns proportional to the amount of water it receives (Arguedas 2002: 163). These ethnographic details highlight a commitment to upholding precepts based on a proportional model of justice based on reciprocity, agreed on with the landscape beings themselves. The understanding that ritual payments must be exact ties in with a model of justice based on attention to ensuring exacting compliance. Social relationships in Andean communities are marked by rules about how personal services should be exchanged, where completed cycles of exchanges cancel out debts (Mayer 2002: 108–110). Failure to apply the traditional justice system based on proportional punishments would have been seen as making penalties from the ancestors inevitable.

The Entablo tells us that the punishments at Casta's champería were proportionate with the *falta* (failure). Once the canal labor was complete, workers were assessed. The instructions for the Friday and Saturday accounts note that the elders approved punishment scores entered on the *planilla* "report list." Each *planilla*, one with the men's scores, another with the women's, was followed by a corresponding (gendered) reprimand roll-call administered through a khipu board *padrón*. Each performance score was signified by a number on the *planilla*:

WOMEN
Rebel—365
Fulfilled—11
Surpassed—15
"Owes 2"—352
"Owes 1"—351

MEN
Rebel—355
Fulfilled—12
Surpassed—5
"Owes 2"—352
"Owes 1"—351

It appears that scores beginning with a "3" indicate a debt, the value of which follows the "5." Note that the "3" at the start of the rebel scores appears to "invert" the idealization of "5." While a "5" is the highest score, a "5" prefixed with a score beginning with "3" indicates the poorest result. Prefixing a number value with a "1" appears to be positive or neutral. A single score of "5" is the ideal score for men, and "15" for women. It is unclear whether the scores of "owes 1," "owes 2," and so forth indicate the number of lashes to be given as punishment or whether the numbers correspond to different kinds of punishment represented by a number. The fact that the "debt" scores are the same for men and women may indicate that men and women were equally accountable in matters of justice.

Clearly, before approaching the huaca ancestors to submit a claim for water, the functionaries in Casta needed to cancel out any personal debts that might jeopardize the success of the claim submitted to the group's shared ancestor(s).[42]

At the *huayrona*, the January ceremony for the balancing or settling of the community accounts (*balance económico*), members must emerge in "perfect" order in time for the functionary "purification" ceremony to proceed a fortnight later. As Doña Anselma Bautista Pérez explained, punishments in her youth were drastic because they were geared at canceling out imperfections in a person's record: "para recibir el año ya, tenían que salir perfectos" (to bring in the new year, they had to come out perfect).

Sitting on the doorstep of her granddaughter's house overlooking Cuhuay, Doña Luzmila Salinas Bautista, granddaughter of the Entablo's *gobernador* Nemesio Bautista, recalled the good old days when severe punishments meted out at Cuhuay on the Friday of the *champería* drew a crowd:

Ooooh, antes era bien bonito. Antes había realmente ... ¡reglamento! El que no cumplía: ¡látigo! ¡Castigo! ¡A veces nos burlábamos todos! [gesticulating toward the area of Cuhuay where the cross is located] A veces mirábamos.

Ooooh, before, it was real nice. Before, there were proper ... regulations! Anyone who didn't fulfill their duties: whip! Punishment! Sometimes we'd all laugh! [gesticulating toward the area of Cuhuay where the cross is located] Sometimes we'd go watch.

Although Doña Luzmila lamented the decline of the strict regulations in her lifetime, her grandfather and his contemporaries a century ago would likely have deemed it a crisis. Any threat to the quantitative system based on the absolution of individuals for the sake of community well-being would undoubtedly have contributed to community tensions in Andean communities, potentially deepening any generational conflict.

As the Entablo makes clear, the application of justice was carried out at ancestral sites, presided over by the elders (Hyland, Bennison, and Hyland 2021). Therefore, any failure to acknowledge the ultimate authority of these

---

42. This logic underpins potato-sowing rituals in Huaquirca, Peru, where number-based divination rites determine whether individuals must "save themselves" by submitting cuttings from their clothes, which are then interred underground so that they reach the ancestors who determine the fertility of the crops (Gose 1994: 150–151).

sites is tantamount to undermining the legitimacy of the group's existence, because the huacas governing the sacred sites are the beings who likewise govern the climatic conditions upon which human production depends. For this same reason, the increasing legal, economic, and moral importance of Lima in the early twentieth century could have undermined the authority of the ancestral sites, the huacas, and the elders as representatives of the ancestral past. Drawing on Bolin (1998), Cushman (2015: 108) explains: "The disruption of a person or community's relationship with place and the carefully timed rituals that allowed them to thrive in a locale could mean the difference between prosperity or poverty, life or death, reproduction or extinction of an ancestral line."

In early colonial Huarochirí, disasters such as illnesses, landslides, and floods were deemed to be direct outcomes of *falta de costumbre* (ritual failure) (Bennison 2016). In the Huarochirí Manuscript of 1608, the author contemplated the decline of the Yunca group following colonization, which he attributed to a recent abandonment of a collective Yunca pilgrimage to the *apu* (sacred mountain being) Pariacaca:

> Regarding this worship, it may be that the Yunca don't practice it anymore, or that not all the Yunca do. But they do perform it away from their own places.
>
> When they don't do it people speculate, saying, "It's because of that fault of theirs that the Yunca are becoming extinct."
>
> And the Yunca, speaking for themselves, say, "The highlanders are getting along all right. It's because they carry on our old way of life that their people flourish so." (Salomon and Urioste 1991: 75)

It is clear that fully carrying on the customs from ancient times was deemed pivotal to societal success and that failure to do so would bring on destructive climatic conditions and social decline. Nearly a century ago, the Huarochirí-born archaeologist Julio C. Tello (1923: 187) attributed weather storms to the canal-creating water deity Wari, who was said to make his force felt when enraged. He described Wari's temperament as ambivalent:

> Wari . . . is in the ocean, in the lakes, and in the snow-capped mountains, he produces and controls the rains and, when he becomes wild, cries out or roars, unleashes his rage over the land in the form of

hailstorms, lightning storms, and strikes of lightning and thunder. (Tello 1923: 188)[43]

Those in charge of rituals had the responsibility of satisfying and pacifying each individual huaca or *apu* associated with the respective canal trajectory. The identity of the overarching principal deity worshipped during the *champería* in Casta has been subject to debate. Although Tello and Miranda claimed that Casteños perform their *champería* in honour of Wallallo, others maintain that the *champería* honors the huaca Suqta Kuri (e.g., Llanos and Osterling 1982: 117–118). Today, Suqta Kuri (also spelled "Suqta Curi," meaning "Six Children of Lightning" in Quechua) is one of the principal huacas in Casta and is described by villagers as a powerful "King" who founded the local lineages in ancient times. He is said to bring on the rains today. Throughout the twentieth century, Casta's villagers, who structured their daily routines around protecting those vulnerable to his demands, evidently feared Suqta Kuri.

Surrounded by her three daughters, *yachak* Catalina Olivares explained that Suqta Kuri manifests as lightning and is a rapist ("Es violador"). Agreeing enthusiastically, her daughters explained that until fairly recently, women would avoid his attacks by refraining from walking in the lands above the village after one o'clock in the afternoon. So great was the risk posed by Suqta Kuri to women that staying within the confines of the village in the afternoons was obligatory: "¡Eso ha sido legal!" ("That was the law!"). Catalina's grandmother, who was the *yachak* before her, told Catalina that Suqta Kuri demanded that beautiful maidens be given to him in sacrifice. She explained to Catalina that when the community refused to keep sacrificing innocent young women, instead offering Suqta Kuri a llama as a substitute for a maiden, he was not satisfied. This observation may have made it all the more important that the annual *champería* be carried out properly, according to ancestral law, in order to pacify Suqta Kuri. During my 2022 visit to Casta, Suqta Kuri reportedly made an appearance, bringing the rains; when discussing a recent loud thunderstorm with Catalina, she asked me "¿No escuchastes que vino Suqta Kuri anteayer? ¡Tak, Tak, tak! " ("Suqta Kuri came the day before yesterday, didn't you hear? Tak, tak tak!"). These

---

43. "Wari ... está en el Océano, en las lagunas y en las cordilleras nevadas; produce y controla las lluvias, y cuando se embravece, brama o ruge, descarga su cólera sobre la tierra en forma de granizo, relámpagos, rayos y truenos" (Tello 1923: 188).

accounts suggest that Suqta Kuri has been an important force in the lives of Casteños throughout the last century. It therefore seems peculiar that Tello and Miranda placed more importance on the huaca Wallallo in their account of Casta and its *champería*.

Today, Wallallo (also spelled "Huallallo"), is remembered as having resided in Casta in remote times, however his current dwelling is said to be located in between the nearby hamlets of Huinco and Cumpe (both annexes of San Pedro de Casta today) where there is a site named Wallallo. Wallallo has presumably been associated with this nearby hamlet since pre-hispanic times. Casta's Auto Redondo manuscript (1711–1808) mentions a site located three quarters of a league from Casta called "Huallallo" in a list of ancient settlements that in 1808 were no longer populated (CCSPC 1711–1808: f.62v). It would therefore make sense for the Casta *champería* to have some persisting features of Wallallo worship (as I shall explain later, the alternative name for the *champería*, *walla-walla*, suggests an association with Wallallo). Nevertheless, Tello and Miranda's claim that Wallallo was the most important deity in 1920s Casta (1923: 510) and their related claim that the entire ceremony was performed in devotion of Wallallo (1923: 523) are misleading. In fact, many of the supposedly Wallallo-focused traditions mentioned in the 1923 article are described in Tello's unpublished field notes as Suqta Kuri–focused traditions (Tello n.d.: f.3r–f.7v). In the published article, which draws on these very field notes, the authors (or presumably Tello) claim that Casteños confuse Wallallo with Suqta Kuri (Tello and Miranda 1923: 514).

The discrepancy between the information presented in Tello's 1922 field notes and his 1923 article coauthored with Miranda makes it difficult to ascertain which elements of local knowledge the authors overwrote or misrepresented in their published account of the ritual. The extent to which Wallallo reverence featured in the *champería* in the 1920s is therefore unclear. Nevertheless, it is important to note that today, multiple huacas are honoured throughout the weeklong ceremony at the various key ceremonial sites along and nearby the irrigation system; this would have also been the case in the 1920s.

Various ethnographies testify to the multiplicity of sacred beings honored in canal-cleaning ceremonies in the Lima highlands (Llanos and Osterling 1982; Ráez Retamozo 2001a; Tello and Miranda 1923). Ensuring the full participation of all community members in ritual was vital to appeasing the huacas: it is for this reason that the Concha ethnic group of San Damián, Huarochirí, submits a list of irrigators' names to the ancestral lake-owners during their annual lake-damming *champería* each February; historically they submitted a khipu account as well (Salomon 1998).

These same lake-owning ancestors, who feature in the Huarochirí Manuscript of 1608, are understood to demonstrate and demand good moral behavior from their Concha descendants. As a collaborator explained during my doctoral fieldwork in San Damián, "Nos enseñan como comportarnos" (They teach us how to behave). The ancestors are said to either approve or reject the list of irrigators; if they approve, they will "grab" the submitted list, pulling it deep into the lake's waters. When I attended this *champería* in 2012, a collaborator named Doña Dometila described the practice of submitting the list of irrigators on a "boat" or block of *champa* (sod) at noon:

> Hacen una champa así cuadrado como ésta y en medio del barco va la lista, así como una banderita hacen y va la lista de toditos los comuneros del Concha . . . y allí le envían el barco con todo, la lista, le juegan su carnaval, su serpentina, su coca, su pisco que ellos quieren, ¿no? Su regalito, y envían todo allí en el barquito, le ponen todo allí. Y le sueltan el barquito, el barquito solito se va, nadando, nadando, nadando, nadando, nadando, y arriba ya al llegar ya al justo . . . para llegar al la capillita eso, eh, y solito se . . . la lista, o sea el papelito se funde sol-i-to. O sea el barquito, la champita solo . . . ese partecita que está allá, esa solita se flota ya, ya se va. Se queda flotando en cambio el papelito se hunde allí, entonces se quiere decir o que según creencia que Pedro Batán y Mama Campiana recibe a todito su lista de sus comuneros.

> They cut a sod block into a square like this and in the middle of the boat goes the list, they make it like a little flag, and on it goes the list of all the Concha *comuneros* . . . and [from] there, they send the boat out to them with everything on it, the list, they play carnival with it for them, it gets its carnival paper ribbons, its coca, its pisco [grape brandy]. The things that they [the lake owners] want, isn't that so? Their gift. And they send all that there in the boat, they put everything on it for them. And they release the little boat for them and the little boat goes out all on its own, swimming, swimming, swimming, swimming, swimming, and at the far side, exactly at the spot . . . where it reaches the little chapel on its own . . . that little section over there, that floats there all on its own, off it goes. It keeps floating, whereas the little bit of paper sinks there. This means, or according to the belief it means, that Pedro Batán and Mama Campiana accept the entire list of their *comuneros*.

The approval of the ancestors is required so that they may grant the Concha people access to water in the coming year. In this sense, the effort made by the ritual participants written on the list is factored in ("registered") by the ancestors. The degree of effort and energy shown by ritual participants was historically known as *callpa*, and the ancestors were known to possess *callpa*, a vital animating force central to Andean notions of causality (Taylor 1987: 26; Topic 2015: 370). The Entablo instructions are informed by such an understanding. The *nómina* accounts—whether cord or paper—of each work party possibly were submitted on the final day of the *champería*. Echeandia Valladares (1981: 151) explains that the production of crafts, crops, and chicha to be submitted during the *champería* was geared at pleasing the ancestors. A collaborator told him that Casteños started preparing their work contributions in September. The elders would go about asking people if they were preparing their maize, potatoes, and guinea pigs, making sure they were getting their *carismantas* "and all the necessary items ready to please our parents the *aukis*."[44] The term *aukis* (*awkis*, *auqis*) refers generally to the sacred ancestors, who are honored at sites associated with the pre-Hispanic local populations (Dedenbach-Salazar Sáenz 2017).

The elders' surveillance over the progress of skilled work prior to the *champería* is not explicitly mentioned in the Entablo, but it does provide a general assessment of these offerings. During the Padrón de Huallque, each household is obliged to display its finest *curiosidades*: skilled crafts displaying knowledge-forms that the ancestors respond to, including intricate brightly colored ritual bags called *huallques* (also *huallquis* in the Entablo).[45] These submissions were recorded on a khipu board, which suggests that the general productivity of the group was thought to be taken into account by the ancestors. Were khipus and khipu boards used to submit offerings of *callpa* to them?

I was repeatedly told in San Damián that a failed ritual is the responsibility of the functionary in charge. Thus, anyone who seeks to innovate, alter, or omit any section of an ancestral ritual will have these *faltas* (omissions or failings) noticed. Even one *falta* could have serious consequences for the

---

44. "Y todo lo necesario para agradecer a nuestros padres los aukis" (Echeandia Valladares 1981: 151). *Carismanta* is an alternative spelling of *calashmanta* (also *calashmanta*, *kalashmanta*), referring to the brightly colored striped carrying cloths used to carry loads on people's backs.

45. The standard method of making a *huallque* uses linked spiral stitching (see Emery 1994: 45) to build outward from a central spiral base. The stitches on each row link minimally with the previous row before the row is closed off with a loop. I am grateful to Anselma Bautista Pérez, who generously (and patiently!) taught me this method. More novel approaches appear to use looping techniques (without linking stitches) (Emery 1994: 45). Women are taught to make *huallque* bags as children by their mothers and grandmothers. One collaborator recalled her mother slapping her hand as a child for producing "ugly" messy stitches.

FIGURE 1.14. *A* huallque *(wallki, huallqui): a small bag in which men carry an* eshcupuro *(gourd to store lime), coca leaves, and cigarettes, elements associated with male labor. Photo and caption: Luis Miguel Silva-Novoa Sánchez.*

entire community (Bennison 2016: 168). Don Eugenio Anchelia Llata, who had been a *curandero* in his younger years, went through childhood in the 1920s and explained social change in the village during his lifetime on various occasions. He described the ways the ancestors castigated ritual omissions by inflicting illness, causing drought, and frightening ritual functionaries by appearing along the canal trajectory as ghost-like beings.

Don Eugenio took great amusement in recounting the difficulties of a *guardia* (state police officer) who attempted to loot the mortuary structures at a local Pre-Hispanic ritual complex, Llaquistambo. He failed to acknowledge the sacred ancestors with a ritual "payment" and became unwell five days later. After he broke out in a rash, could not sleep, and wet himself, he consulted a village elder, Don Albino, who advised him to comply with customary law (*costumbre*). Only when the *guardia* returned to Llaquistambo to submit his offerings, guided by Don Albino, did the ancestors relieve him of his affliction (Bennison 2016). Eugenio appeared to find it humorous that the *guardia* tried, but failed, to circumvent customary law.

Don Eugenio summarized the logic behind the moral code, which dictates that rituals should be carried out fully and to the letter: "Aca se registra eso. Hace daño para el abuelo" (Here this is officially taken into account. It causes harm to the ancestor) (Bennison 2016: 27). As Abercrombie (1998: 175–176) writes, "Inca, and more generally, Andean forms of social memory were 'registered' in multiple and intersecting media."[46] This is true of Casta in the early twenty-first century, where the Entablo apparently complemented the use of khipu boards. Eugenio never spoke to me about khipus or khipu boards, but his words about "registering" commitment to ritual succinctly convey the logic behind the *padrones* of the Entablo and indeed the Entablo itself. The degree of respect and effort shown to the ancestors in ritual acknowledgment is quantifiable, measured, and judged. The functionaries in Casta oversee bringing about optimal conditions for a successful ritual within this ancestor-focused network of dependency.

The central role of traditional authorities in managing social and climactic contingencies is illustrated clearly in the case of Rapaz. An authority known as the Vendelhombre (*bien del hombre*: human welfare) guards the community's sacred khipu housed in a precinct known as Kaha Wayi, meaning Treasury House (Salomon 2016: 185). According to Salomon (2016: 192), the Vendelhombre is called that because "his influence with the 'owners of rain' is the only defence against drought." As Salomon explains, locals in Rapaz regard the community khipu to be a powerful conduit between themselves and the nonhuman owners of rain. As such, any ritual failings or behaviors deemed to be a threat to the efficacy of the khipu human-ancestor negotiations reflect negatively on the Vendelhombre, whose performance is scrutinized by the community if rains do not come when expected (Salomon 2016: 192).

A recent paper by Hyland (2021: 127) draws on this Entablo research, arguing that the Rapaz khipu recorded calendrical information relating to the community's annual festivity cycle. Melecio Montes, the Vendelhombre in Rapaz, explained that the Rapaz khipu "determines all that happens" (Hyland 2021: 147). Andean records determining ritual schedules are substantive because the matter contained within them dictates how and when the onward flows of all other matter must be mobilized in and through ritual. They provide structure to a world characterized by permeability (Itier 2013: 75–76), where the channeling of substances according to their instructions requires expertise in transmission.

---

46. In Inca khipu administration, census and tribute data were synthesized and transferred between different levels of accounts (Urton and Brezine 2005).

Social Change and Intergenerational Conflict in the Early Twentieth Century

Roadbuilding in the Huarochirí province in the Lima highlands between the 1920s and 1950s increased the "allure of modernity" among youths.[47] When roadbuilding work began, young local men left their villages to fulfill their roadbuilding conscription duties. This brought working-age Huarochirano men increasingly physically and ideologically closer to the city of Lima.[48] The increased articulation with Lima resulted in young people bringing new political and economic ideas to the village, including capitalism and communism. They challenged the autonomy and power of the *mayores* (elders) (Soler 1958: 180–181).

Mayer (1989: 40) observed the same phenomenon in Laraos in the Cañete valley (Lima highlands) in the 1970s. Changes impelled by liberal thinkers between approximately 1900 and 1950—including to water and land rights—were the result of a rebellion organized by a youth group called La Quinta Internacional, which likewise succeeded in conquering power in its community. Similarly, Gow and Condori (1976: 23) note intergenerational conflict in Pinchimuro, Cusco, which was under the hacienda system until 1970. They observed that its abolition resulted in tension: "The elderly folk still try to live the old way, fulfilling their obligations and being respectful, and they feel resentful to see themselves displaced by the new independent youth. The youths are searching for their own pathway. They still believe in the laws dictated by the *apus* [sacred mountain deities] and in the old regime, but they are also beginning to believe in themselves."[49] As de la Cadena (1989: 99) points out, conflicts between communal and individual interests are common in Andean communities. These develop and are resolved in different ways by political, ritual, and economic means according to the dynamics of local contexts. Howard-Malverde (1990: 69) notes that rebellion and nonconformism

---

47. As the work of Drinot (2011) demonstrates, political discourses relating to industrialization in Peru from the 1920s onward were based on the premise that labor and indigeneity were incommensurable and placed value on a modern, non-Indigenous workforce.
48. Augusto Leguía's conscription law passed in 1920 meant that men between the ages of eighteen and sixty were obliged to provide six to twelve days of labor a year in building and repairing roads in the province in which they lived (Harvey and Knox 2015: 28).
49. "Los ancianos tratan todavía de vivir a la antigua usanza, cumpliendo sus obligaciones y siendo respetuosos, y se sienten resentidos al verse desplazados por la nueva juventud independiente. Los jóvenes buscan su propio camino. Creen todavía en las normas dictadas por los apus y en el orden antiguo, pero también empiezan a creer en ellos mismos" (Gow and Condori 1976: 23).

within Andean communities are deemed to impede community well-being, indicating a lack of agreement and unity.

Dissonance in Andean communities can have serious economic consequences, because the maintenance of irrigative infrastructure requires high levels of ideological cohesion to enable labor cooperation (Bennison 2022). For instance, a group of youths in the highland Lima community of Lampián (Canta province) in the 1930s voiced their discontent with their low rank. They were expelled from their community, charged with "rebelling against the community's *costumbres* and traditions" (Alberti 1972: 99),[50] and reported to the Ministerio de Fomento, Dirección de Asuntos Indígenas (Ministry of Development, Directorate of Indigenous Affairs), for provoking disorder. Through this expulsion the community lost the membership and labor of thirty youths and was unable to maintain the irrigation systems during a period of drought (Alberti 1972: 104). Similarly, community authorities in San Pedro de Huancairé (Huarochirí) in the 1930s reported some of its youths to the district authorities, accusing them of Communist ideology (Soler 1958: 181). Clearly, the rejection of traditional hierarchies was a radical stance incompatible with community life in the early twentieth century, calling into question the traditional prestige hierarchy. Such ideologies clashed with the humiliation and strict punishments of noncompliant young people by elders during rituals (Bennison 2022). Did the growth of progressive ideologies in the Peruvian highlands play a part in impelling changes to ritual record-keeping?

Early twentieth-century social change brought on by educated, Spanish-speaking youths in Huarochirí appears to have been expressed, managed, and prevented through normative written accounts, with variable outcomes in Huarochirano communities. As noted earlier, a ritual specialist explained to Tello in the 1930s that the youths had insisted on shifting from khipus to paper accounts in preceding decades in Anchucaya (Hyland 2016: 496).

Soler's account of intergenerational conflict in a Huarochirí community is important for understanding the kinds of conditions that could have brought the elders in Casta to produce a written account of ritual regulations and responsibilities to which all community members were bound by legal agreement. By the 1950s, intracommunity generational tensions in San Pedro de Huancaire had escalated to a crisis point: the authority of the community elders came to be challenged by the liberalized young, whose strict punishments for doing so were meted out publicly during rituals by the elders

---

50. "Acusándolos de rebeldes a las costumbres y tradiciones de la comunidad" (Alberti 1972: 99).

(Soler 1958). This resulted in a youth rebellion in 1940, which revolutionized community life and resulted in a more equitable distribution of lands and power, with more power being conferred to the young (Soler 1958: 180).

In this case, the liberal ideals of the young led to the creation of numerous cultural and sporting initiatives that brought men and women into closer social contact; prior to this, social relations were informed by Catholic dogma and strictly controlled by the elders (Soler 1958: 180–189).[51] A Sandamianino couple I visited in Sydney, Australia, explained that elderly *comuneros* would hit young people and children who did not greet them when passing by in public during their childhood and youth in San Damián. According to the oral testimony of an elderly woman from the Casta district, local authorities punished the parents of children and young people who failed to show respect (Ediciones Flora Tristán and CENDOC-Mujer 2002: 28). Many elderly Huarochiranos today lament the *falta de respeto* (lack of respect) of younger generations. In some communities, youth resistance in the early twentieth century resulted in profound infrastructural changes in community life, which may have exacerbated existing intergenerational tensions.

The manner in which youths in San Pedro de Huancaire achieved change, seizing power from the elders, is particularly revealing. On December 31, 1939, the youths held a secret meeting in the house of a man who had recently returned from a trip to Lima. They attended the January 1 change of authorities the next day and realized that their rebellion had been successful when they managed to seize the community books during the meeting (Soler 1958: 182). This powerful case illuminates the central role of written accounts in the ordering of community life.[52] That is surely why the elders in Casta deemed it appropriate to use a community book to address the poor ritual performance of the functionaries in 1921. In doing so, they criminalized social change from the seat of community power and authority. Given that the *champería* relies on the *comuneros* to acknowledge the authority of the elders and the functionaries to be carried out successfully, the canal system became the domain in which communal tensions played out (Bennison 2022).

---

51. In 2018 elderly Casteñas described the strict moral policing of unmarried women in their lifetimes. During the annual change of authorities at New Year (*huayrona*), they were lined up so that their breasts could checked for signs of lactation, which authorities would consider evidence of an illegitimately conceived aborted infant. For further information on the surveillance of romantic relationships and women's reproductive health in Huarochirí in the mid- to late twentieth century, see Ediciones Flora Tristán and CENDOC-Mujer (2002).
52. It is surely relevant that khipus were used to mobilize community uprisings: Pimentel (2014) shows that an Aymara khipu was interpreted to communicate the phrase *nos levantaremos* (we will rise up).

The early twentieth century saw significant social and political changes throughout Peru. Various scholars have shown that nation-building in Peru in the early twentieth century was premised on racialized terms and specifically on the project of de-Indianization (de la Cadena 2000: 6; Drinot 2011: 15). The Indigenous population was seen to be incommensurable with the national goal of civilization and modernization (Drinot 2011).

The content of the Entablo challenges the broader context of dominant perceptions of indigeneity at the time, which associated Indians with backwardness (de la Cadena 2000; Drinot 2011: 13). Whereas elites in Lima saw industrialization and modernization as the key to national progress and civilization (Drinot 2011: 1–15), the makers of the Entablo saw the upholding of ancestral Indigenous customs relating to local water management as a moral-political obligation necessary for well-being. The ritual instructions set out in the Entablo elucidate the sheer amount of organization, accountancy, and physical labor required during the *champería*.

The Linguistic Environment and the Spanish of the Entablo

The Inca era–aligned laws set down in the *champería* instructions in 1921 were written primarily in Spanish, the language of the state and Lima. The manuscript features the Quechua lexicon as well as lexical elements from other languages, including Jaqaru (an Aymara language) and Latin. It is possible that both Jaqaru and to some degree Quechua were spoken conversationally in the Huarochirí province, where Casta is located (Bennison 2019), at the time the Entablo was written.

In making this claim, my understanding of language sensitivities and language transformation in twentieth-century Huarochirí villages differs from the views of other scholars. Llanos and Osterling (1982: 116) state that in 1979 Casta was a Spanish-speaking community with no recent Quechua history. According to Salomon and Niño-Murcia (2011: 23), the main period of language shift from Quechua to Spanish in Huarochirí villages probably occurred between the late nineteenth and early twentieth centuries. Nevertheless, Indigenous languages were likely to have been spoken in Casta to some degree in the early to mid-twentieth century, particularly during landscape-focused rituals (Bennison 2019).[53] Likewise, Gushiken (1972: 151) carried out fieldwork in Carampoma, a village close to Casta, where

---

53. The persistence of Indigenous language use in Huarochirano water customs is also evidenced in Salomon's work (Salomon 2002a, 2004).

a collaborator in his sixties said that he remembered hearing older women speak Cauqui when he was a child.[54] Although Indigenous languages were still spoken in Huarochirí villages in the early twentieth century, linguistic diversity is associated with older periods. A collaborator in Casta told Echeandia Valladares (1981: 20) that in former times groups within Casta could not understand one another and had to communicate through sign language.

Similarly, a collaborator in 2018 sang a short Quechua song to me, explaining that the song is sung each January during the *pirwa* ritual rain dances.[55] The collaborator who sang the song did not wish to be named, which goes some way in demonstrating the understandable sensitivities surrounding the speaking or singing of "old words." The reluctance to discuss Quechua words is the result of a long history of language stigmatization. Nevertheless, Indigenous-language words can fulfill social and economic functions in landscape rituals, in that they possess ontological strength and can communicate the force of the land in ways that non-Indigenous Spanish cannot (Bennison 2019; Course 2018).

Julio C. Tello, the famous Huarochirano archaeologist, and/or his coinvestigator Próspero Miranda, heard participants in the *champería* in Casta address the huaca Wallallo (or Suqta Kuri?) with invocations in Quechua in 1922 (Tello and Miranda 1923: 527). This aspect of the *champería*, which is referred to only briefly in the Entablo through the Quechua word *waqay* (spelled *huajay* in the text, meaning "to weep," "to wail," or "to cry out"), relates to the Inca-era practice of crying—as children of the Inca—in order to implore the powerful royal huacas for rain (Bennison 2019). In this respect, the Entablo does feature laws associated with the Inca era. However, as I discuss later in this introduction, the ritual regulations that the Entablo offers as instructions are highly influenced by Peru's colonial history. Moreover, just as in many Andean communities today, the water ritual in Casta in the 1920s involved elements of Catholic worship. Beside the expressions of Catholic worship detailed for the *champería* in October, the manuscript also includes a section setting out the duties of the church staff during Holy Week (from f. 26v).

The Spanish of the Entablo is characteristic of Andean Spanish. The high degree of lexical idiosyncrasy in the manuscript is reflective of the highly localized domain of ancestral landscape ritual. According to Andrade (2016: 32), Andean Spanish is a concept whose definition is rarely ever agreed upon in the linguistic literature. Nevertheless, he identifies three common

---
54. I am grateful to Sabine Hyland for recommending Gushiken's article.
55. Rösing (2010: 121) defines a *pirúa* as a storeroom where potatoes and corn are kept. The word *pirwa* is associated with maize (and potatoes) in Casta today (Bennison 2019).

conceptual notions that run through scholarly work on Andean Spanish. The variety is marked by regional variation, social variation, and phenomena rooted in language contact. The work of Mackenzie (2017) likewise highlights the broad applicability of the concept. "The term 'Andean Spanish' is commonly applied to the spectrum of speech types, from interlanguage to indigenously influenced monolingual Spanish, that are encountered in the highland area stretching from the equator to the Tropic of Capricorn."

The language of the Entablo is marked by grammatical and lexical influences from the Indigenous languages of the Lima highlands, notably Quechua and Jaqaru. The manuscript emerged in a context of "Indigenous multilingualism" (Vaughan and Singer 2018). This term refers to the development of preconquest and postconquest language ecologies in their various manifestations, accounting for regional variation (such as in this region of the Andes) (Vaughan and Singer 2018). As Rostworowski de Diez Canseco (1978) demonstrates, Huarochirí has a multilayered history, resulting from multiple conquests by diverse ethnic groups. This human geography is reflected in the diverse linguistic history of the province: Spanish was incorporated into an already diverse linguistic environment in the early colonial era. Analysis of the early colonial Huarochirí Manuscript by Adelaar (1994: 140–149) suggests that two varieties of Quechua were spoken in the province (Central Quechua, also known as Waywash Quechua, and a local variant of the Inca Empire Quechua *lingua franca*, known as the *lengua general*) as well as an Aru language (such as Jaqaru).

Significantly, Taylor (2008: 11–17) demonstrates that this diverse linguistic history is evident in the Quechua Huarochirí Manuscript of 1608. Jaqaru was the native tongue of its narrator. His analysis of the text suggests that the information transcribed in the manuscript in the Quechua *lengua general* was originally collected in Jaqaru and local varieties of Quechua, given that the narrator's Jaqaru substrate emerges throughout the manuscript. It is likely that three different languages were spoken in early twentieth-century Casta: Jaqaru, Quechua, and Spanish (Bennison 2019). Hardman (1966: 15) points out that Jaqaru was spoken in a neighboring province of Huarochirí at the turn of the twentieth century: "there were still a few speakers in Canta, north of Lima." This statement could be expanded to some Huarochirí villages for the early twentieth century, given the presence of adult native speakers of Jaqaru in Huarochirí in 1920.

According to a descendant, Tello was a native speaker of Cauqui (Jaqaru) (Padilla Deza 2018: 241). Furthermore, middle-aged and elderly collaborators in San Damián associate Jaqaru words used in daily parlance today with their grandparents' ways of speaking, before the introduction of "time" (capitalist clock-time) in the village. Similarly, a collaborator in Casta explained that Quechua language is associated with village life up to a specific moment in history. A village elder, Don Porfirio, described singing during Holy Week in Casta: "La Semana Santa las señoras cantaban en Quechua y en Latín. Pero esas señoras ya no están. Desde los 1800s, ya no hay esa gente. A veces cantamos en Quechua y en Latín sin saber de qué se trata la letra" (In Holy Week, the women would sing in Quechua and Latin. But those women are no more. Since the 1800s, those people no longer exist. Sometimes we sing in Quechua and in Latin without knowing what the lyrics are about).[56] Echeandia Valladares (1981: 169) describes the lyrics of the songs sung during the *champería* in the 1970s as sounding very old. Although he offers no etymological analysis of the lyrics sung, Tello and Miranda (1923: 527–529) report the speaking and singing of Quechua in Casta in 1922 during a secret night-time ritual preceding the *champería*. A ritual authority known as the Wachik,[57] together with the functionaries, sang a number of Quechua songs in unison during the secret ritual but did not understand the meaning of the lyrics that they had learned mechanically through the generations (Tello and Miranda 1923: 529).

Although Quechua was spoken (in ritual contexts, if nowhere else) in Casta in the early twentieth century, Don Porfirio's statement that locals sing in Quechua today without understanding the Quechua lyrics is the first time I have ever heard anyone from Huarochirí acknowledge any degree of Quechua language use in the province.[58] It is noteworthy that Quechua songs are sung in Casta during rituals described as secret (Bennison 2019).

As Don Porfirio explains, linguistic diversity in Casta also includes Latin language practices within liturgical contexts. The ubiquity of the Latin lexicon in sacred domains is evidenced by the Latin-derived terms in the Entablo. From the colonial period onward, sacred ceremonies such as *champerías* are likely to have been multilingual, involving speaking and/or singing in some

---

56. Speakers in Huarochirí avoid a personal association with the speaking of Indigenous languages. This is an understandable legacy of historical and ongoing language discrimination, which has no doubt contributed to a decline in Indigenous language use in Huarochirí villages.
57. The term *wachik* (*wachiq*) is an agentive verb form; the Quechua verb root *wač'i* or *waĉi* can mean "to plant seeds using a foot plow." In this particular ritual context, the agentive form can be translated as "the one who pierces." I explore the term *wachik* in greater depth elsewhere, in a discussion of ritual wailing and earth breaking in Inca and contemporary Andean rainmaking rituals (Bennison 2019).
58. As Arguedas (2002: 162) points out, participants in the canal-cleaning ritual in Puquio in the 1950s referred to water with the Cusco Quechua word *unu*, which they do not otherwise use in daily speech.

or all of the following languages: Spanish, Latin, Jaqaru, and Quechua. The variety of Andean Spanish spoken in Casta and in other Huarochirí villages emerged following a long period of language contact from the colonial period. In this respect, linguistic diversity in early twentieth-century Huarochirí is reflective of other rural Andean communities articulated with urban centers.

Mackenzie's (2017) description of interlanguage crystallization is relevant in considering the variety of Spanish spoken in Huarochirí today and presumably earlier in its history:

> Language contact between Spanish and indigenous Andean languages (Quechua throughout the region and Aymara in southern Peru and Bolivia) has been long-lasting and intense. In many areas stable forms of interlanguage Spanish have been in use for centuries and it is likely that the speech of some monolingual speakers—especially in the remoter urban centres, such as Puno or Juliaca in southern Peru—represents a crystallization of such hybrid systems.

Within the spectrum of speech types represented by the term "Andean Spanish" (ways of speaking in Huarochirí communities today), the variety of Spanish is a fossilized interlanguage in the sense described above.[59] Varieties of Spanish spoken in Huarochirí today are influenced by the diverse linguistic history of the province. Communication between Huarochiranos and Limeños may at times be unintelligible. A collaborator in San Damián wondered how I adapted to monthly visits to Lima and described her own difficulties there: "En Lima es otro castellano. ¡Otro castellano hablan! A veces no nos entendemos" (In Lima it's another Spanish. They speak another Spanish! Sometimes we don't understand each other) (Bennison 2016: 185).

Nevertheless, the formalized language written in the Entablo may be described as an "indigenously influenced Spanish" per Mackenzie's definition above. There is a conscious effort to use Spanish words for landscape features and functionary roles wherever possible, resulting in multiple instances of in-text glossing of Indigenous terms. The instructions for the Sunday preparations for the *champería* dictate: "el [Alcalde] Campo a voz popular nombrará sacsaneros o revisadores de la acequia" (the [Alcalde] Campo will publicly announce the names of the canal Sacsaneros or Supervisors; CCSPC 1921: f. 5v).[60]

---

59. An interlanguage is a language or language variety with features of two or more languages.
60. The hispanicized Quechua word *sacsaneros* can be translated into English as "the ones to be satisfied." The Quechua *saqsay* means "to be satisfied or sated," so the Spanish *revisador* (reviewer) does not convey the full sense of the term being glossed.

Likewise, the instructions for Wednesday state that the functionaries should perform a "secret ritual" at Cumau Waterfall: "Despues de pocos momentos bajan a la acequia a hacer una ceremonia secreta en la Paccha o Chorro" (After a short moment, they go down to the canal to do a secret ceremony in the Paccha or Waterfall) (CCSPC 1921: f. 9r).[61] Descending water is ritually significant throughout the Andes. Arguedas (2002: 181) notes that participants in the canal-cleaning ritual in mid-twentieth century Puquio submitted offerings of *llampu* (a red ceremonial powder made from cornmeal) at the foot of small waterfalls, beneath large stones. The term *paccha* is onomatopoeic, referring to a space where the descent of water is audible. In the Andes, the sounds produced by water pummeling rocks at the base of a waterfall are said to inspire musicians to compose melodies for *huaynos* (songs associated with the rainy season) (Stobart 2006: 19).[62] It is for this reason that musicians place their musical instruments beside waterfalls or streams at night, so that the *sami* (vital energy) known to be present in such places can be passed to the instruments and thereby regenerate their owners' energy too (see, for example, Allen 2002: 33).

As Dransart (2006: 12, 14) points out, a *paccha* (*paqcha*) can be constructed. This is the term given to a vessel from the pre-Hispanic period that was likely used to pour liquids directly into the earth during planting rituals. As Allen (2002: 35) explains, *sami* is transferred when liquids are poured into the ground or flicked into the air, so a *paccha* is a lively, generative, and enlivening site associated with fertility and production. The term *pacchha* (also *paqcha* and *pakcha*) is likewise given to the concave depression in stones formed by descending water (Dransart 2006: 12), so it is fitting that Cumau Waterfall is noted for its large recess formed by the continuous bubbling descent of the waters (Tello and Miranda 1923: 524). The degree of impact between the powerful water and the stone base makes *pacchas* ritually significant and the focus of offerings.[63] Collaborator Kedwin Obispo Bautista

---

61. The Quechua term *paccha* means "waterfall." Many of the water customs are likewise described in Casta as "secret." A collaborator explained that the New Year *pirwa* ritual to bring on the rains takes place in the middle of the night because locals had to conceal the custom during the early colonial era. Given that Casta is well known for the persistence in rituals of pre-Hispanic origin, the concealment of these rituals is surely a contributing factor. Furthermore, it is likely that the continued use of khipu boards upholding the customary laws has contributed to this persistence.
62. Likewise, participants in the *champería* in Casta invoke landscape beings associated with music at a drum-shaped stone at the site of Chuswa (Chusgua) (Tello and Miranda 1923: 531).
63. For the same reason, seafoam brought to Casta from the coast each January must be collected from Lima's *agua más bravo* (wildest waters), at specific sites where it pummels

explained that a concave stone taken from the base of Cumau Waterfall has been tucked into a recess at the top of the waterfall. During the *champería*, the functionaries fill it with offerings of chicha beer. He believes that this natural *canterito* (little jug) is very old: "El canterito es de los antiguos, pe" (The little jug is from the time of the ancients).[64]

The older authorities reading the Entablo each year undoubtedly would have known the meanings of words such as *paccha*, and many other words of Quechua etymology that are not glossed. Despite the internal status of the text, these instances of in-text glossing, where the Spanish "synonyms" follow the Quechua words that have already been written, suggest that the producers of the Entablo found it more natural to describe ritual discourse and features or characteristics of the landscape in Quechua but felt under pressure to facilitate comprehension of a Spanish-speaking readership. Perhaps the functionaries and elders who wrote the Entablo had a state institutional readership in mind. They may have made a conscious effort to have the manuscript in Spanish wherever possible, according to state legislation obliging legally recognized communities to keep records in Spanish.

For instance, in a section added to the Entablo in 1939, a contributor explained that the manuscript would be given to a state official from the newly created Ministry of Health, so that its contents could be officially approved. Perhaps the manuscript's producers had a future (monolingual Spanish-speaking) functionary readership in mind. Elders from the three ayllus in Puquio told Arguedas in the 1950s that young community members would return from the coast after short stays and complain that they could not understand the older people, who "speak a language they no longer understand." Furthermore, they explained that younger members tried to exclude the elders from community assemblies and withdraw their right to irrigation water (Arguedas 2002: 153).

Although the elders in Casta appear to have been able to assert their power to a certain extent, it is likely that they and the senior authorities were under some degree of pressure to "modernize" the modes of communication that were central to community organization: the beginning of the Entablo tells us that some functionaries who did not fulfill their obligations claimed that

---

the cliffs. The bubbles in the seafoam from these sites are said to be filled with air that can "mobilize" Casta's springs. The mixing of the two distinct waters is said to produce clouds that generate rainfall.

64. A *canterito*, which he described as a concave stone taken from the base of the waterfall, is placed in a recess at the top of Cumau Waterfall year-round so that during the *champería* the functionaries can fill it with chicha beer. Other collaborators explained that the Cumau customs also involve divining the coming year's rainfall using coca leaves.

"without there being a written record" they had diminished responsibility ("no haber constancia y menos fuerza de ley") (CCSPC 1921: f. 2r).

A Life Force: The Music and Water Songs of the *Champería*

Music is a key structural element of Andean ritual (Romero 2001; Stobart 2001). As Stobart (2001: 96) shows, music in Andean rituals influences the atmospheric conditions by generating a rhythmic force and melodies and by the strict structuring of harmony. The influence of music on the atmosphere of the *champería* is demonstrated very clearly in the Entablo. Like other elements of the *champería*, the ritual soundscape is structured along dual lines (as explored later). In the same way that the khipu-board *padrones* are carried out at specific sites at specific times (Hyland, Bennison, and Hyland 2021), the varying forms of *champería* music must be played or sung at specific sites at the relevant points in the work parties' movement along the canals.

The sounds generated during the ritual are functional and are produced with the understanding that they play a key role in generating the conditions for claiming rights to water from the ancestors (Bennison 2019). As a collaborator in San Damián told me, members of the Concha group celebrate and dance to music during their annual lake ritual because "eso es lo que ellos quieren" (that is what they [the ancestors] want). As Gelles (2000b: 200) points out, *hualinas* "are dedicated to sources of water and to the ancestor heroes who built the canals and reservoirs." The strict regulation of the *champería* music and its specific social location at ancestral sites like the canals reveal its socioeconomic function. For example, the instructions for Wednesday read:

> Despues de pocos momentos bajan a la acequia a hacer una ceremonia secreta en la Paccha o Chorro y despues [torn]—partó los funcionarios soñando un cuhete hasta el lugar [torn] "Cumau" a donde continúa una ceremonia secreta y sus [torn] un cuhete esto es al pie de chorro grande de "Cumau" al mismo tiempo parte por la misma acequia hasta el lugar de "Huancaquirma" llegando al lugar salen los funcionarios a entrevistarse y saludar a la parada de "Cumau" con sus entonaciones correctas como son hualinas tono de Chirimías que cantan al son de los cascabeles.[65]

---

65. The *chirimía* or *chirisuya* is an oboe of Arab origin, brought to Peru and other Andean countries in the colonial era (Robles Mendoza and Flores Yon 2016). The condor is con-

FIGURE 1.15. *The* cura *(traditional healer and ritual specialist) Jorge Salinas Obispo plays the* chirimía *in the office of the* gobernador *(governor) at the 2022* champería.

After a short moment, they go down to the canal to do a secret ceremony in the Paccha or Waterfall and afterward [torn] the functionaries ... sounding off a flare until the site of [torn] "Cumau," where the secret ceremony continues and their [torn] ... a flare. This is at the foot of the big waterfall at "Cumau." At the same time, they set off along the same canal until they reach "Huancaquirma." When they arrive at the site, the functionaries come out to meet with and greet the "Cumau" *parada* with [them playing] the correct kinds of tunes such as *hualinas* [and] the tune of *chirimías* and they sing to the sound of the bells. (CCSPC 1921: ff. 9v–10r)

Clearly, *chirimía* and *hualina* songs are associated with flowing water and in the *champería* capture the "correct" mood for the fast-flowing waters of Cumau or perhaps the mood from the waterfall itself.[66] Villar Córdova

---

sidered to be a sacred bird in Andean society, so the insertion of the condor feather reed in the Andean oboe "indigenized" the Arabian oboe when introduced to the Andes in the colonial era (Hyland, Bennison, and Hyland 2021; Kuss 2004: 318; Robles Mendoza and Flores Yon 2016: 105).

66. In Casta it is said that unborn babies whose mothers hear a loud waterfall will make the same sounds as the waterfall when born (Haboud de Ortega 1980: 81).

FIGURE 1.16. *Cumau waterfall.*

(1935: 344) describes the oral narratives of Jicamarca, Huarochirí, where local residents hear rushing water at night, the sound of *chirimías* and the noise of the *hualina* (*walina*) water rituals at an abandoned canal.

On the Thursday, "encontrándose en este lugar o paraje los Michcos ejecutarán las chichas a los camachicos así como también las banderas y cajeras[67] de ambas paradas ésta exijencia será por los Michcos en voz alta y fuerte del lugar de 'Taquina'" (gathered together in this place or spot, the Michcos will carry out the chichas for the Camachicos and likewise also the flags and *cajeras* of both *paradas*. This requirement will be carried out by the Michcos out loud in a loud voice [befitting] the site of "Taquina") (CCSPC 1921: f. 11v).

The end of the *champería* is officially signaled on the final Monday of the festival, when elderly participants return from a sacred site:

> los viejos y viejas unos con la bandera y otras con la caja sevan hasta "Gotogoto" y de ahí regresan con las banderas desarmadas y las cajas destempladas y regresan al pueblo cada uno à sus huaironas o paradas

---

67. *Cajeras* are women drummers who play the *tinya* (a traditional leather and wood drum) for their *parada* while singing fast-tempo ritual songs called *kashwas*.

FIGURE 1.17. *Taquina (Singing Place).*

con una alegría muy distinta con lo que se dió término la presente memoria de nuestras costumbres.

The elderly men and women set off for "Gotogoto," returning from there with their flags lowered and their drums out of tune. They come back to the village, all going to their *huayronas* or *paradas* with a very different sense of cheer. This brings an end to this memory of our *costumbres*. (CCSPC 1921: f. 17v)

According to the Entablo, joyous, animated songs should be routinely paused whenever the functionaries decree solemn moments of silence and prayer. Dualism also characterizes the mood of the water songs sung alternately throughout the week: *hualinas* (*walinas* or *warinas*) and *yaravíes*. Although both songs are highly emotional and associated with the past, *hualinas* are a cheerful genre, while *yaravíes* tend to foreground themes of sadness such as heartbreak and loves lost. The term *yaravíes* is a hispanicization of the Quechua *arawi* or *harawi*, a genre of songs and poetry popular during the Inca era, when the songs "could be sacred or profane in function, joyous or profoundly sad in tone and historical or personal in content" (Butterworth 2014: 108). According to Mannheim (2015b: 227–228), these were songs about separation and absent loved ones. Tschudi (1847: 343), who heard Quechua *yaravíes* being sung in Peru in the 1830s, seems to have been struck by the beauty of the melancholic songs: "A foreigner, who for the first time hears one of these Yaravíes sung, even though he may not understand the Quichua words, is nevertheless deeply moved by the melody... no other music is at once so dismal and so tender."

Nevertheless, in the Entablo the *yaravíes* are associated with the joyous cheer of the *hualinas*, although the function of the *yaravíes* is distinct: they are sung throughout the *champería* when groups must reunite. In this respect, the *yaravíes* are sung to end a period of separation, to draw the distant party to gravitate toward the party in song. The use of sound to call absent loved ones to a certain point in time and space follows the logics of Inca-era water customs, where ritual crying was meant to attract the attention and guardianship of the ancestors (Bennison 2019). This Inca custom, *waqayllikuy*, persists in the Casta *champería*: on the Wednesday, participants must cry "¡huajay!" (Quechua *waqay*: "to weep" or "to wail") at the sites of Otagaca and Mashca (Mashka), where Wallallo (or Suqta Kuri?) is invoked. As Tello and Miranda (1923: 540) explain, the *mayoralas* would sing *arawis* when they could see work parties finishing their work and advancing, which are "answered" with the *walla-walla* or Wallallo song. Evidently, the singing of *arawis/yaravíes* functioned to reunite work parties and awaken Wallallo (or Suqta Kuri?), so children accompanied the singing of the *arawis* with cries of "¡waxay!" (*huajay*). It is likely that *hualinas* and *yaravíes* were sung in Quechua in the 1920s; in the 1980s, while the *hualinas* were composed and sung in Spanish, the *yaravíes* were still being sung in Quechua (Gelles 1984a).[68]

Andean water songs are in themselves mediative domains: Arnold and Yapita (1998: 48) describe the *huayno* genre of song associated with the rainy season as a liminal, intermediary domain between life and death. In the same way, *hualinas* are also associated with the ancestral past. The members of the four *parcialidades* mediate between the present and the deep past by singing annually adapted *hualina* lyrics conveying their appreciation for the water sources that sustained their ancestors who maintained the reservoirs and canals for future generations. Perhaps because local music genres are associated with the lived landscape and the past, they are assigned a moral value that nonlocal music forms are not.

During my doctoral fieldwork in San Damián, elderly collaborators lamented the loss of respect for community elders and declining commitment

---

68. In the 1990s, songs called *kashwas* blended Quechua and Spanish lyrics (Ráez Retamozo 2001b: 6). In 2022, the *kashwa* "Michikuykunki Tayta" mixed Quechua and Spanish lyrics.

to *costumbre*. They identified the introduction of *bailes sociales* (social dances) organized and attended by young people in the mid-twentieth century as a key factor in the breakdown of community cohesion. These events were enabled by road construction, when large brass instruments for playing *cumbia* music—then popular on the coast—could be transported to the village on trucks. Brass bands play at *champerías* in San Damián today, navigating steep mountain verges with their instruments on their backs to set up at reservoirs and beside water sources.

When I attended the canal cleaning at the Ayshipa canal and reservoir of the Concha group, a participant approached me to make sure I noted that the brass band set up beside the reservoir did not technically belong in the *champería*, according to tradition. He regarded the brass band as a corruption of a tradition he described as "una herencia" (a heritage). Musical innovation was not permitted in Casta to the same degree as in other villages throughout the twentieth century. Fernández (2003: 138) notes that *hualinas* in the 1990s were accompanied only by the *chirisuya* and *tinya* drum and/or bells (cascabeles). This is also true today.

The Cosmopolitics of Consumption

Drinking chicha (maize beer) is an integral aspect of Andean irrigation customs. Chicha production is dependent on adequate access to water, because maize cultivation requires substantial irrigation during early growth (Mayer 1989: 45). As Williams et al. (2019: 2) explain, in pre-Hispanic rituals: "The practice of drinking *chicha* invoked the flow of mountain water and represented the shared desire to exert supernatural control over the most precious resource—water." Furthermore, chicha drinking is understood to have encouraged social and political cohesion not just between deities and the groups that honored them but also among different social groups (Williams et al. 2019). This was also the case in early twentieth-century Huarochirí, where residents brewed drinks containing local produce from both the highlands and the low-valley wine-producing regions of Carapongos and Lunahuaná.[69]

The Entablo reveals the extent to which alcohol consumption was regulated during the *champería*. On the Wednesday, participants should consume "un pequeño almuerzo que contiene de diferentes clases de comidas incaicas" (a little lunch that contains different kinds of Inca foods) (CCSPC 1921:

---

69. I was told that the practice of transporting large quantities of Lunahuaná wine to Casta ceased around forty years ago.

INTRODUCTION   69

f. 9v).⁷⁰ The functionaries would need to draw on their networks in order to provide the specified food and drink obligations, which places pressure on the households of the authorities. Salas Carreño (2018: 207–208) explores excessive communal commensality in Andean rituals and festivities:

> it also constitutes a powerful embodied experience of celebrating the community as a group of related people who feed and care for each other, and who collectively are able to satisfy all their members fully, and even to excess. These events of communal commensality are overstatements of what regularly, and in a more partial way, happens in everyday life via the different networks of cooperation at work within the local community.

Chicha is a key element in the promotion of good cheer throughout the *champería*. Numerous ethnographies of the Andes have pointed out that women, who are responsible for chicha production, submit an expected number of jugs (Isbell 1978: 171). It was important to have an abundance of chicha for public gatherings in pre-Hispanic Huarochirí, so the *cántaros* (pitchers) for storing the chicha needed to be sized accordingly, with generous proportions.

Chapter 5 of the Huarochirí Manuscript tells of a poor man called Huatya Curi who entered a drinking contest with a powerful lord named Tamta Ñamca. When it was Huatya Curi's turn to dole out the chicha, he was ridiculed for the size of his pitcher: people asked, "How could he possibly fill so many people from such a tiny jar?" (Salomon and Urioste 1991: 58). Chapter 7 of the Huarochirí Manuscript describes how members of the Cupara ayllu honor the huaca called Chuqui Suso during their annual canal-cleaning ritual. The manuscript recounts how they drink an abundance of beer in her honor, dancing and addressing her as their mother. A section of this chapter entitled "How Those Cupara People Revere the One Called Chuqui Suso Even to This Day" reads:

> All the Cupara people, as we know, make up a single *ayllu* called Cupara.
>
> These people now live in San Lorenzo, where they remain forcibly relocated right up to now. There is within this *ayllu* a patrilineage that bears the name Chauincho.

---

70. Today, the consumption of Inca-themed goods includes cigarettes; any brought to the ritual must be "Inca" brand.

Chuqui Suso was <crossed out:> [a woman of] a member of the Chauincho *ayllu*.

In the old days, in the month of May when the canal had to be cleaned (as is done today, too), all these people went to the woman Chuqui Suso's dwelling; they went with their maize beer, *ticti*, guinea pigs, and llamas to worship that demon woman.[71]

In worshiping her, they built a *quishuar* enclosure and stayed inside it for five days without ever letting people walk outside.

It's said that when they finished that, and accomplished everything else including their canal-cleaning, the people came home dancing and singing. They'd lead one woman along in their midst, reverencing her as they did the huaca and saying,

"This is Chuqui Suso!"

As this woman arrived at their village, we'd see some people awaiting her, laying out maize beer and other things and greeting her:

"This is Chuqui Suso!"

On that occasion they say people celebrated a major festival, dancing and drinking all night long.

In fact that's why, when the late lord Don Sebastián was still alive, during Corpus Christi and the other major Christian holy days, a woman used to proclaim,

"I am Chuqui Suso!"

And give maize beer from a large gold or silver jar with a large gourd to everyone in rank order, saying,

---

71. Many *champerías* today still take place in May, ahead of the long dry season. The scheduling of Casta's *champería* in October may be indicative of historical compliance with the Inca calendar in Casta: October was the month for water worship in the Inca era (Bennison 2019; Guaman Poma de Ayala 1615/1616).

"This is our mother's beer." (Salomon and Urioste 1991: 64–65).

In a related vein, the Entablo mentions that a specific *padrón* was used to record the submissions of chicha during the *champería*: the Padrón de los Veinte Cántaros (Padrón of the Twenty Pitchers). Using this device, the pitchers were collected from each *parada*, with a total of twenty being submitted. The following numerical breakdown was used on Wednesday to specify the minimum number of pitchers that each *parada* was obliged to submit, in the following order:

6: Carhuayumac
6: Cumau
4: Yanapaccha
4: Ocshayco (also known as Ocusha)

This section of the Entablo apparently replicates information recorded on the Padrón de los Veinte Cántaros, given that the Wednesday section mentions these specific figures as well as the following instructions, which indicates that readers could cross-reference the instructions with the *padrones* themselves:

> Despues de la invitación resarà una oración y en seguida ordenará el Sr. Campo las mesas o banquetes que se encuentra servido terminado estos actos los cuatro Michcos llaman a la colecta de los veinte cántaros o mas que han distribuydo en la mañana y entrega a los camachicos los que han llevado en seguida del padrón el Sr. Rejedor en precencia de los camachicos una vez terminado recoje sus cántaros las Srs. mujeres de Yacapar segun como llaman sus padrones.

> After these [food offerings] are given out, they will recite a prayer and promptly after the Campo will call for the tables or banquets to be served. Once these deeds are finished, the four Michcos call for the twenty pitchers or more that were distributed in the morning and that they have been carrying to be handed back in to the Camachicos. Promptly after the *padrón*, the Regidor, in the presence of the Camachicos, collects their pitchers from the married Yacapar women according to how the *padrones* dictate that this be done. (CCSPC 1921: f. 10v)

The dictation of the amounts of chicha necessary for the *champería* in the *padrones* underscores the importance of chicha consumption during

FIGURE 1.18. *The Yacapar* huayrona *(group premises). A mural by the entrance depicts an* añaz, *the Andean skunk associated with the high-altitude puna.*

irrigation rituals. These ritual logics account for the preferences of the ancestors: as Allen (2002: 33) explains, since the sacred ancestors are the ultimate sources of food, drink, and clothes, they "watch human consumption jealously and demand their part in it."

There are two groups or *parcialidades* in Casta, Yañac and Yacapar, each of which has its own *huayrona* (premises for meetings and events).[72] These groups were formerly known as ayllus. Yacapar is associated with the puna and its products: yucca, sweet potato, and fruits, whereas Yañac is associated with the coast and its flora and fauna: foxes, the Andean skunk, garlics, and medicinal herbs (Llanos and Osterling 1982: 118). Yacapar may represent a former *llacuaz* group, whereas Yañac may represent a former *huari* ethnic group. Yañac and Yacapar have been Casta's only ayllus since 1752, when San Pedro de Casta had only Yacapar and Yañac listed as ayllus in the *visita* (colonial inspection) accounts. They had five ayllus listed for the *visita* in 1725: Yacapar, Yanac (Yañac), Binquiguamo, Allauca, and Guallacocha (Gentille Lafaille 1977: 88).

---

72. Echeandia Valladares (1981: 26), who carried out fieldwork in Casta in the 1970s, records alternative *parcialidad* names: "Yañica" and "Yacapara."

Casta has four kin groups, which regroup within the context of the *champería* to assemble as work parties known as *paradas* (Fernández 2003: 136). These groups are activated only for the *champería*. Each is led by a special *mayordomo* known as a *michco* or *varayoc* (*varayuq*/*varayoq*). The *parada* groups appear to be subdivisions or moieties of the Yañac and Yacapar *parcialidades*. According to Gushiken (1972: 151), the two *parcialidades* in neighboring Santiago de Carampoma were historically further subdivided into "small ayllus."

During the assigning of work groups on the Sunday night by using maize kernels (the *conteo* or *graneo*, described on f. 7v of the Entablo), the kernels representing individuals are divided into the two *parcialidades* before being divided once again into the four *paradas* (Echeandia Valladares 1981: 16).[73] The Entablo also explains that the women are divided according to their "*parcialidad* or *cofradía*" (*parcialidad*, or religious confraternity). The fact that these terms are used synonymously suggests that these two institutions at some point may have shared or merged their account-keeping practices and/or records.[74]

The four *paradas* in Casta are Carhuayumac (Carguayumac), Cumau, Yanapaccha, and Ucusha (also referred to in the Entablo as Ocshayco, Ocusha, and Ucucha).[75] Each *parada* is responsible for cleaning its respective reservoir: Laclán, Chuswa, Hualhual, and Pampacocha (Fernández 2003: 136). Collaborators explained their sense of belonging to their respective *parada*. As the current *yachak* (highly regarded ritual expert; the Quechua term *yachaq* means "knower"), Doña Catalina Olivares, told me, people resist if the authorities attempt to assign them to a *parada* other than their own.

---

73. This "count" is discussed further in Hyland, Bennison, and Hyland 2021. The 1995 ethnographic documentary *La Fiesta del Agua* by Ráez Retamozo illustrates this procedure: http://videos.pucp.edu.pe/videos/ver/cac4468752bbf59317df9b013e866320.

74. As Soler (1958: 171–172) describes in his ethnography of the Huarochirí village of San Pedro de Huancaire, local ayllus were developed into *cofradías* during the early colonial era. Although the ayllus became known as *parcialidades* (sectors or portions) in the eighteenth century, the term "ayllu" was still in use in the 1950s (Soler 1958: 171). The repackaging of ayllus into *cofradías* would have facilitated the persistence of ritual adoration of huacas and ayllu-focused traditions under a veil of Christianization.

When might the *cofradía*-based organization and regulation of sacred events have ended? In Huayopampa in the Chancay valley (Lima), community authorities were regulated by the members of the *cofradía* Adoradores del Niño Jesús until the 1920s. A seminary was then set up by the archbishop of Lima to form a new generation of community authorities (Whyte 1969: 167). Further research on the *cofradías* in Casta may shed light on the antecedent regulations for community rituals and illuminate the extent to which the *cofradías* regulated ayllu law.

75. Cumau is also known as Cumaupaccha or "Comaopaccha" (Fernández 2003: 136).

When I showed her the illustration of the Casta khipu board (the Padrón de Huallque) in Tello and Miranda (1923), she explained that today individuals are assigned to a *parada* on Sunday, with the *paradas* announced during the *champería* on Tuesday:

> "¡Pasen a la cuenta todos los comuneros!" ... Sale Carhuayumac, Cumaopachha, Yanapacha y Hualhualcocha. Eso está en el padrón. [imitates shouting] "Tal fulano, le toca tal parada. El otro, tal fulano se va a Carhuayumac. ¡El otro se va a Hualhualcocha!" "¡No!" dice, "¡yo estoy tronco Carhuayumac!" [laughs]. Es éste. Está divido ya allí pue[s].

> "All the *comuneros* come to the account!" ... They come out [as] Carhuayumac, Cumaopachha, Yanapacha, and Hualhualcocha. That's in the *padrón* [imitates shouting] "That guy, he's in such a *parada*. The other guy is going to Carhuayumac. The other is going to Hualhualcocha!" "No!" he says, "I'm Carhuayumac to the core!" [laughs]. It's this! It's divided up there.

The Entablo regulations for the Monday describe the Padrón General de los Asistentes a la Faena (General Padrón of the Work Party Attendees) at the site of Chuswa (Chushgua), where the *mayordomos* in charge of each *parada* charge each man a fee of 1 *sol* and each woman 50 cents.[76] The regulations for the Tuesday describe the use of the Padrón General de los Asistentes al Trabajo (General Padrón of the Work Attendees), which is likely the same *padrón*.

The *paradas* function within a hierarchy of lineages: Carhuayumac and Cumau (Comaopaccha) are described as the most ancient "mother" *paradas*, while Hualhualcocha (also known as Ochaico, Ucusha, and Ocusha) and Yanapaccha are the "daughter" *paradas* (Echeandia Valladares 1981: 165–166). This hierarchy is reflected in the Entablo in the order in which the *paradas* are listed as well as in the specified quantities of chicha to be submitted by the respective *paradas* on the Wednesday: six pitchers or more based on the amount due from Carhuayumac, six pitchers or more for Cumau, four pitchers or more for Yanapaccha, and four pitchers or more for "Ocshayco or Ocusha" (f. 9r). Competition among these work groups drives the labor: the four *paradas* represent teams, whose members and functionaries compete for

---

76. Gelles (2000b: 199) glosses *faena*: "communal work service; a kind of labor tax required of community members." At certain points during the *champería*, the "mother and daughter" work groups reunite (Echeandia Valladares 1981: 166).

prestige in a dramatic, dangerous, and high-speed horse race that generates billowing dust clouds along the pathway parallel to the canal trajectory on the Wednesday.[77]

A collaborator in Casta explained that the night before the horse race functionaries from each *parada* enter a running race along the canal, to predict which team will be more successful in bringing water through the canal. Each team has its own color: green for Carhuayumac, yellow for Cumau, white for Ucusha (also known as Hualhualcocha), and red for Yanapaccha.

It is unclear whether *parada*-level records are based on the performance of individuals throughout the *faena* work. It appears that the recording of obligations on the *padrones* is always done in public and predominantly when all groups are together, such as in the case of the "general *padrones*." I observed in 2022 that there are moments when different *padrones* are (more or less) simultaneously being carried out for different work groups; the elders had their "Huallqui *padrón*" at Atagaca (Otagaca) on the Monday around the same time the general work party had theirs nearby below at Huanca Acequia. Nevertheless, I was unable to observe the proceedings from the Wednesday, when the *parada* work teams fully "activate."[78] Given the competitive nature of the *parada* system, it is logical that records would be made when all groups are united, in order to incentivize productivity and compliance throughout the work. This appears to be the case for the general padrones (for men and women, respectively) described in the Entablo.

Salomon (2004: 5) describes the way in which Tupicocha's khipus represent friendly inter-ayllu rivalry. Tupicochanos refer to their khipus as *equipos* (which he translates into English as "teams"). As I explained earlier, Casteña Catalina Olivares likewise referred to a khipu from Casta that she was shown as a child as an *equipo*. While the *paradas* of the Casta *champería*, like Tupicocha's ayllus, are "teams" engaging in competition, the Spanish word *equipo* has connotations relevant for khipus: it could also refer to the gathering of tribute or material obligations.[79] The verb *equipar* (to equip) conveys the sense of furnishing the equipment necessary for a specified task. In this sense, my interpretation of the pun of referring to khipus as *equipos* differs slightly from that of Salomon (2004: 5), for whom Tupicocha's ayllus

---

77. The climactic horse race is still performed today.
78. Although the *paradas* activate on the Wednesday, *champería* participants don a neckerchief in the color of their team on the preceding days. I was generously gifted a white neckerchief by Catalina's family, so that I could be assigned to Hualhualcocha, which new participants without existing familial or marital ties in Casta are expected to join.
79. I am indebted to the anonymous reviewer who suggested that I give greater consideration to the interpretation of *equipos* in its Tupicocha usage.

represent *equipos* (teams), in that they "furnish a team in the complex array of crews who, in friendly rivalry, do the village's basic infrastructural work."

Casta's Irrigation System

Casta's water sources are fed by three springs. The most important of these is Cunya spring, which is said never to dry out. Described as "la mama" (the mother) by Casteños, it is the source of life itself: "Cunya nos da la vida" (Cunya gives us life). The spring's crystalline waters feed into Carhuayumac, Casta's matrix or "mother" canal (Gelles 1984b).

The following summary of Casta's irrigation system is adapted from the highly detailed description of Casta's irrigation system by Tello and Miranda (1923: 523–525). It charts the key landmarks of the *champería*, supplementing the toponyms provided with their corresponding spelling(s) in the Entablo.

Casta's principal canal is Carhuayumac, used since the pre-Hispanic era. The Carhuayumac canal is fed at the Carhuayumac River intake by waters from the following springs: Cunya, Bitama, and Saywa. The canal runs almost horizontally, crossing the Pitic Gorge. It enters the gorge before reaching the Chakian branch, which comes off Marcahuasi (a rocky plateau southeast of Casta, today a popular tourist site). From there the canal enters the gorge that separates this section from the Mashca (Mascha) branch. It descends from its highest part, crossing the recess at Chuswa (Chusgua) before reaching the principal branch of Kishka K'umo. There it breaks off into different branches that channel the water to Casta's most far-flung lands.

At the bottom of Pitiki Gorge, seven kilometers from the canal intake, is the Olacocha reservoir (called a "lake" in the Entablo). At the center of this section, on the outermost edge of Kuri Pata Hill, is Cumau (also Comao, Cumao) Waterfall, which stands around twenty meters tall. Two kilometers along from this waterfall, the canal runs into Huanaquirma Waterfall. This waterfall has three sections formed by rock platforms situated at different heights. At the tract of canal between Huanaquirma Waterfall and Cumau, the ancient settlement of Soculún sits a short distance above the canal. Between Huanaquirma and Olacocha, the Ocshayco and Huanca-Shilca (Wanka Ilka) clearings sit a short distance above the canal. Huanca-Shilca is located at the start of the dip. Ocshayco (Okshaiko) is in the deepest section, which is a continuation of the Pitic Gorge.

Once it traverses this recess, the canal reaches the Chakian offshoot, which descends from Marcahuasi. Above this offshoot are clearings at Laco

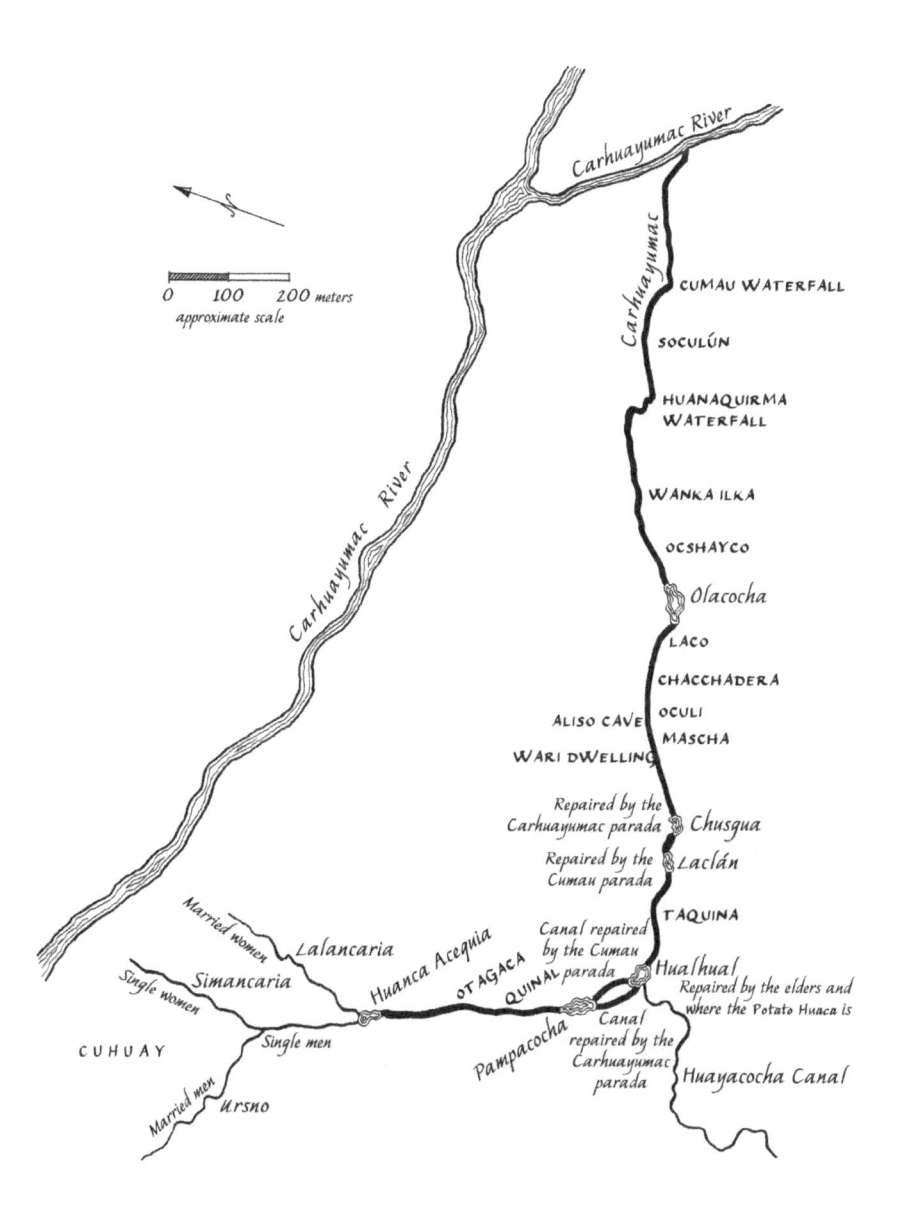

MAP 1.1. *Canal system in San Pedro de Casta in the 1920s. Map created by Molly O'Halloran, based on Tello and Miranda (1923: 524).*

and Chacchadera.[80] From Chacchadera it enters another recess between the branches at Chakian and Mashca (Mascha). From there it ascends toward Mashca, where there is another ancient settlement containing mortuary structures. Oculi is located at the lowest part of the ravine and Mascha at its highest part, which is six kilometers from Olacocha.

From Mashca, the canal traverses a large recess where it supplies water to the nearby lands as it descends. It reaches the hill at the Kishka K'umo branch then continues for a short distance. At the highest part of the canal is Pokle "Lake" (reservoir), around three kilometers from Mashca. At the lower section are the Chushwa (Chusgua) and Laclán "lakes" or reservoirs, located around two hundred meters apart.

Three different canal branches descend from the Pokle reservoir: first, Waya Kocha, which irrigates the lands toward the southeast section of Kishka K'umo Hill. Then two smaller canals, which channel the water a hundred meters away from Pokle reservoir to the one at Pampacocha. The canal continues from there toward Quinual, some four hundred meters from Pampacocha. It then changes direction approaching Huanca-Acequia, splitting off into two branches, Lalancaria and Mulupu. The Lalancaria canal irrigates the lands on the northern section of the hill, and the second continues toward Casta before splitting off into two branches, Simancaria and Urno (Ursno, Uhsno), not far from Cuhuay (Coguay, Cohuay). Simancaria passes through the northern side of the village, irrigating the lands located toward that side, and the Urno irrigates the lands below Mulupu.

The Organization of Work during the *Champería*

Much of the *champería* labor involves the ritual work of engineering proximity to the ancestors who are said to own and control the canals. Certain actions must be performed at certain sacred sites. Songs are sung at Taquina (Singing Place), and announcements must be loud. A special ritual word in Quechua is shouted at Mashca (Lookout) to invoke the attention and pity of Wallallo, to beg him for water, while everyone awaits signs of his "reply" (Bennison 2019). In early eighteenth-century Carampoma, not far from Casta, a ritual specialist who organized ritual wailing ceremonies to beg for rain was called the *masqayoq* (from the Quechua *masqay* or *maskay*: "to seek

---

80. "Chacchana" means "coca-chewing site" in Quechua. The toponym used throughout the Entablo is the hispanicized form "Chacchadera." It was presumably known by both terms in the 1920s.

FIGURE 1.19. *The elders clean the road on Monday morning to clear the way for Wednesday's horse race at the 2022* champería.

or search for"; Spalding 1984: 264). A secret delegation of functionaries keeps watch at Mashca on the Sunday prior to the start of work, waiting for signs of Wallallo's presence and willingness to cooperate (Tello and Miranda 1923).

Before the waters are released along the freshly cleaned canals, Casteños need to engineer the conditions that will allow the water to be released. They must draw various ancestors to the respective sites that they "own": where—and when—their presence and full attentions are needed. This ritual work is not always placatory. At times, it involves provocation: flares used at *costumbre* sites serve the purpose of rupturing the ancestors therein, so they can be tapped into and, once receptive to the needs of their descendants, convinced to release their waters.

The Entablo's regulations set out how the irrigation system maintenance work was structured in time and space. The *champería* was a marathon-like test of endurance. Although the labor was carried out in a spirit of jolly confraternity, it was arduous, with no time for slacking. Workers took breaks at the designated locations only after they had made timely and sufficient progress. They were obliged to maintain a speedy walking pace from site to site, covering a considerable distance on foot in the space of a week. Coca

FIGURE 1.20. *The functionaries of the 1979* champería *chew coca leaves during the Saturday proceedings at the ceremonial site of Cuhuay.* © *Julio Erhart, courtesy of Julio Erhart.*

leaf—a highly valued stimulant—was distributed regularly throughout the *champería*, helping everyone to get through the work.

The map of Casta's irrigation system in the 1920s (Tello and Miranda 1923: see map 1.1) illustrates the division of work in spatial terms. On the Monday and Tuesday, the first two *faena* (communal labor) days of the *champería*, the cleaning work began on the canal branches closest to Casta. The workers were grouped according to gender and social status. Each of the four groups was assigned a *mayordomo* (steward or auxiliary) to lead the laborers to their corresponding site and guide the work.

The labor for these days was structured in the following way:

Ursno—married men
Wanka-Acequia to Simancaria—single men
Simancaria—single women
Lalancaria—married women

Beginning on the Wednesday, the *mayordomos* adopted the title and identity of *michcos*, special traditional authorities whose role came into play with the formation of the four work groups known as *paradas* on the same day. After being elected on the Monday, the *michcos* pledged their allegiance to the ancestors (Tello and Miranda 1923: 535). According to Gelles (1984b: 313), these authorities have an intimate association with water and fulfill important roles throughout the year, beyond the *champería*. It is therefore significant that they take up their duties on the days when the water must start to flow.

The preparations for "receiving" the water began on the Wednesday. The functionaries carried out a series of ritual ceremonies at various key sites along the canal, while the *michcos* led the grimy and sweaty work of cleaning out mud from the reservoirs—referred to throughout the Entablo as "lakes." Wednesday's work consisted of cleaning of the four "lakes" closest to Casta and cleaning and repair work on the surrounding canals. While the functionaries were responsible for the proper enactment of the Wednesday sacred rituals, responsibility for overseeing the labor and driving the water forward through the freshly cleared irrigation system fell on the *michcos*. The work was structured in the following way:

Cuswa (Chusgua) Lake—Karwayuma [Carguayumac] *parada* (also spelled Carhuayumac)
Laklan (Laclán) Lake—Komao (Cumau) *parada* (also known as Cumaopaccha)
Hualhual Lake—Ocshayco/Ocusha/Ucusha *parada* (also known as Hualhualcocha)
Pampacocha Lake—Yanapaccha *parada* (also spelled Yanapacha)

A horse race on the Wednesday brought an end to the day's activities.

On the Thursday, the waters were released from the high intakes and channeled through the canals. The *michcos*, accompanied by their respective *paradas*, successively "pass" the water along the canal system, so that each of the reservoirs is filled in turn. Friday and Saturday were devoted to the moral accounting ceremonies of the community members. First, the public ceremonial punishments of the functionaries were carried out. Then the performance scores of all the workers were registered on the khipu-board accounts. These were reviewed by the council of *mayores* (elders), who issued instructions on the appropriate punishments, relative to the crime or moral failing committed.

Notes on the Transcription and Translation of the Entablo into English

Transcription
The Entablo forms part of a living archive, so its condition has deteriorated over a century of use as an object of study. The navy leather surfaces on the front and back covers bear the traces of multiple layers of tape used to

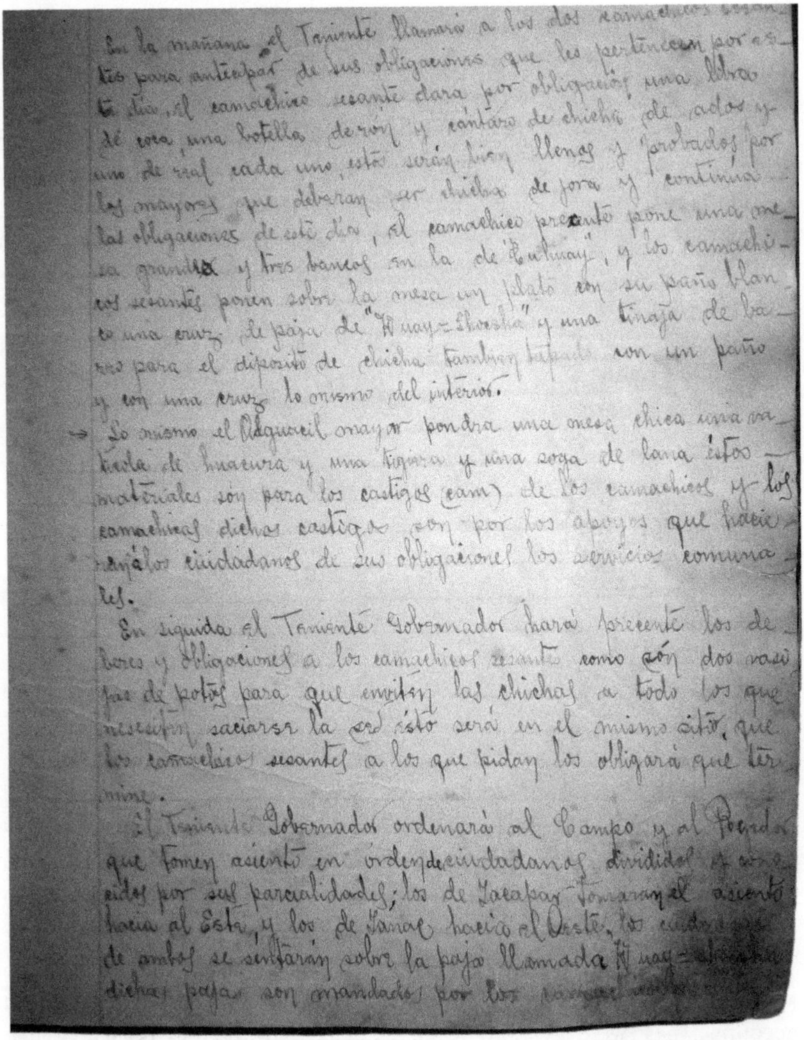

FIGURE 1.21. *The well-thumbed pages of the manuscript after a century of use.*

compensate for a spine that deteriorated over the years. Some pages threaten to break away or crumble mid-page, while most of the 101 pages in the jotter have softened, fuzzy corners and edges. The bottom corners are darkened and well thumbed, and a number of them are split or torn. I indicate such instances in the inscription in square brackets. In sections where the ink has faded, some short sections are illegible. Most omissions of words in the transcription, however, correspond to the darkened sections where words run into a crumbled corner.

While the flowing handwriting of the various scribes can be read by some Casteños, others reported finding it illegible. I have likewise indicated instances where words are illegible or unclear in the transcription. My diplomatic transcription retains all perceivable features of the document, including nonstandard punctuation such as quotation marks on place names and periods in mid-sentence, the use of equals signs for hyphens, and so forth. The only exceptions are the pencil lines where readers have marked their progress in the margins while reading; these markings are not easily replicated.

The transcription includes marginal notes, because these illustrate the role of the text as an object of study and/or disagreement as well as containing a great amount of detail that the functionaries have evidently pored over closely each January.

Moreover, the original spellings have been maintained for political reasons and because they offer the opportunity to contribute to linguistic studies of Andean Spanish and interlanguage, particularly for vowel and consonant variation. The spelling is nonstandard throughout in terms of vowels and consonants. The letters "e" and "i" are often used interchangeably, as are "b" and "v" and "s" and "c." Where a functionary title is spelled (or capitalized) variably throughout the text, these alternative orthographies have been maintained. For example, "Regidor" is also spelled "Rejidor," "Rijidor," "Rejedor," and "Regedor" and "camachico" is also spelled "kamachico" and "cama chico." Grammatical idiosyncrasies that are characteristic of Andean Spanish and forms of interlanguage have been respected for the same reasons. Finally, because the Entablo forms part of a living archive that continues to be referenced, the transcription presented here reflects the manuscript as I observed it in 2018.

Translation

The manuscript is a set of regulations, so its content is prescriptive and sequential. For this reason, my translation into English seeks to maintain the authoritative and instructive tone of the original Spanish. To support reader comprehension and provide additional references for topics of interest, footnotes in the English translation offer further context. Because the functionary roles are tied to the landscape of Casta and its spiritual workings, the original Spanish and Quechua role titles have been maintained in the English translation. Translating these terms into English would suggest semantic equivalence when it would be difficult to translate some of the Indigenous terms concisely. Unlike the major functionary titles, the junior titles tend not to be capitalized in the manuscript, making the functionary hierarchy manifest in the written presentation of the regulations. My translation capitalizes all the functionary titles, however. Conversely, the names of some musical instruments and songs are inconsistently capitalized in the manuscript. I retain the original Spanish and Quechua terms in lowercase italics in the translation for consistency.

The functionaries are referred to throughout the manuscript, albeit inconsistently, with the respectful title prefix "Sr." (Mr. in English).[81] Similarly, the women participants are often referred to as "Sras. mujeres" (Madam women). These marks of respect do not tend to feature in written English, so they have been omitted in the translation. However, it is important to note that the junior functionaries (*alguaciles* and *camachicos*) are not given these marks of respect: their *cargos* are probationary, so they have not yet earned the status to merit such treatment.

The pronouns in the transcription do not always match the nouns in terms of number (plural or singular) and gender agreement. For this reason, it is sometimes difficult to comprehend who is doing what. In such instances, I have added alternative interpretations in the notes. Spanish sentences tend to be longer than English sentences, so the English translation sometimes breaks longer sentences into smaller ones.

The Structure of the Manuscript

- 1921: The main corpus of the text details the duties corresponding to the *champería*. An entry at the end of this section mentions that the 1921 regulations took three years to be approved. Therefore the undated signatures of the community members may have been added in 1924. The objection entered in pencil on f. 19v (presumably by "Notario SC") may have impeded the approval of the Entablo as official *constancia*.

---

81. This is reflective of the depth of mutual respect between individuals and between people and the animate landscape in Andean rituals. In her research on the rituals of herders from Chillihuani, Peru, Bolin (1998: xv) observes that "without respect, no society, no civilization, can flourish for long. Without respect, humanity is doomed and so is the earth, sustainer of all life." From this perspective, the care and commitment to upholding interpersonal respect in the Entablo can be understood as part of a cultural framework wherein respect is conducive to production. Fernández Osco (2000: xxix) has noted the use of titles as marks of respect in addressing ritual functionaries, which he takes to be indicative of ethical-moral norms in Bolivian ayllus. Soler (1958: 216–217) notes the use of the title "señor" in the 1950s, followed by a person's job title or authority role, as a mark of respect in the Huarochirí village of San Pedro de Huancaire and its use in all written documents, often out of courtesy.

- 1939: Reform of the regulations following the creation of the Ministerio de Salud Pública, Trabajo y Previsión Social (Ministry for Public Health, Work, and Social Security), responsible for Indigenous affairs. The 1939 reformation demonstrates the impact that national-level legislation had on community life and specifically on functionary obligations. The New Year and Carnival duties and obligations are added, based on a unanimous decision to add the secondary duties of the functionaries whose respective duties for the October traditions are detailed in the existing entries. These regulations may have been transferred from another set of regulations corresponding to New Year and Carnival Season.

- 1947: The regulations are reformed again to include the obligations of the *alguaciles menores* for the costumbres in October and at Carnival in February. Regulations are also entered for the road-cleaning work to take place in December and the *costumbres* and *visita* inspections taking place in January in the nearby hamlets in the district of Casta. Both reforms are entered in January following the New Year *huayrona*, the annual accounts ceremony.

- 1952: The final entry in the main body of the Entablo manuscript is added in January 1952 by Gabino Obispo and Juan Obispo, who were presidents at the time of writing. The addendum details the New Year traditions and includes an inventory of ritual items. These include a number of stones, with one representing the Sami Dios (Sami God), a fortune deity who was consulted to divine rain conditions in the coming year at the sacred progenitor stone Purpito Mama during the *pirwa* ritual.

- Undated (February 1921?): A sheet attached to the Entablo is used to record matters relating to community accounting in February. A piece of plain paper taped to the back of the booklet features an accounting chart to determine the fees to be paid in February for animal grazing. Analysis of the handwriting suggests that this entry was penned during the early life of the manuscript: it matches the handwriting of the 1921 section. This entry, like all entries in the manuscript, was probably written by the community secretary in office at the time of writing.

  The grid features nineteen names (both men and women), and table sections record which kind of animals each person owned and how many, calculating the total monetary value owed to the community coffer per animal owner. It is unclear whether the community also kept khipu records of such data at the likely time of writing in 1921 or whether individuals used khipus to keep track of their livestock. Tschudi (1847: 344), who observed herding khipus being maintained by shepherds in the high puna during his expedition to Peru between 1839 and 1842, writes: "On the first branch of string they usually placed the numbers of the bulls; on the second, that of the cows; the latter being classed into those which were milked, and those which were not milked; on the next string were numbered the calves, according to their ages and sizes. Then came the sheep, in several subdivisions." There are various accounts of twentieth-century herding khipus, where tallies recorded by individuals were then entered onto a group-level record (Mackey 2002; Soto Flores 1950).[82] Salomon (2004: 218) was told by a collaborator in Tupicocha that its ayllus historically kept track of livestock and other property by using khipus.

The page featuring the livestock data also has an accountancy note apparently made in the 1930s describing community expenses for different *faena* events in February. The handwriting matches that of the 1939 scribe. This sheet may have been attached to the Entablo in the early 1990s; a signature by the 1990–1993 community secretary Jesús Salinas Rojas is featured on the page, suggesting that he may be responsible for attaching it. In summary, the data recorded on this page are the kind of information also likely to have been recorded on khipus either at the time of writing or in the past. Thus it is fitting that the page has been appended to the Entablo.

- 1990–1993: The last dated entry was made in 2018 beneath the accounting chart by the community secretary Jesús Salinas Rojas, who signed his name in blue ballpoint pen: "Secretario de 1990–1993 Jesús Salinas Rojas." He may have attached this record to the Entablo during that period.

The manuscript features countless notes and traces of readership, including:

- "Tick" marks.
- Multiple sections marked "ojo" ("NB" in English), where readers over the last century have highlighted sections of importance.

---

82. For a detailed description of the herding khipus used in Laramarca in the mid-twentieth century, see Soto Flores (1950).

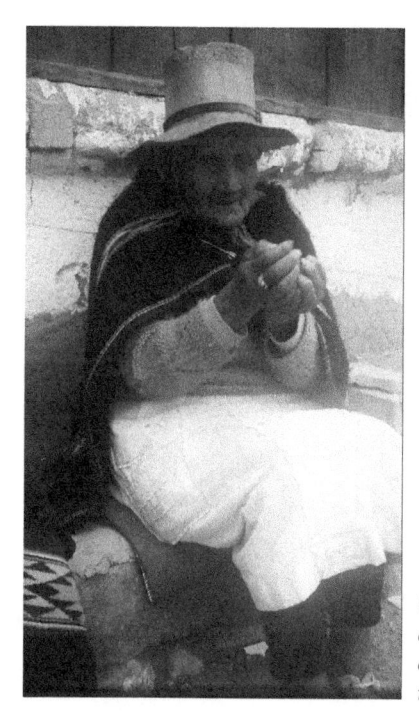

FIGURE 1.22. *Nemesio Bautista's granddaughter, Doña Luzmila Salinas Bautista, demonstrating how a sacred stone inventoried in the Entablo is held.*

- Pencil marks, where readers have guided their progress through the pages with a pencil in their hand.
- Folios 51–52 of the Entablo have been torn out, leaving slim shreds of the pages at the spine.
- Evidence of account stock-taking, with inventory notes appearing within the book. On folio 30v, in the section beginning in 1952 (written in blue ink), a note written with a darker blue ballpoint pen has been entered in the top margin: "27 hojas en libro del Entablo" (27 pages in the book of the Entablo). This note shows that the content of the Entablo was being monitored over time: even this text, designed to set out ritual measurements, was itself subject to being measured and revised according to the stringent monitoring logic that it sets down as imperative within its core content.[83]

---

83. Likewise, community authorities in Tupicocha annually take stock of their account books (Salomon and Niño-Murcia 2011).

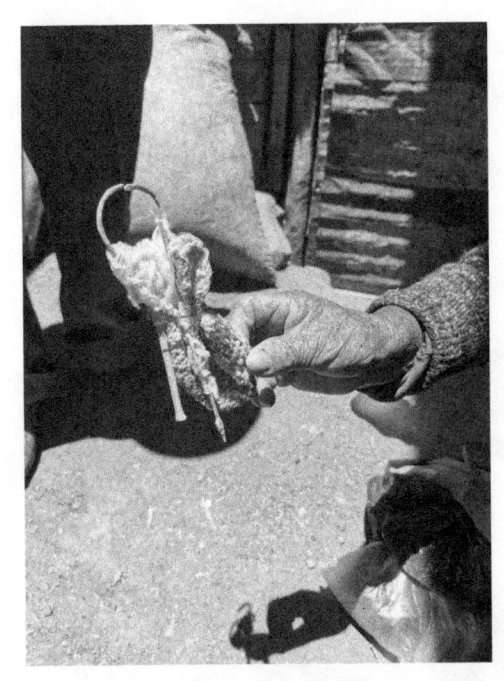

FIGURE 1.23. *Catalina's* puchka *and* shicra: *items used by women in the January rainmaking rituals.*

The Entablo is an exciting source for the study of Andean society and religion, providing rarely offered insights into a community's water customs from an inside perspective. The manuscript is important not only because it contains knowledge about the ritual use of khipu devices in relatively recent history but also because the descendants of those who created it and have studied its contents deem it so. A hundred years after the 1921 version of the agreement was set down, the book is regarded by locals today as an account of the community's inception. These ritual regulations help us to understand why Casta's *champería* has maintained such a notable status, attracting many scholars over the last century.

As a founding constitution for the community, the pages of the Entablo allow for a deeper understanding of the ways in which the fundamental principles of Casta's economic, philosophical, and political outlook are all expressed and performed through the axis of water ritual. Of all the work written about the *champería* in Casta over the last century, the words of the ritual experts provide us with a unique viewpoint, allowing us to reenvisage this well-documented Andean ritual and perhaps also to reenvision our understandings of ancestral ritual and literacy more broadly. While much has been written about the *champería* by outsiders, we can now appreciate that the ritual has been documented in even greater detail in the community books for a hundred years, if not longer.

Epilogue

The disastrous effects of the COVID-19 pandemic in 2020 in Peru—which suffered one of the deadliest outbreaks in the world—did not fully spare Casta. The pandemic brought significant disruption to village life. For most of 2020, movement in and out of Casta was either banned or subject to restrictions.

Tourists were not permitted to travel to Casta for over a year on the orders of both the Comunidad Campesina and the municipality. This was a significant blow to the local economy, which has become increasingly reliant on tourism in the last decade. The village suffered a three-month power outage early in the pandemic, which affected telecommunication and internet access when locals were unable to charge their cell phones. Children were unable to take classes virtually, and perishable foods could not be refrigerated.

By October 2020 electricity had been restored, but the village was still in quarantine, which impacted the *champería*. The ceremony that year was carried out partially. In the words of Carlos Alberto Olivares Bautista, the president of the Comunidad Campesina de San Pedro de Casta in 2021, "un cuarenta por ciento hemos hecho, pe" (We did forty percent of it). For those who were not in Casta prior to the start of October, however, the *champería* was canceled entirely. Days before the *champería* was due to commence, the Comunidad Campesina announced that the ceremony was canceled, meaning that visitors and returning migrants were not permitted to come to Casta for the event. The decision was made collectively through a community assembly, with the aim of protecting local lives.[84]

In the first days of October 2020, migrants outside of Casta took to social media to share photographs of ceremonies from years past, to pledge allegiance to their *parada*, and to deliver greetings to their *parada* kinfolk back in Casta. To the delight of many, a handful of distinguished singers of *hualinas* based in Lima recorded videos of themselves singing freshly composed songs in their finest ceremonial garb. They had evidently spent considerable time preparing these contributions. Embroidered cloths or *manteles* and brightly colored *huallque* bags that never made it to Casta formed carefully curated backdrops so that their intricate needlework could be displayed and admired, regardless of the circumstances. The eventual arrival of a vaccination program in the Lima highlands in mid-2021 brought hopes that Casta's beloved *champería* might be carried out more fully later in the year, if all went well, perhaps even "un ochenta por ciento" (at eighty percent). Some Casteños

---

84. Tragedy could not be averted: a small number of Casteños did lose their lives to the coronavirus in 2020, although most or all were staying in Lima. Locals report that, thankfully, the virus did not break out in Casta.

described the 2021 ritual as more or less back to normal. After all, family members living outside of Casta could come back for it this time around.

The *yachak* Catalina Olivares was not completely satisfied that the 2021 *champería* was performed in accordance with ancestral law. Nevertheless, as we sat on her porch sharing a bundle of sacks to sit on for comfort, she asserted that 2022 would be the year the *champería* would make a full comeback. "¡Este año vamos a hacer lo legal, ya!" (This year we're going to do it the legal way!). Although 2022 was the first time I had been able to attend myself, at that point the *champería* appeared to be in full swing once again. With barely any face masks in sight, people danced, sang, and passed around drinks in the customary way, sharing gourd cups.

Clothes vendors from the central city of Huancayo showed up with their wares, knowing Casteñas might be keen to buy a shiny new apron to wear. The village really buzzed: women were busy washing clothes, arranging for their hats to be professionally cleaned, and sitting out in the sunshine, finishing off their embroidered cloths to show on the Monday. People multitasked and made preparations even while working. When I took a ride in Beto Bautista's taxi, he was listening to a recording of himself singing his *parada*'s *hualina* in order to learn the lyrics. Functionaries did not linger for long in the days approaching the big event. Their wives were busy too, amassing food. The weather had changed: the bright blue skies of the previous week were now replaced by looming gray clouds. It seemed like even the sky was getting ready. Restaurant owner and chef Kedwin Obispo Bautista remarked to a friend: "¡Como cambia el clima para champería, pe!" (How the weather changes for the *champería*!).

Researchers from Lima's Catholic University and Columbia University arrived in Casta during the 2022 ritual. A film production crew from Mexico turned up in a four-by-four with big cameras, various sorts of camcorders, and a drone to record the proceedings for a documentary. The word in Casta was that the *champería* was going to appear on Netflix. On the Monday when the elders rested at Chuswa waiting for the workers to finish and meet them there, the film crew recorded Catalina singing a *hualina*. As she burst into song, it began to rain.

The whereabouts of the Entablo manuscript were uncertain in 2022. In October community elder Don Gregorio Ríos deemed the text to be long lost, stating that he would not be convinced of the Entablo's continued presence in the community without seeing it "con mis propios ojos" (with my own eyes). Doña Catalina Olivares also lamented the loss of the manuscript. Don Gregorio was surprised I had been able to see the manuscript myself as recently as 2019, because he thought it was already gone by then. In the days following this conversation, I made some gentle inquiries to the community secretary about the possibility of consulting the Entablo. I had been keen to check the manuscript during my 2022 trip, to scan it for any edits or other changes. I had not expected to hear that the text might have been lost. But my subsequent meeting with the secretary was not especially reassuring. After checking and confirming that the Entablo was indeed, as he had thought, not in the Comunidad Campesina's locked storeroom annex, he explained that the text had reportedly been given to last year's *principal*, whose whereabouts were currently unknown. Given the significance of this sacred book and the burden of responsibility placed on the secretary and other authorities for its safekeeping, I would be very surprised if it failed to reemerge.

2
THE ENTABLO

[Cover:] ENTABLO

78
COMMUNITY ENTABLO[1]

[Inside cover—in black ballpoint:] 92

[f. 1r] [in pencil:][2] Book No. 8

9

[written upside down:] Severino Crisós[tomo?][3]

[in red ink quill script:] Notes to the reader

This legendary book detailing all the internal customs of our community, from the Teniente down to the final clergyman, must be the object of study in the first days of the month of January; by the "Campo" or the Principal so that they know the obligations. Casta, 10.-15.-of the year 1947.[4]

---

1. Rather than using "community" as a closer translation of the adjective form, *comunal* could also be translated as "communal" or "internal." The word *entablo* is also written in capitals on the matte tape used to replace the absent spine of the notebook. The tape runs from the back cover to the front. Thus "Entablo" is written on the front cover three times—the result of repeated inventorying. I am grateful to Frank Salomon, whose review of this book pointed this out. Salomon and Niño-Murcia (2011) describe the inventorying practices of Tupicocha's community archive.
2. This inventory number appears to have been written by the notary who wrote short notes in pencil at the beginning and end of the Entablo, the latter expressing his ownership of the book.
3. Could Severino be "Notario SC"?
4. The majority of the page had been left empty until 1947 when the anonymous *alcalde*

93

The A. Campo[5]

[A flourish beneath the signature covers a section of the note in pencil below.][6]

[in pencil:] I hereby make it known within this *entablo*[7] that I do not agree, because it is [representative] of so few at this point.[8]

[f. 1v] [in blue ballpoint on a fresh white sheet adhered to the back of f. 1r:]

#92 Because of having lost [it] and then appearing with its photocopy.[9]

[f. 2r][10] CHAMPERIA 1921

[in blue ballpoint:] ENTABLO

92

Champeria

[f. 3r] [a flourish in pencil in the top margin may have been made by Notario

---

campo made this entry. The empty space at the top of the page contains a scribble in red ballpoint and other faded scribbles.
5. "A. Campo" is an abbreviation for *alcalde campo*. Also referred to as "Campo."
6. The *alcalde campo* who added this introductory note also entered a note in the instructions for the proceedings on Monday, instructing the reader to consult page 51.
7. The use of the demonstrative pronoun "this" (*este*) suggests that the practice of *entablo*-keeping may have been widespread.
8. This means that all the community members had not signed it in agreement yet. This skeptical and cautionary note left by the notary highlights the collective nature of producing an *entablo* agreement and illustrates the complex process that its producers went through. The process of approval would require negotiating disagreements among community members and gaining the official approval of local stakeholders who would scrutinize its content and its degree of representativeness and accuracy. Undoubtedly, the notary was committed to ensuring that this particular *entablo* fulfilled his expectations of the criteria for an *entablo*. Rengifo de la Cruz (2018: 34) transcribes this note differently: "I do not agree with this book because it is the work of so few [people]" ("No estoy de acuerdo con este libro porque es obra de pocos"). He also interprets the note differently, regarding it a curious, irreverent opinion added later.
9. This entry was made between 2015 and 2018 when the adjacent folio (folios 2r and 2v) became lost.
10. Between 2015, when Hyland was loaned the Entablo for analysis, and 2018, when I consulted the text, the page for folios 2r and 2v became lost. The note on the adjacent page suggests that the loss of the folio was spotted during an audit or on the return of the book after it was studied by a functionary or someone else with access to it.

SC]¹¹ "Internal regulations for the (*citizens*) [underlined and put in parentheses, with "comuneros" written above in red]¹² during the *faena*¹³ on the first of October of each and every year for the canal cleaning starting from this village up to the Carhuayumac canal intake,¹⁴ which begins on a Monday through to the next Monday."

"The citizens of Casta"_____

In light of the many interventions and disagreements concerning the obligations from the Teniente right down to the last functionary, which is the Camachico, the functionaries are not fulfilling their duties and obligations. They have agreed to collectively set down¹⁵ an official record, under [the jurisdiction of] our signatures so that they are obliged to fulfill their duties. They must fulfill them in a punctual manner and cannot give the excuse of taking on their roles without there being a written record and claiming diminished force of law.¹⁶ Since we all submit ourselves to this *regim*,¹⁷ as it

---

11. Notaries in Peru have a long habit of embellishing documents with authenticating rubric marks (Burns 2010: 76–77).
12. *Comuneros* means members of the peasant community. While the Entablo was written during a period of intensive nation-building, this edit suggests reluctance by a reader in a later period to accept the collective identity of community members in Casta as "citizehs." These edits in faded red ink were likely made by the *alcalde campo* in 1947.
13. Gelles (2000: 199) glosses *faena*: "communal work service; a kind of labor tax required of community members." As explained in the introduction, the *champería* is both a ritual and a *faena* labor event.
14. The *toma* (intake) is the point at which water is channeled from an existing source and diverted along a canal system. Gelles (2000b: 205) glosses the Spanish term *toma* as "intake from river to system of canals." The Carhuayumac canal is the principal canal in Casta, channeling water from the Carhuayumac River (Gelles 1984b: 310).
15. The verb used here is *constar*, which has connotations of completeness, precision, and legality. Salomon and Niño Murcia (2011: 25) explain the importance of *constancia* records in Tupicocha, Huarochirí: "*Constancia* ('document of record') is an omnipresent word. If asked why one must write down so many details, Tupicochans usually answer, 'Para que conste' ('So it will be on record'). The word *constancia* connotes durable knowledge, a defense against errors, falsehoods, and forgetting. Producing *constancia* is the culmination of every collective function. The function is not considered done without it: the document is not *about* the deed but *is* the deed." They define the word *constancias* in local usage as "consubstantial records. *Constancias* trump all oral testimonies in cases of dispute." In this respect, *constancias* replicate the functions of khipu accountancy.
16. The role of the Entablo in remedying community discord is testimony to the centrality of collective decision-making in highland Andean communities. This set of repeatedly updated regulations is a perfect example of the fact that Andean irrigation management involves the continual ratification of collective-choice rules by users of the system (Trawick 2001: 13).
17. The use of the term *regim* may reflect linguistic influences from European liturgical or philosophical texts.

is the fundamental basis of the water and life source of [the place] where we live and quench our thirst from birth until the final moment of our death arrives, we hereby submit ourselves to the task of signing in this book.[18] Our aim is that the expert knowledge and judgment[19] dictated by the community and three notable elderly men should remain as an official record for future years. At the end, their names will have been recorded.

Passed[20] on the [torn] government under the presidency of [torn]

[f. 3v] [Three lines in pencil have been drawn here:] ///co *personero*[21] Don Máximo Calistro [signature]

———————

———————

Casta, eighteenth of October of nineteen twenty-one.

Nemesio Bautista [signature with flourish]

We also hereby note that the *faena* must be on the first day of the month of October and, in the event that the work is not finished, a shift system will be set up to avoid running into difficulties with said work.[22]

Máximo Calistro [signature with flourish]

[f. 4r] Sunday Afternoon

The obligations of the functionaries and their duties in said *faena*.

---

18. The process of signing the names (recording the identity of each person) is directly linked with the "fundamental basis" of the local economy, which hinges on irrigation water.
19. The word used here (*dictamines*) has legal connotations and refers to good judgment and expert opinion. It can also refer to a ruling and resultant report. Here it refers to the Entablo as a set of moral codes.
20. The use of the phrase "dada en" indicates an intent to replicate state legalistic language, as the expression is used when promulgating state laws.
21. A *personero* is a community member responsible for documents and land litigation (Isbell 1978: 254).
22. The theme of fairness runs throughout the instructions for the *champería* set out in the Entablo. In his account of the canal cleaning in Huaquirca, Gose (1994: 95) notes: "The cleaning of the canals is noteworthy for the calculated egalitarianism displayed in the organisation of the work process."

[Note in the margin: First 1] To commence the canal-cleaning *faena*, on the day before, which will be the Sunday eve before the works, the political corporation composed of all the functionaries, presided over by the village's Mister Teniente Gobernador, shall meet together in a private or secret convention in the house of the Alcalde Campo along with the Regidor Mayor, Regidor Campo, Alguacil Mayor, the four Menores,[23] and finally the two Camachicos, for the purpose of observing all the procedures related to the work of the following day, Monday.[24] In this, in this private meeting, all the precautionary measures will be dictated and they will draw up plans, above all, concerning the fulfillment of obligations using a traditional and expert formula.[25] So that the Camachicos shall be ready ahead of time with all their corresponding obligations; for example, the Camachicos must submit three *toritos*,[26] as we are accustomed to calling them, and the citizens will supply these to the Camachicos. They will use these in the appropriate places: first, where they need to announce the commencement of the men's work, which is behind the (church and the school), another at Quinituca, another at Mashca.[27] Together, the functionaries will carry out a collective inspection

---

23. The four *alguaciles menores*.
24. It is worthwhile reflecting on the reference to the ritual party as a "political corporation." Given that the functionaries are tasked with upholding the ancestor-focused rituals, their work is "cosmopolitical": it acknowledges and embodies the power and agency of landscape beings (de la Cadena 2010) and polices change.
25. This procedure involved the use of maize kernels for calculating the division of work tasks (Ráez Retamozo 1995; Tello and Miranda 1923).
26. *Toritos* literally means "little bulls." Village elder Eufronio Obispo Rojas explained that the *toritos* mentioned in the Entablo are small guinea pigs used in rituals. The writer of this section acknowledges the idiosyncratic local usage of the term. The Huarochirí Manuscript mentions the practice of sacrificing guinea pigs immediately before the Allauca ayllu began working on its irrigation canal and before the Concha ayllu began the work to dam up its lake (Salomon and Urioste 1991: 135, 142). The guinea pigs were used for divination purposes (Echeandia Valladares 1981: 157; Tello and Miranda 1923: 526–528). According to *yachak* (knower) Doña Catalina Olivares, the color of the guinea pig is important: a *toro negro* (black guinea pig) will not do; it should be a *toro shoq* (also *toro shoquito*: red guinea pig).
27. In other words, the *toritos* will be sacrificed or used for divination purposes at these key sites. The site behind the church and school where the men commence work is known as Ursno (Llanos and Osterling 1982: 127). Animal sacrifices are performed in Huarochirí villages today when beginning development projects on or close to the irrigation systems. An account by Vera Delgado (2011: 148) on the canal-cleaning ceremony (Yarqa Haspiy) in Coparaque in the Colca valley is helpful in understanding why a red blood sacrifice at the beginning of the worksite would be fitting: "The red colour means a very active spirit (energy) for users for working and cleaning the canals. . . . The blood of the vicuña symbolises the fluidity and velocity of water, also expressed in the local saying 'water must run like a vicuña.'"

with all the people gathered in the places where they are to work on the canal, setting off together from the small plaza site named [torn: Cu-?]

[f. 4v] -huay until they reach Llauli, from whence they will return to the Campo's house. This journey will go along the route of the canal, fulfilling the tasks required at the site of Huanca Acequia[28] and also Pampacocha and other points, as directed by the one who knows and represents.[29]

[The writing continues in faint, possibly diluted, ink.]

[In the margin: Second =] Monday: First thing on Monday morning, all the political functionaries unanimously, such as the Campo, Regidor, Regidor Campo, Alguacil Mayor, two Camachicos, and the Alguaciles Menores, will reunite in the house of the Teniente Gobernador, with everyone extremely well organized and well prepared to set off to work on the *champería*.[30] In this meeting, the functionaries will bring out their obligations for this day. The Campo will give a pound of coca, a bottle of rum, two packets of cigarettes of any quantity, and two starter flares; the Regidor Mayor will give the same obligation. The Regidor Campo will give half a pound of coca,[31] half a bottle of rum, one packet of cigarettes of any quantity,[32] and a flare. The Alguacil

---

28. The toponym Huanca Acequia can be translated literally as "canal of the founding ancestor petrified in stone" (Duviols 1973: 163). As Howard-Malverde (1990: 64) explains, *wanka* (*huanca*) standing stones are thought to be formerly human and "to possess fertilising and protective powers as field or village guardian, according to religious practices prevalent in the Central Andes in ancient times and still attested to this day."
29. Tello and Miranda (1923: 527–531) describe a set of secret and elaborate customs carried out by the functionaries on Sunday night under the guidance of a ritual expert called the "Wachik." The Wachik invokes the deity Wallallo in Quechua at the site of Mashca and uses one of the guinea pigs to divine whether the ancestors are accepting the functionaries (527). Because Tello and Miranda observed the 1922 *champería*, we should assume that these customs were also carried out at the time this section of the Entablo was written in 1921.
30. Note the reference to "political functionaries"; the *champería* is referred to as a political-legal event with political functionaries delegating and overseeing the work and submission of related obligations.
31. The coca leaves submitted by the functionaries will be distributed among the attendees before they set off to work, so that they may chew the leaves. When lime powder is added to the wad of coca leaf kept in the cheek, the mild stimulant properties of the coca are activated, assisting with physical labor. Furthermore, coca-chewing has an important social function, creating an atmosphere of solidarity and confraternity (Mayer 2002: 177; Salomon 2004). For further information on the use of coca in Andean ritual, see Allen (2002).
32. The Spanish reads *cigarros* (cigars) but this word is also used for cigarettes, which are a standard feature of irrigation rituals in the Andes.

Mayor will give the same as the Regidor Campo. The Camachicos will collect from the stateswomen,[33] whether widow or widower, or, rather, from all people who do not have a turn of water, some 20 pitchers of chicha *de jora*, or chicha made from black maize, calculated in quantities of one *arroba*[34] for each pitcher.[35] And with these objects all brought together at the site [in the margin in blue ballpoint: X] of Cohuay, having all collected the obligations in their own branches, these functionaries, along with the Camachicos, will then show their obligations to the workers in legal weights and satisfactory measurements.[36] For this procedure, all the men and women will be brought to this place, having been verbally called there by the functionaries. Straight afterward, the Campo . . . [faded] and among the workers, [he] will name

[f. 5r] three Mayordomos for the works, and these Mayordomos will be [delegated], one for the men and two for the women.

[The handwriting and ink differ from this point.] Right away, all the functionaries will proceed to give out from their obligations[37] the necessary amount of coca leaves to all the workers, but not the bottle of rum and the cigarettes, which they will keep behind for the *chaccha*[38] at Huanca=Acequia. This was,

---

33. The phrase "Señoras mujeres de estado" (Madam stateswomen) is unclear. This could refer to the wives of the political functionaries. However, individuals without a turn [ration] of water (widows and widowers) can also fall into this category. Perhaps the "stateswomen" are the wives of the elders?
34. An *arroba* is an archaic unit of weight equivalent to 25 pounds or 11 kilograms and 502 grams. Isbell (1978: 249) glosses it as a "weight of 25 pounds; liquid measure varying from 2.6 to 3.6 gallons."
35. Note the irrigation water rights status of widows and widowers: they do not receive a "turn" (ration) of water. An account by Hall (2014: 33) of the ritual duties of "young men" at *faenas* in Llanchu resembles the description of the duties of the *camachicos*: she notes that the first *cargo* for young men is to prepare and serve chicha, an activity that is closely linked to learning the hierarchy and marks of respect. Notably, she explains that a young man must serve 40 liters of chicha prepared by his wife in full view of everyone. It is clear that accounts of communal labor in other places than Casta also specified the quantities of chicha to be submitted.
36. Much importance was placed on the collective public approval of the weights and sizes of the ritual submissions. Such procedures ensured transparency and safeguarded against the risk of conflict. On the Monday a traditional Andean balance scale called a *huipi* is used today by the *principal* to publicly weigh and approve the *camachicos*' coca submissions. Further information on the *huipi* balance and the weighing procedure is in the notes to the regulations for the Saturday of the Carnival Season customs.
37. "Obligations" refers to the functionaries' own contribution stock, which they have had clarified in advance on Sunday evening and perhaps by other means of instruction.
38. Coca-chewing ceremony.

or is,[39] at the time when the functionaries come out once they have fulfilled their assigned obligations.

One of the following, whether it be the Regidor-Campo or Alguacil Mayor, will leave the following for the work of the elders: ½ a pound of coca, ½ a bottle of rum, and a packet of cigarettes and a flare. The Camachico will leave a pitcher of chicha. With all of this duly submitted, the Campo will set off a flare and the men will go out to work. [tick mark in blue ink]

Once [the men are] at the work site, which is behind the church, the Mayordomo will then name a work measurer and they will proceed to measure throughout the entire distance of the day's work,[40] on those[41] within which they will proceed to position all the men doing their respective jobs in numerical order; beginning with the men behind the church, and some of the married women at Lalancaria and some at Simancaria [Seman Karia], where their respective Mayordomos check the work.

Meanwhile, the workers carry out the canal-cleaning work behind the church along to Huanca-Acequia; then the functionaries will set off all together from Cuhuay toward Huanca-Acequia, to the site where the men's tasks started, [in the margin: an arrow in blue ballpoint] where the functionaries will set off another flare. Here one Camachico and one Alguacil Mayor will stay behind with the elders. In this way, [with the proceedings] harmonized by a *chirimía* which will be played by an experienced person, as they are arriving at the site of Huanca-Acequia, the functionaries will join up with the three Mayordomos. Upon meeting up, the Mayordomos will be offered a glass of liquor[42] and the Camachicos will be offered a glass of chicha by the functionaries, taken from their provisions.[43]

---

39. The default tense for talking about ritual protocol is to have recourse to the past. The memory regeneration process of the three elders comes through clearly here.
40. That is, the work along the course of the canal.
41. "El mayordomo nombrará un medidor de tareas que procederá à medir en toda la distancia del trabajo del día, en los que se hiran colocando todos los hombres en sus respectivas tareas en orden numérico." There is no indication of what the definite article "los" refers to. Are recording devices being used to track the work performance? The omission of a noun invites speculation. The khipu-board *padrón* accounts, which we are later told record similar information, are expressly identified as *padrones* or *cuentas* (accounts) throughout.
42. I have translated *una copita* as "a glass" rather than "a drink" because of the preoccupation with specifying quantities of ritual goods throughout the Entablo.
43. The Spanish term *fiambres* (provisions) refers to a picnic of cold cuts or, in modern-

THE ENTABLO 101

Promptly afterward, the Campo will lead the party along with the Mayordomos, getting the people to gather together at the site already pointed out, "Huanca-Acequia," to take some coca leaves and glasses of chicha. In this place, a cross will be placed on the altar base that has existed since very ancient times;[44] this will be ordered by... [illegible, darkened paper]. Once the people or the *lamperos*[45] are all gathered in this place... [illegible, darkened paper]

[f. 5v] women will go across to the sites of Laco, the ones at Semangaria and the ones from Lalangaria to Olacocha. They will await the Mayordomos at these sites.

For this reason, along with the men who are at Huanca-Acequia, the functionaries will proceed to share out the coca [leaves], the liquor, and the cigarettes from their obligations,[46] which will be distributed by the Alguaciles of each one, beginning with the Campo.

In this place, while the workers are in this period of rest and tranquility, they will begin the Padrón de Huallque y Poronguitos Labrados [Padrón of Huallque Bags and Decorated Drinking Gourds],[47] which must be some *curiosidades*[48] that demonstrate the handicrafts of each person from their household, consisting of a *taleguita*,[49] which should be made to a high level of detail, with different colored threads, and the *poronguito* should also be

---

day parlance, a "packed lunch." In this particular context, *fiambres* can be translated as "stocks of alcohol carried on someone's person." I have translated the term as "provisions" throughout. Today a *fiambre* consists of a bottle or bottles of liquor such as aniseed liquor or pisco, with a *puchu* (also *putu*, *potito*, *mate*: hollowed out gourd) from which to drink.
44. In the original Spanish: "la peana que existe desde tiempos muy antiguos." Throughout the Entablo, certain aspects of the ritual proceedings are referred to as having emerged in ancient times; these are largely pre-Hispanic traditions. It is noteworthy that a colonial feature of the ritual is also talked about in this way.
45. *Lamperos* can be translated "spade workers."
46. That is, from their "obligatory contributions."
47. As the following section explains, this *padrón* records the skilled craft submissions of individuals. It is possible that the individuals are listed on the *padrón* by household, given that the instructions mention the household as an organizing factor in the grouping of individual submissions. As Mayer (2002: 100) shows, handicrafts were a way in which households in the precolonial era deployed skills and capabilities as a powerful productive unit.
48. "Curiosities." In Huarochirano parlance today, expertise and skills are described as *curioso* if they are local, ancestral forms of knowledge (Bennison 2016: 273; Hyland, Bennison, and Hyland 2021).
49. A *taleqa* or *talega* is a bag similar to a *huallque* but larger, designed to hold bottles of alcohol.

made to a high standard, according to the liking of each person. In the same way, those who know how will be ordered to play the *chirisuya* or *chirimía* instrument, with everyone under the threat of being reprimanded and punished right there on the spot [should they refuse].[50]

[in the margin, a note in the same red ink as the 1947 entry: Reformed in 1947—turn to page = 51. The note alerting the reader to the reform was written in response to the following section:]

And in this way, the Mayordomo [in charge] of the men will carry out the *padrón* with the functionaries from the Campo right down to the last Alguacil.[51]

Promptly afterward, the Camachico will proceed to give chicha to all the workers in satisfactory proportions, and in the same way the Campo's two Alguaciles and the Regidor will give out liquor to everyone from their stocks, and this will be at the cost of the Campo and the Regidor Mayor.[52] This will cost one-third of a bottle brimming with liquid, and after a moment the Camachico should repeat giving out the chicha, which is for setting off to work. During this gathering, the Campo will publicly announce the names of the canal Sacsaneros or Supervisors[53] for the two groups of married women, who will be told by their respective Mayordomos when they can drink among themselves. The Mayordomos will promptly stand to attention with their folks and set off to work, each returning to the place where he had left off his work, or rather, one of the Mayordomos [goes] to Laco; and another to Olacocha. All the functionaries remain in the site of Huanca-Acequia for some time until the workers come around the hill at Otagaca. At this point, everyone will set off in the direction of Pampacocha and in this place, at Quinual, at the

---

50. The *champería* regulations illuminate the ways in which flows of *camay* were generated in ritual through khipus. *Camay* is related to ideas about obligation and the capacity of an individual (human or object) to fulfill an assigned role or task in society (Taylor 1987: 29). The logics of *camay* permeate the Entablo through frequent references to *obligaciones* (obligations) and *deberes* (duties).
51. This appears to be a *padrón* that holds the functionaries themselves to account.
52. An account of the ritual duties of "young men" in work parties in Llanchu, Peru, by Hall (2014: 20) corresponds with the duties of the *camachico*. She explains that distributions of food and drink within rituals and work events are ways of indicating hierarchy: the first *cargo* for young men is to serve chicha. As Hall explains (20), the chicha is made by the wife of a young man, who must serve out forty liters of beer in full view of those present.
53. As explained in chapter 1, the hispanicized Quechua term *sacsanero* is not fully equivalent to the Spanish term *revisador*. The Quechua root *saqsa-* is related to satisfaction.

moment of reaching the Mayordomos, the Campo and all the functionaries will offer a glass of liquor from their stocks. The Camachico will offer the Mayordomo[s] a [obscured by tape residue]

[f. 6r] chicha, and the functionaries will set straight off to meet with the married women and the Mayordomos of the married women. The work is such that the married women do the first part. The functionaries will offer [drinks], from their stocks to those they fancy, and the Mayordomos and the Camachicho will do the same, offering the chicha that he carries with him. [dark-blue ballpoint tick]

From this place, Huanca-Shilca,[54] and when they meet the married women, the functionaries will offer [drinks] from their stocks, and from this place all the functionaries will return together with all the women to the site of Chushgua. In this place the male elders wait; in this case the *lampero* men, seeing that the functionaries are already coming, will then leave the work where it is; but it should not go beyond the place "Oculi" because they will also gather together at the site of Chushgua. In this place, once all the women and men are gathered together, they will proceed with the Padrón General de los Asistentes a la Faena [General Padrón of the Work Party Attendees], charging or assigning a fine of 1 *sol* for the men right then on the spot and 50 cts [céntimos] for the women so that the Mayordomos will take stock of the people who have been working for them.[55] During this meeting, the functionaries will proceed to share out the expenditures that are left over from their obligations and their stocks and will finish all the leftovers until the cloaks containing the coca are shaken out empty and the pitchers of chicha are empty.[56]

Straight away, the Campo will proceed to order that they put up the crosses on the following day, in all the places where there are altar bases, those that go from the canal intake or from Casta-Cuhuay at the sites located along the canal and that [faded] up to the intake at "Carguayumac." For this purpose,

---

54. This toponym was recorded by Llanos and Osterling (1982: 135) as "Huankailka."
55. It appears that the monetary contributions of each individual are recorded on this *padrón* as they are submitted. This *padrón* would be based on the Sunday night division of the workers into *paradas* (work parties). It is likely that the cords would have reflected the four respective colors of the *parada* "teams."
56. In addition to remarks on the "maximizing," "plentiful" nature of the *champería*, it is clear from this section that exhaustion of the goods is also required. Everything must be "spent" and offered up to the group.

all the single youths will be stood two by two in order of relation and responsibility,[57] and in the same way the Mayordomos will order that the cross at "Lacsa" be taken down by the people that they have at their disposal and once everything is ready. [tick in black ink]

One of the principal elders will announce the names of the new elected political functionaries who will hold office in the next incoming year, from the Teniente Gobernador right down to the Alguacil Mayor.

And then once all this has been announced and completed, he will order that all the people move along to the village, cleaning all sections of the path from Chushgua to Casta on their way.

[f. 6v] The tasks for Tuesday

Tuesday: On this day, as early as possible, all the functionaries will gather in the house of the Teniente Gobernador, from the Campo right down to the last Alguacil and the two Camachicos, who will all have with them their respective obligations [ritual offerings], which they will have carried with them the previous day. This way, they will submit their obligatory expenditures: a pound of coca, a bottle of rum, two packets of cigarettes, and two flares. [From] the Campo and Regidor Mayor, ½ a pound of coca [leaf], ½ a bottle of rum, one packet of cigarettes, and one flare [from] the Regidor Campo and Alguacil Mayor, respectively.[58] [tick in dark ink]

From here, with everyone gathered together from the Campo right down to the last Alguacil and Camachico, they will set off for the gathering at

---

57. That is, the youths will be lined up according to their hierarchical status in relation to one another. Hall (2014) points out the importance of linear files in the representation of social hierarchies and the recording of these hierarchies in khipu devices, while Arnold with Yapita (2006: 267) highlight the importance of linear furrows in the making and reading of khipus.

58. The collaborators of Echeandia Valladares (1981: 166) told him in the 1970s that historically Tuesdays were the day when "messengers" representing different roles, including the *camachicos*, would be sent to urban sites and neighboring villages associated with the tasks expected of them, such as Matucana, Chosica, Carampoma, Otao, and Huachupampa. These tasks resemble those associated with the Inca-style khipu used in neighboring Anchucaya until the 1940s (Hyland 2016: 493–494). A functionary in Casta in 2018 explained that junior functionaries today get sent on far-flung secret missions at night. On their return, they must fulfill their mission by bringing back specific items to Casta such as handfuls of earth from the fields of neighboring villages, or stones.

"Mashca." For this, they will send out a warning signal with a flare for the people at the site of or rather at the hill of Otagaca. On this signal, the people will set off to gather together, men and women, in the place indicated earlier: "Mashca." [note in black ballpoint: 2]

At this place, once everyone is gathered together, the Padrón General de los Asistentes al Trabajo [General Padrón of the Work Attendees][59] will resume and right away, the obligations[60] indicated above according to weight and legal measurement will be shown.[61] In the same way, the Camachicos will hand in from their collected stocks twenty pitchers of chicha *de jora*, each pitcher containing an *arroba*.

[In the margin in blue ballpoint: X] Immediately afterward, the married women leave in the direction of Huanca-Shilca at the place that the work party reached the day before. Meanwhile, as they are walking, the married men drink or chew[62] coca, and they warn the Mayordomos to proceed in a lawful manner with the workers with respect to their tasks and to give their expenditures for the work as on the previous day. The canal Sacsaneros or Supervisors will do the same as the day before.

And, leaving behind expenses for the elders as on the day before, all the workers will leave under the authority of their Mayordomos, while the functionaries stay behind in this place for a while, chatting with the elders.[63]

---

59. If we translate *seguirá* as "will resume," then this is the same *padrón* as on the day before, Monday (Padrón General de los Asistentes a la Faena). If the same *padrón* resumes, this suggests that multiple entries would have been made on each cord for the recording of attendance. If *seguirá* means "will follow," then two separate *padrones* record the work party attendees on Monday and Tuesday, respectively.
60. That is, the submissions.
61. A later section of the regulations provides helpful context. The Carnival Season regulations describe the use of a traditional balance known as a *huipi* (f. 24r). These devices were used to publicly approve the weights of coca leaf tribute submissions.
62. The original Spanish reads "mastican o chacchan coca"; the use of the two equivalent terms (Spanish and Quechua, respectively) indicates linguistic tension.
63. The degree of respect shown to the elders includes privileges such as being offered food and drink.

Thus, the men will begin the work at "Oculi,"⁶⁴ the site that the earlier work party must reach, and the married women who left the work at "Olacocha" at the stream will go along to Huanca-Shilca and [in the margin in blue ballpoint: an arrow] inner Socalun; and the ones who left off the work at Huanca-Shilca will go along to the canal intake. From the intake, they will come back cleaning [the canal] until they meet with those who are working their way up from Huanca-Shilca.

[f. 7r] This is the point at which the functionaries at "Mashca" go to the site of Chacchadera,⁶⁵ and, on setting off, send off a flare. They will set out along the path, taking up the canal [work] from "Oculi." Once they reach "Chacchadera," the functionaries will have a meeting with the Mayordomos in the same way as the day before. The functionaries will order that they leave their tasks and gather together in the aforementioned place and will proceed with all the obligations and the same *padrón* as the day before.⁶⁶ Once it [the *padrón*] is finished, the functionaries will set off, setting off along the canal until they reach the foot of the waterfall at "Comau." In preparation for this, as he did the day before, the Camachico will leave behind the [amount of] pitchers of chicha that the Camachicho deems fit, and according to the number of workers who may have had or have already had some.

---

64. A petrified ancestor known as Juan is said to reside in a cave at Oculi. Offerings were left there during the *champería* in 1974 (Echeandia Valladares 1981: 155). Describing the deeds of this ancestor, Doña Catalina Olivares referred to him by his full name, Juan Rojas. She explained that Juan does not preside over the Oculi canal alone; he is accompanied by the canal's other owner: his wife, María Cascanti. They still demand offerings today. Anyone who upsets Juan and María by walking along their canal during the *champería* must bring them a rag doll, blessed water, and a red guinea pig (*toro shoq*) to appease them. According to Llanos and Osterling (1982: 125), a stone at Oculi represents the husband of a stone known as the *mujercita* (little woman), which is located lower down the canal, close to Mashca; perhaps this stone is María('s stone).

As I have explained elsewhere (Bennison 2019), the *abuelos* are said to respond only to strong, direct language and the *curandero* has had to have strong words with Juan in particular, chastising him for punishing "innocent children." Juan himself has his own ways of speaking; he is said to threaten people with a promise to *shokurqur* them. Doña Catalina explained that this word is used by the *abuelos* and refers to their method of punishing people by inflicting harm. She described an incident during one *champería*, when a racer was thrown off his horse at Oculi during the Wednesday horse race and later died from his injuries. She attributed the incident to Juan's wrath, explaining that a racer who falls off a horse during the *champería* has been thrown down for "not believing in them" ("por no creer").

65. "Place for the ritual chewing of coca leaves."
66. That is, the Padrón General de los Asistentes al Trabajo.

THE ENTABLO 107

On setting off, the functionaries will set off a flare. This is at "Chacchadera," and they will leave behind a flare for the workers. [note in dark ink: 2]

Promptly after the functionaries leave, the workers will proceed to finish their tasks which, according to [note in the margin beside "according to": customary law], they are responsible for up to "Laco."

In this place at "Laco," once the *faena* part of the *champería* is complete, all the *lamperos* go out to the place where the luncheon is carried out on Wednesday. On this day, Tuesday, the cleaning of the traditional site will be carried out in a lawful, strictly hygienic way, having arranged the seats for all the guests, and immediately after the cleaning is finished they will proceed to have their meals or provisions, this happening while the functionaries [in the margin: *return] from the site of "Comau" along with the married women.

For that reason the elders will arrive at this location, and once all the people arrive at this place here called "Laco" they will begin the *padrón* just as they did the day before,[67] and once it is finished they will bring themselves back, cleaning the road that is dirty on their way, right up to this village of Casta.[68]

[Note in the margin in blue ballpoint: NB] And once they are in this village, the functionaries will all come over together to this village to the house of the Teniente Gobernador to carry out the *cuenta* [account] in the way established since very ancient times.[69]

[f. 7v] For the account, the Teniente will submit from his obligations an *arroba* pitcher of chicha de *jora* as it is called, one pitcher of four [*arrobas?*], one bottle of rum, and a pound of coca. In this *cuenta*, the Camachicos will figure out the number of pitchers that have been invested in the days that have passed and will see how much is left over to distribute in the days to come.[70]

---

67. Might this mean they continued the Padrón General de los Asistentes al Trabajo?
68. The account by Gose (1994) of the canal cleaning in Huaquirca, Peru, notes the assigning of four days for the canal-cleaning activities and an additional fifth day for work to be carried out on the roads, to smooth them. In this respect, Casta is not unique in having road maintenance work form part of the extended canal-cleaning work. Gose writes: "in this way, the work on the canals mixes with other kind of labour tribute, and does not form a special category of its own" (95). Canal-cleaning rituals are focused on unblocking pathways of transmission, which includes social and spiritual communicative pathways.
69. While all the villagers are cleaning the roads on the way back, the functionaries are privately carrying out this ancient account in the *teniente gobernador*'s house.
70. Prior organization by the *camachicos* is required in the days leading up to this day,

This is when it will be reported verbally[71] to all the women, including widows, married women, and single women, to all the women[72] who have a turn[73] of [irrigation] water, and including the widowers and single men, in this *relación*,[74] which shall continue to be voiced out loud, they will go about setting the married women into their *parcialidades* or their *cofradías*.[75] For this, they will be divided up in a verbal fashion [note in the margin: X] by two very judicious people. At the call of the Regidor Mayor, the ones who have been named will answer by specifying or classifying the *cofradía* to which they belong and at the same time will carry out the *cómputos*[76] of the pitchers of chicha so that they end up as numbers of kernels. The Regidor Mayor will put a tablecloth on the floor and the kernels for this.[77] Promptly after, he will proceed with the classifications and distributions of the inhabitants according to *paradas*. For this, two further people will be elected to classify them [the inhabitants] in grains, setting them out among the *paradas* of "Carguayumac," "Cumau," "Yanapaccha," and Ucucha. For these acts, the Alfereces of the *paradas* will already be present with their obligatory compliances[78] and likewise

---

to work out how many pitchers will be left over for this specific chicha account-taking procedure. Did the *camachico* have a portable method of accounting for the fluctuating numbers of chicha pitchers?

71. The report will not be read by the irrigators themselves; it will be publicly read out from the "written" report.

72. The gender of those being categorized here is ambiguous; the original Spanish reads: "todas los que tienen turno de agua."

73. *Turno de agua*: a ration of irrigation water.

74. A *relación* is a report written up and shown to authorities, but the term has other meanings that are relevant for this context. Implicit in the word *relación* is the idea that the report will be constructed from various data sets or will be compared to another data set. According to the Real Academia Española dictionary, a *relación* is the "result of a comparison between two quantities expressed in numbers" ("resultado de comparar dos cantidades expresadas en números") (Real Academia Española [1726–1732] 2014: s.v. "relación").

75. Each *parcialidad* had its own respective *cofradía*, so these are presented as equivalent terms.

76. *Cómputos* means a calculation or set of calculations. According to the Real Academia Española ([1726–1739] 2014: s.v. "cómputos"), the term refers to a set of calculations necessary to determine movable fiestas. Determining both numerical and calendrical data through sequences of calculations would have been integral to khipu accountancy.

77. Mayer (2002: 128–129) observed similar rites in Tangor, Peru, in 1969. Pebbles representing individual people were set out on top of a poncho and the enumerations relative to labor contributions were memorized by two men commissioned by a *varayoq*. Mayer concludes that the practice represented khipu accountancy.

78. *Cumplimientos*: fulfillments or compliances (in other words, the goods that people are obliged to bring or submit).

the Michcos, as we call the ones who are going to replace the Campo, Regidor Mayor, Regidor Campo, and Alguacil Mayor, which makes four Michcos.

On this same day, with all the functionaries gathered together after the *padrón*, the Alcalde Campo is the one among them all [that is, the functionaries] who has the obligation of walking through the streets, announcing to every person their corresponding *parada*: "Carguayumac," "Cumau," or "Yanapaccha," "Ocucha."[79] Once the walkabout is finished, they all gather once again, giving an account[80] [?] of their compliances.

Straight away, the Alcalde Campo will elect a *cantor*,[81] giving by way of compliance ½ a bottle of rum, and the Regidor will put on his bell. The Regidor Campo will take a palm shoot stick and then [torn]

[f. 8r] From the gathering, they will set out on the walk, led by the Campo, who will give by way of compliance rum, coca, and cigarettes and followed in turn by the Regidor Mayor, the Regidor Campo, and the Alguacil Mayor. Once all these obligations are completed, they will go together to the house of the Teniente Gobernador. The fans and young horse riders will ask for permission from the elders. Once they have been accepted, they should go to the office of the honorable council at that moment or rather the next day go and get their respective licenses. Then the youths, finding themselves cheerful, will accompany the elders on foot with their enlivening tunes or *hualina* songs and bells.

~Wednesday~ [wavy underlining]

---

79. Mayer (2002: 129) notes that two men commissioned by a *varayoq* to oversee the pebble-based division of labor enumerations in Tangor in 1969 "were not only counting, they were memorizing the names and the services rendered. Their memories constituted the record, and they remained available as expert witnesses in case of disagreements." Llanos and Osterling (1982: 124) describe a secret *padrón* simulation carried out during the Sunday night proceedings in 1979. The *campo* was ordered by the *cura* (Casta's principal male ritual specialist and healer) to carry out the *padrón* at the sacred site of Kuway (Cuhuay), where he listed all the *comuneros* from memory. As Platt (2002) points out, khipu authorities were apparently capable of memorizing the information held on accountancy khipus. In such cases, the public demonstration of khipu accountancy logics legitimized and gave authority to the foundations of their knowledge practices. The memory *padrón* in the *champería* seems to confirm Platt's argument.
80. The section reading "dando cuanta de sus cumplimientos" is unclear.
81. A *cantor* is a religious functionary whose role is to compose canticles and psalms.

Its duties and obligations

On Wednesday morning, the Alcalde Campo will serve up breakfast for the entire community. Once this is ready or served up, he will give a signal by sending out a call with a flare.

And the Regidor Mayor will do the same, also announcing the call with a flare.

The same [for] the Regidor Campo and also the Alguacil Mayor.

Once these tasks are completed, the Alcalde Campo will supply for their replacements[82] [substitutes] a *manta tarmeña*,[83] a clasp or brooch, a staff, and a *corredor*.[84]

The Regidor Mayor, the Regidor Campo, and Alguacil Mayor will do the same and, having finished that, will submit them to the Michcos. These elected Michcos will supply a certain amount of *mate*[85] in order to collect or receive the coca leaves from the functionaries, and these same Michcos will each supply a *manta* in which to receive the coca. Then, straight afterward, the Michcos will take up tenure, carrying the measure so that the elders [darkened: approve them?]. Right away they will begin to collect the coca from the functionaries: first, from the Campo then, second, from the Regidor Mayor

[f. 8v] They will give a complete measure to each of their substitutes.

The Regidor Campo and the Alguacil Mayor will give, halfway through, every single one of their obligations to each of their substitutes.[86]

---

82. In other words, the *michcos*, who are the substitutes for himself (the *alcalde campo*), the *regidor mayor*, the *regidor campo*, and the *alguacil mayor*. Through passing on these items, these functionaries are conferring authority upon the *michcos*.
83. A *manta tarmeña* is a brown poncho worn as formal attire by community authorities in the central highlands. Thanks to Frank Salomon, who helped contextualize this vocabulary in his review of this book.
84. *Corredor* means "runner." It is unclear what this item might be.
85. A receptacle made from a dried hollowed squash. These items are also known as *putus* or *puchus* in Casta today. A few days before the 2022 *champería*, I observed a functionary showing a *mate* to some elders, asking if it was an appropriate size and explaining that he did not fancy getting punished. After the elders reassured him that his *mate* was adequate, he hurriedly went on his way.
86. "Substitutes" refers to the Michco functionaries who are coming in to replace the functionaries.

This being finished, the Michcos will progress to the ritual sacred site of "Cuhuay" and will notify the Campo and the rest of the functionaries. At the same time, the functionaries, from the Campo right down to the last functionaries, which are the Camachicos, will get their horses ready and in good order and properly saddled up and have the horses nicely decorated with ribbons and flowers and also with bells. Their staffs should also be well decorated to the taste of each person. Once all the functionaries are gathered together on horseback in the house of the Alcalde Campo,[87] they will take up tenure in order, each person with a *chonta* [palm shoot] staff, with pieces of silver in his right hand. Behind them, the horse [race] aficionados will make their way or follow. After gaining permission from the Teniente, they all go to the *costumbre* [obligatory ritual] site of "Cuhuay," everyone on horseback. At this place, everyone will dismount and will go to the place where order is maintained, greeting the public who are there in that place. [Note in dark ink: 2]

The Alcalde Campo, after having fulfilled his moral duties and prudences, will put forward a *cantor* and the Alfereces of both *paradas*[88] will hold up a multicolored flag well adorned with bells and feathers and will continue the *hualina* song. In this ceremony, the Alfereces of both *paradas* will give their compliances to the elders. In the same manner, the Michcos will offer [in the margin: a tick in blue ballpoint] coca to the elders. [Two lines have been added in the same blue ballpoint: //]

Once this is done, they will set off for the site of "Otagaca" and from there an announcement will be made with a "Huajay," which will gain the attention of the spectators.[89] Then the functionaries, along with the aficionados,[90] will halt the *hualina* and proceed to establish a sense of order. Once order is in place, they will kneel down and recite a number of prayers so that things go well, commending themselves with full-hearted faith as they end their prayers to God. After fulfilling all their duties, all the functionaries and aficionados will

---

87. If they are on horseback, the functionaries presumably enter the *alcalde campo*'s courtyard rather than his house.
88. The regulations repeatedly refer to "both *paradas*," although there are in fact four. This may reflect difficulties of expression in the Spanish language or perhaps a tendency to conflate the two "daughter" *paradas* with their two respective "mother" *paradas*.
89. It is not clear specifically which functionary will make the announcement, but the *alcalde campo* is responsible for shouting out during the January traditions (Bennison 2019).
90. The jockeys are probably referred to as *aficionados* in the Entablo because as skilled and highly respected amateurs, they participate in the challenging and dangerous horse race in a nonprofessional capacity.

112   THE ENTABLO MANUSCRIPT

[?] their horses and ent[er] [torn page]

[f. 9r] in formation, lining up in order with the Alcalde Campo first and next the Regidor Mayor and so forth, with the rest right down to the very last aficionado.

The Teniente will give a speech, explaining and emphasizing the responsibilities they must fulfill and overseeing the peace and tranquility of the trajectory and ensuring that the people who committed any kind of disorderly behavior are captured as conspirators and disturbers of the public order. Once put into my charge, I will pass [them] to the judicial authorities so that the due legal process can continue. [Note in black ballpoint: X]

After this event, the Teniente will count, in numerical order, starting "one, two, three." On finishing the last number, the party on horseback will set off for "Taquina" [note in black ink: *NB] [corresponding note in the margin in black ink: *Here the Regidor Mayor will set off a flare, since the *parada* belongs to him], where the Michcos shall wait. Once they have arrived at the place, they gather together, first the functionaries and then the aficionados, and continue the *hualina* cheer among everyone. In this way, after the Michcos meet the functionaries, they will set off for "Mashca." From there, they [the Michcos] will alert the functionaries and aficionados with a cry of *huajay*.[91] At the same time, the Campo will set off with everyone and the Alguacil Mayor, for his part, will send off an exit flare when setting off toward the site of Laco, where where [*sic*], they will rest or gather together again. The functionaries and the aficionados will continue the same cheer with the flags of both *paradas* and the Michcos will demand the submission of the twenty pitchers or more from the Camachicos. The chicha pitchers must be collected from the married women of "Yacapar." [Note in blue ballpoint: X over scribbles in red ballpoint]

Once these twenty pitchers or more are complete, they will be divided up by the Michco of "Carguayumac," six pitchers or more based on the amount due to Carguayumac and six more pitchers or more for "Cumau."[92]

---

91. *Waqay* in Quechua means "to weep," "to wail," or "to cry out."
92. Note the numerical breakdown of the submissions of chicha: 6 + 6 + 4 + 4 = 20. A "Padrón de los Veinte Cántaros" (Padrón of the Twenty Pitchers) similar to the one described in the regulations for Thursday may have exhibited such a breakdown.

Four pitchers or more for "Yanapaccha" and, finally, four pitchers or more for "Ocshayco or Ocusha."

This being finished, the party will set off, led by the Michcos and the functionaries, who will carry forward the cheer until a certain moment and the functionaries and aficionados will set off on horseback. At this place or setting-off point, the Regidor Campo will set off a flare [for the group's departure] toward "Huanca-Shilca." In this place [faded]

[f. 9v] and the "Cumau" *parada* with the *caja* or *tinya* drum and with the *yaravíes*[93] tunes sung by the Mayoralas of the said *parada*. Once everyone is gathered, everyone will be offered a bit of excellent lunch in the open air, first [it will be offered] to the authorities and functionaries and other people who are present. During this same event [moment?], the Alfereces of that *parada* will give out a glass of champagne.

Promptly afterward, the functionaries proceed to the site of Soculún, where they will await the "Carguayumac" *parada* with the same *tinya* drum and *yaravíes* tunes, accompanied by the singing of the lovely Mayoralas. This happens while everyone gathers together for a little lunch, which contains different kinds of Inca foods.

Once this is finished, the Michco sets off for the canal intake, joined by his workers who have arrived at the intake where the water is released. The Michco gives the workers a bit of coca and they chew it. Once this ceremony[94] is finished, the workers get to work. While the Michco and his workers are doing this, the functionaries proceed on foot toward the intake to be given their work. The said functionaries go along carrying their provisions such as coca, rum, cigarettes, and their flares, which will be put to use in the *costumbre* sites, beginning with the site of "Pariapungo."[95] After this secret ceremony, the functionaries proceed to the intake, where they meet with the Michco and the functionaries drink a toast from their provisions, beginning with the Campo right down to the last, which is the Camachico.

---

93. Andean songs sung to lament or end a period of separation (see chapter 1).
94. Coca chewing is referred to as an *acto* (ceremony). In all the irrigation rituals that I have attended in Huarochirí, coca leaves are distributed while standing or sitting still in a circle and always at sites considered sacred.
95. "Pariapungo" is the name given to an ancestor said to reside in a grotto here, where offerings are left (Ráez Retamozo 1995).

And straight away, the functionaries embark on their return journey along the canal, checking the work up to the site of "Silguerito," where the *parada* awaits them with the cheer of the *tinya* drum and *yaravíes*.

After a short moment, they go down to the canal to do a secret ceremony in the Paccha or Waterfall[96] and afterward the functionaries [torn] setting off a flare until the site of [torn] "Cumau," where the secret ceremony continues and their [torn]

[f. 10r] . . . a flare. This is at the foot of the big waterfall at "Cumau." At the same time, they set off along the same canal until they reach "Huancaquirma." When they arrive at the site, the functionaries come out to meet with and greet the "Cumau" *parada* with [them playing] the correct kinds of tunes such as *hualinas* [and] the tune of *chirimías* and they sing to the sound of the bells. After fulfilling all these duties, they wait to receive the water that the Michco from Carhuayumac hands over to the Michco from "Cumau" (received by him). Once this is fulfilled, the two *paradas* and Michcos welcome in the water with many rounds of dynamite, flares, small fireworks, and other explosives that embellish the reception. Once these duties have been fulfilled, the functionaries set off along the same canal until they reach "Yanapaccha," the place where they do a secret ceremony. They proceed until they reach the hill at "Huanca-Shilca," where they meet with the two Michcos from "Yanapaccha" and "Ocucha." Here they partake of some glasses of Carapongos Lunaguaná[97] and Malt Callao and Lima exports from their stock of tasty provisions.

[a blue ballpoint place mark: —] Right away, they set off along the same canal, setting off a flare with the same [sense of] cheer until they reach "Ocshayco," from whence they leave the canal, going out along the path. This is before they arrive at the hill at "Ocshayco," where the Palangana functionaries[98] and [?]

---

96. "Paccha" (the Quechua term for "waterfall") is glossed in Spanish here, indicating a conscious effort to have as much of the content presented in the Spanish language as possible.
97. Carapongos and Lunaguaná (Lunahuaná) are wines produced in the warm valleys between Casta and Lima: Carapongos from the Rimac River valley and Lunahuaná from the Cañete River valley.
98. Today *palangana* means "cocky," "clownish," or "foolish." According to village elder Eufronio Obispo Rojas, the term tends to be used disparagingly. Elderly villagers in San Damián recall the former presence of clown-like functionaries in local *champerías* prior to the mid-twentieth century. These clowns would insult the female huaca Mama Capiama out loud, to anger her. The *palangana* functionaries referred to here are probably the *michcos*.

take their horses and await the aficionados before setting off, guiding in an orderly fashion until they reach the *costumbre* site of "Ocshayco," the pampa where a cross is located.

At this spot, both *paradas* await them and they carry on fulfilling their obligations. Once the *paradas* have finished, they set off for the site of "Piscatambo," the site where they await them with the tunes of the *yaravíes* and *tinya* drum. While they are arriving, the functionaries remain there with the cheer of the lovely *hualina* tunes. After a short moment, the functionaries set off for the site of "Laco." (h)[99] Before starting off, they make an announcement that the aficionados should set off in a line, two by two on their horses, being careful as they familiarize themselves with their challenge.

Once everyone is gathered at the site of "Laco," the Mr. Alcalde Campo (and the)[100] will call everyone to a public banquet that is so excellent, decent, and of the very highest standards [faded]

[f. 10v] with the gaieties fully underway, halfway through the banquet, the Camachicos will get up with their compliances and wearing a *shicra* bag[101] on their chest, they will proceed to offer some [coca?] to everyone who is seated at the celebration. They [the Camachicos] will return to those who receive[d] some [coca], giving them more, plus a *biscocho* [*bizcocho*: sweet bread], which they keep in the bag they carry. They will start off at each end of the seats, crossing in the middle, happily and decently.

After these are given out, they will recite a prayer and promptly afterward the Campo will call for the tables or banquets to be served. Once these deeds are finished, the four Michcos call for the twenty pitchers or more that were distributed in the morning and that they have been carrying to be handed back in to the Camachicos. Promptly afterward, the *padrón*, the Regidor, in the presence of the Camachicos, collects their pitchers from the married Yacapar women according to how the *padrones* dictate that this be done. Once this is finished, the *paradas* set off for the site of "Machca" and the functionaries stay in "Laco" with the cheer or song of the *hualina* with all the horse aficionados. Once the *paradas* reach the hill at "Mashca," they

---

99. This inclusion appears to be an error.
100. In an apparent error of omission, the functionary who must collaborate with the *alcalde campo* here is not specified.
101. *Shicra* bags are made with plant fibers using a manual looping technique (Del Solar 2011). They are no longer worn at Casta's *champería*; however, some Casteñas still make them.

suspend the cheer and order them all to organize themselves in order facing the cross to recite a mystery or some religious prayers. They commend themselves to the male saints and female saints of the court of heaven so that through them our divine providence attends to them [our prayers].[102] Preferably, they will recite two "Our Fathers" and two "Ave Marias" for the patron saints of this village ("San Pedro")[103] and "San Antonio." [in the margin in red ballpoint: an arrow]

Having completed these religious deeds, the Mr. Alcalde Campo will call out: "Get ready!" to the entrants on their horses, who need to get onto the racetrack.

Once this is (finished) ready,[104] the Cam-

[f. 11r] po will call all the horse-race aficionados to fall into line. Once this has been ordered, the Campo will set off on horseback to the level section of ground where he will assert all his power to bring about a sense of order, based on the number they are assigned in the council's list. It [the starting mark?] will be drawn out along a vertical straight line, and the Campo will make an announcement, asking if they are ready or not, to which they will respond with a "yes" or a "no" to give more time so they can finish [getting ready].

During this dangerous act, the Alcalde Campo, with tears in his eyes, will tell the entrants to make sure that none of them, absolutely none of them, should get trampled, nor should they trample anyone else while at the starting point or during the race. Having fulfilled all these duties, the Alcalde Campo once again checks over the straight line of horses, to check whether they are positioned in the right place or not. He will go over it again, going up and down the line. Afterward, he retreats by three or four meters toward the cross and gives a call to get ready, counting the numbers "one, two, and three" out loud, announcing that this final one is the real one, and finishes saying the

---

102. Mashca is the site where the functionaries perform a secret ritual in honor of the deity Wallallo (or Suqta Kuri?) on Sunday night (see chapter 1). The regulations for the public ceremony given here place an emphasis on Christian worship, whereas Tello and Miranda (1923: 526–529) describe the speaking of Quechua during invocations to Wallallo at Mashca. It is likely that the saint-focused "mysteries" referred to here are Quechua invocations, in line with the other secretive practices associated with Wallallo's (or Suqta Kuri's?) cult.
103. Brackets added by the same hand with the same ink. The quotation marks have been added in blue ink.
104. The word "ready" appears to supersede "finished," with brackets added by the same hand.

same words, "one, two, and three, may God be with you." The very moment they set off, the Alguacil of the Campo sets off a flare. This is provided by the Campo. Once all the entrants have passed the hill at Mashca, the *paradas* and spectators enter the pathway; but before that, the Mayoralas and the most enthusiastic aficionados sing the *yaravíes* tunes at all the most visible sites and set locations. Depending on how they come [how long it takes for the racers to pass them], they gather together and get themselves along to the village with the *tinya* drums and the four Michcos until they reach the house of the Teniente Gobernador. Once these people are on the property, the Michcos shake out their *mantas* in front of everyone. Then the Teniente calls for a pause until the following day. Right away, the Alfereces from both *paradas* beg the Teniente and the elders for their permission to go out and celebrate until the time indicated. Meanwhile, the aficionados entertain themselves in the house of the win-

[f. 11v] -ner or the [rider of the] first horse. With this, the duties and obligations of (while) [*sic*] Wednesday are finished.

~Thursday~

The duties and obligations for this day

The Alcalde Campo, Regidor Mayor, Regidor Campo, and Alguacil Mayor will prepare a delicious breakfast, each one in his house, and it will be made by their Alguaciles. They will announce [that it is ready] to the village with a flare. Once they finish breakfast, each one of the Michcos will set off to collect the coca from each functionary in the same way as the day before, in the same *mate* or *collo*.[105] That is, each functionary will hand [these to] their substitute or Michco. Likewise, they will ask for their compliances for [neon pink highlighter place mark: —] entering, sitting down, moving, and exiting. Once this is finished, the Michcos set off in the direction of the scared ritual site named "Taquina."

While gathered together in this place or spot, the Michcos will carry out the chichas for the Camachicos and likewise also the flags and *cajeras*[106] of both

---

105. A *collo* or *qollo* is a bowl-shaped container. It is unclear if the terms *mate* and *collo* are synonymous or whether they refer to different kinds of receptacles. As such, this *collo* could either be a hollow gourd bowl (like a *mate*) or an alternative kind of bowl.
106. As I explained earlier, *cajeras* (women drummers) play the *tinya* drum while singing *kashwa* songs for their *parada*.

paradas. This requirement will be carried out by the Michcos out loud in a loud voice befitting the site of "Taquina."

While gathered together at the site where the Michcos are, the Camachicos will submit the twenty pitchers[107] or more to the Michcos.

The Michco Mayor will distribute [the chicha] to each *parada* in the same way as the previous day and then from that place each Michcos will set off to his work tasks with his respective workers. The Michco Mayor will go to Chushgua Lake. The Segundo will go to Laclan Lake[108] and the two Menores [to] "Ocusha" and "Yanapaccha." Each one of them will go to Hualhual Lake at the start of the work,

[f. 12r] [and?] giving [out] their *chaccha*[109] from the *manta* that they keep in their power.

Once they are halfway through the work, the functionaries leave the site of "Taquina," setting off for the site of Chushgua to receive the finished work. The said functionaries will go inside the reservoir to receive the work to the [sound of the] harmony of the *chirimía* and the *cantor* and, in this way, these functionaries will begin to give their compliances out to all the workers.[110] All the functionaries, right down to the last Camachico, [should do this]. Once the reception of the work is over, they leave, setting off a flare, and once they are at the edge of the reservoir, they will do a loop, spreading the cheer with the canticle[111] of the *hualina, yaravíes*, and drum. Straight afterward, they will get themselves to the site of "Laclan Lake [reservoir]," where they will perform the same ceremonies. Having finished the reception ceremony with the same cheer, they will get themselves to the site of "Hualhual" Lake [reservoir], where they will meet with the two Michcos. They will go in[to the reservoir] to receive the work, where the compliances begin. Once all this is finished, the Michcos leave for the site of "Pampacocha." At this point, the

---

107. According to Platt (2002: 246), Bolivian khipus from Aymara-speaking Sakaka referred to in court testimony in the late sixteenth century listed quantities of honey in pitchers (*cántaros*). The pitcher may represent a standardized unit for recording quantities of liquid goods recorded on khipus.
108. The toponym in the manuscript is missing an accent, but it is pronounced "Laclán."
109. Coca for chewing.
110. The "lakes," which are in fact reservoirs, have not yet been filled with water and must be cleaned before the water is released into them.
111. Canticles are hymns taken from the Bible, but the term is applied here to ancestral Andean songs.

functionaries right down to the Camachico stay behind together in "Hualhual" Lake [reservoir], singing their *hualina* canticles. Once the four Michcos [are] in "Pampacocha" Lake [reservoir], they divide up their tasks among themselves and all the Michcos begin the work as follows: the [Michco] Mayor, will carry out the water [work]. First, the Michco Mayor will submit the water, delivering the water to the Michco from "Cumau" accompanied by his people. Then the Michco from "Cumau" will release the intake or sluice from the stream at "Huanaquirma" along with his people and the Michco from "Yanapaccha" releases the water from the stream at "Oculi" alongside his people. They will collect the water inside "Hualhual" Lake [reservoir] for the reception ceremony, whether this is before the banquet or afterward. After that, the functionaries set off a flare as they start off to receive the work, and they carry on with their compliances when they receive the work from each Michco that is done by his workers. Right

[f. 12 v] away, the Teniente will order the functionaries to suspend the harmony and the Campo announces the suspension of the harmonies[112] to all the people, and then they all go out to the little square to take a seat, all the children of the place.[113] The Campo or Regidor will order the youths to collect the *visitas*[114] and will offer them a seat. Once this is finished, the Regidor will summon the two Camachicos to collect the *mesas paños* [tablecloths] or *manteles* [embroidered cloths] made by the single women for the *visitas*, then the Alcalde Campo will summon all the women to stand up with their offerings for the *visitas* until the table is filled with them. Straight afterward, he will summon the same women, telling their [the men's] wives to stand up with the *carhuaymesa*.[115] In the event that the priest is present, a cross will be carried by the village Principal to the chapel, and in case the priest is not

---

112. In other words, the music must be paused.
113. It is common for people in Huarochirí to express their relationship to places in terms of kinship; today many describe themselves as "children" of their village. The pre-Hispanic belief that all groups from Huarochirí derive from the apical mountain ancestor Pariacaca persists. In San Damián, a collaborator exclaimed: "more or less all Huarochirí was born from there [Pariacaca]" (Bennison 2016: 7–8).
114. "Tributes." In the colonial era, *visitas* were inspections focused on monitoring tribute.
115. *Carhuaymesa* (banquet consisting of yellow foods), a composite term combining the Quechua and Jaqaru term for yellow (*qarwa*, *q'arwa*) and the Spanish *mesa* (table, spread or banquet). The foods should be locally produced. It appears that the single women are being asked to help serve up the *carhuaymesa* prepared by the married women. The Spanish reads: "dará a voz a las mismas mujeres que se levanten con la carhuaymesa sus esposas." Today the functionaries' wives are responsible for sourcing the *carhuaymesa* food.

there, a notable person will stand up to give the blessings, and they will say the blessing of the Father, the Son, and the Holy Ghost and then they will continue the banquet. Once the meal is halfway through, the Camachicos will get up with their respective compliances and they will put on a bag or *shicra* on their chest, into which the citizens of the place or the citizens [sitting] at the table will place some *biscochos*. The Camachichos will accept these with goodwill at all the mesas. Once the banquet is finished, the youths or returnees will get up to recite the grace blessing at the table. The Campo or Regidor will announce that the married women should get up to tidy away the meal. Straight away, he will carry out the reception of the water with the utmost happiness, setting off some flares and fireworks. Once this is finished, the Padron de los Veinte Cántaros [Padrón of the Twenty Pitchers] will follow.

The Michcos will submit the pitchers (which they have received during their duties[)]. Once the said pitchers [note in the margin in red ballpoint: X] are collected together, the "Padrón de las Sras. de Yañac" [Padrón of the Yañac Women][116] will begin, according to the *padrón* corresponding to them. Once the *padrón* is finished, the Campo

[f. 13r] will tell the Camachico that he needs to elect two people to hand in the flowers. That is to say that the elected people must be newlyweds and should hand in an *alforja* [woven saddlebag worn over the shoulder] full of flowers each. That is to say, flowers such as *shira shira*, *cumante*, and they will be handed out to all the participants. At this point, the *paradas* will begin with their cheerful celebrations, such as the drum, and right away the elders will take the holy cross and will [in the margin in red ballpoint: an arrow] set off for the village, changing one [cross?] as part of their *costumbre*, as is already known to be part of the tradition. Once the *paradas* arrive at the hill at "Otagaca," the outgoing Camachico gets himself ready with a pitcher or two of chicha from his stocks of obligatory submissions. He will be presented with a *vasija* [jug or drinking vessel] by an older person. The jug should be full, and he will continue to get a Santo Cristo ready in the small plaza [Cuhuay], covering a table with one of the finest cloths, and he will stay in his place, overseeing. This overseer will be accompanied by a whip or *truenador*.[117] The chicha will be enjoyed all the way from the site of

---

116. The Padrón de las Sras. de Yañac is specifically for married women.
117. This is apparently an idiosyncratic term for a whip. *Truenador* literally means "thunderer," perhaps alluding to the thunder-like sound that a whip makes.

"Shamarume" or "Gotogoto" along to the small plaza or "Cuhuay," in front of all the people who are there. Once all the participants are gathered together once again, the Teniente Gobernador or the Principal will tell the village to suspend the harmonies. Then he will call on the four Michcos so that they finish their *mantas*, which he will shake out in view of the public. Straight away, the Teniente will call for the Campo and for the Michco Mayor from "Carguayumac," so that the said Michco hands in items from his *manta*: a staff, a brooch or clasp, and a *corredor*. The Teniente will tell the two of them to kneel down and ask forgiveness for having worked two days as a substitute in favor of the Campo. The Teniente will order them to ask for forgiveness. Before this, he will give out three lashes of the whip,[118] not as a joke but legally, to make them suffer.[119] Straight away, the Regidor and the Michco from "Comau" do the same ceremony mentioned previously. Straight away, the Regidor Campo continues with two lashes of the whip and pardons the Alguacil and the "Ocucha" Michco in the same way as [in] the ceremony discussed previously.[120]

[f. 13v] [in the margin: a red ballpoint place mark: —] Once these sacred customs are finished, the Teniente Gobernador will call for the functionaries to get the Alfereces from both *paradas* to get up with their general compliances.[121] Once this compliance is finished, the Teniente Gobernador says that the cheer is suspended and orders both *paradas* to come into the premises to receive their orders. On arriving at the premises, the Alfereces will enter with their compliances, begging to carry on with their pleasures or gaieties. The Teniente and his elders give permission to the two *paradas*, instructing them about their serious responsibility that there must be no novelties [changes to tradition]. Once this license has been issued, the Teniente Gobernador orders the functionaries to call out to the two *paradas*. Once they are all gathered

---

118. Three is an important number in Andean community justice, so lashes tend to be delivered in sets of three. It is unclear whether this is a pre-Hispanic custom or a tradition that originated during the colonial era. Record-keeping practices for the ritual punishments associate the number three with a moral debt.
119. Andean water rituals feature prescriptive whippings to induce the tears of the young so that the ancestor guardians will attend to the needs of their descendants (Bennison 2019). For example, Arnold with Yapita (2006: 203) observed children in Qaqachaka, Bolivia, being whipped during a rain ritual, while older participants knelt down and beseeched the ancestor mummies as the children wailed.
120. Through receiving the punishments, these junior functionaries are pardoned for the moral crimes they committed during the *champería*.
121. "Compliances" refers to the items submitted by all the ritual participants.

in the premises, they put a stop to the cheer, and the Teniente goes out the door of his premises with the silver fist[122] and then gives his decree for rest [everyone can go home to rest], mentioning his expectation that on Friday all the men have to attend the account. Once this is finished, the teams go home and the village goes quiet. The Teniente and his elders instruct the Alfereces of the *paradas* to go out at dawn playing their *yaravíes* and *hualinas* in the small plaza [Cuhuay] in the manner of someone keeping vigil over the [cross of] Christ, in a very orderly fashion. The outgoing Camachicos are at this vigil, where nobody can enter Christ's side while wearing a hat or cap. As such, the Camachico shall, without any liability, strike with his whip any individual who does not obey this order.[123] These *paradas* or *juntas* will drink hot chicha[124] brought by the *current* Camachicos[125] until dusk[.] Once this is finished, the Alcalde Campo or the Regidor will suspend the cheer to proceed with the account of the men. [in black ink] The note about the word "outgoing" is correct.

[in the margin in black ink by the same hand as the note above:] That is to say, by the outgoing one, not the new one.

[in green ink] Addition: Because this was forgotten, we hereby make it known that on this night, Thursday, the current Camachico will provide the chicha and the outgoing Camachico will heat it up, in the way of someone keeping vigil over the [cross of] Christ.

---

122. *Puño de plata* (silver fist) may refer to the intricately carved silver-topped staff of authority used by the Teniente. In their account of the Thursday proceedings in 1979, Llanos and Osterling (1982: 143) mention that the senior functionaries who addressed the crowds outside the Teniente's premises took turns holding his staff as they spoke. The silver fist could refer to coins held in a closed hand; on Wednesday, the functionaries entered the Alcalde Campo's house, carrying pieces of silver in their right hand and their staff in the other. There appears to be an association between doorways, silver, and staffs.
123. I observed the strict enforcement of rules regarding dress in church ceremonies in San Damián in 2012. Functionaries carried whips into the church for this purpose.
124. In their account of the Thursday night vigil ceremony, Llanos and Osterling (1982: 143) explain that the *chicha caliente* is coffee, which in 1979 was served by the wives of both the current and outgoing *camachicos*.
125. "Puesto por el camachico *precentes*": sometimes the camachico is referred to in the singular when describing the duties of both, indicating that both *camachicos* had to provide coffee. Although a contributor has stressed that the outgoing *camachico* and not the incoming *camachico* should provide the coffee, by the 1970s both the outgoing and incoming *camachicos* provided coffee at the Thursday vigil (Llanos and Osterling 1982: 143). Perhaps they followed the precepts entered below in green ink, specifying that the incoming *camachico* must provide the coffee, while the outgoing *camachico* must heat it up.

[f. 14r] ~Friday~

<u>The duties and obligations for this day.</u> [wavy underlining]

In the morning, the Teniente will call for the two outgoing Camachicos to notify them [the outgoing Camachicos] about what their specific obligations will be for this day. The outgoing Camachico is obliged to give a pound of coca, a bottle of rum, and a [?] sized pitcher of chicha, and another to be royal [sized?].[126] Each of these should be completely full and checked by the elders, and they should be chicha *de jora*. The obligations for this day continue and the current [incoming] Camachico sets out a large table ["or" written here has been crossed out] and three benches in the [plaza at] "Cuhuay." The outgoing Camachicos put a dish with a white cloth on the table and a cross made from "Huay-Shocsha" straw and a large pitcher made from clay for the submitting of the chicha, which should also be covered with a cloth and with the same kind of cross as the previous one.

[in the margin: a red ballpoint arrow] Similarly, the Alguacil will set out a small table with a *huacura*[127] strap, a pair of scissors, and a woolen rope. These materials are for the punishments of the Camachicos and the Camachicas.[128] These punishments are because of the assistance they gave to the citizens when fulfilling their obligatory communal labor service.[129] Straight away, the Teniente Gobernador will make the current Camachicos aware of their duties

---

126. "Cántaro de chicha de ados y uno de real." I reason that the unclear specifications here refer to the sizes of the pitchers, because they must be checked by the elders after being submitted. As we have already seen, the quantities and weights of goods must be approved during the *champería*.
127. Don Eufronio Obispo Rojas defined a *huacura* as *una baticola de lana de soga* (a strap made from sheep's wool). The *huacura* used in the *champería* may be a restraint device or a kind of whip. *Huacura* is also the term given to a weapon made from rope with an attached weight.
128. This is the only reference to *camachicas* (female *camachicos*) in the Entablo. This term is likely used to refer to the wives of the *camachicos*. In Huarochirí villages today, a *cargo* or functionary role is taken on by both individuals in a marriage or partnership, who both have respective duties when either one takes up a *cargo*. It is perhaps for this reason that only men (and widowed women) feature in the community *padrón* in Casta today.
129. It is the role of the *camachicos* to ensure that all individuals fulfill their respective functions and tasks, so for a *camachico* to assist someone with assigned obligations would constitute a moral offense. Taylor (1987: 29) focuses on the Quechua term *camay*, which is related to ideas about obligation and the capacity of an individual (human or object) to fulfill an assigned role or task in society.

and obligations, which are two earthenware jugs so that they can offer the chicha drinks to all who need to quench their thirst. This will be in the same place, with the outgoing Camachicos obliging people to finish up.

The Teniente Gobernador will order the Campo and the Regidor to get everyone to take a seat in the order of citizens, divided up according to tradition in their *parcialidades*. Those from Yacapar will take their seat facing the east, and those from Yañac toward the west. The citizens from both will sit atop the straw called Huay-Shoccha. These straws are provided by the current Camachicos, who send

[f. 14v] two single women to get them.

Once all are properly placed in their respective seats and in their place, the Teniente will command his Campo or Regidor to continue the Padrón General de los Hombres [General Padrón of the Men]. Once this is finished, he will name four staff to correct the mistakes or shortcomings of each person. This reprimand will be in such a way that it will be useful and beneficial for each person.[130]

Once this is finished, he will command that the public *chaccha* [coca-chewing ceremony] continue. Once this is finished, he will call the Secretary—who is provided by the outgoing Camachicos—to the table. The Secretary begins to give the men their *chaccha*, which are coca and rum from their provisions. At this point, the outgoing Camachico prepares a small table and a chair that will be for his Secretary. Once the Secretary has finished his compliance, the elders request the list or *planilla*[131] to approve the numbers of the fulfilled or rebels. The *planilla* officially records[132] the men (qy) who are *originarios*.[133]

---

130. As explained in the introduction, in Andean justice, punishments were decided in accordance to the crime committed.
131. According to the Real Academia Española ([1726–1732], 2014: s.v. "planilla"), a *planilla* is a "form or document with blank spaces for filling in, in which reports are given, legal petitions or testimonies are made, etc., before the state administration" ("Impreso o formulario con espacios en blanco para rellenar, en los que se dan informes, se hacen peticiones o declaraciones, etc., ante la Administración pública." These functions correspond to those of khipus.
132. The verb *constar* is used here in the original Spanish.
133. People with *originario* status were those who could demonstrate an aboriginal connection to the territory in which they were resident. From 1727, the viceregal administration required *corregidores* to list *indios originarios* on separate *padrones* during colonial census inspections (*revisitas*) so that they could be charged tribute (Pearce 2001: 82).

They are the number 355 for a rebel or unfulfilled, 355. __ With the number 352, he owes two __. With the number 351, he owes one. __ With the number 12, fulfilled or obedient. With the number 5, they have surpassed their duties or, if not, have been very obedient. Once this *planilla* has been approved, the Secretary goes to his seat.[134]

Once this is complete, the Teniente commands all his functionaries to get all the people onto their feet in order to carry on with the *cuenta* [account]. The Alguaciles [note in black ink: *] [and] will make an announcement, handing over to the groups of notables. They will begin the Council, this being done by one of them, one of the notables. [in the margin: *The Menores will hear the number that the Secretary mentions]

The person who makes the announcements will publicly announce all the failings[135] of the person kneeling down, especially for the duties relating to the church and for obligations and administration relating to the house and other duties.

Once the reprimand is finished, he will proceed to the Council, where he will kneel down three or four meters away from the elders. The person who has to give them their punishment will ask the councilors what they are guilty of or what amorous encounters they have had[136] and how many [lashes?] they order

[f. 15r] for his punishment.[137]

---

134. While 5 is the ideal number score, 3 signifies a debt. The *planilla* was likely some kind of a khipu device (also see the introduction and footnote 145). In early colonial Huarochirí and today, the number 5 is associated with the deeds of the ancestors (Bennison 2016; Salomon and Urioste 1991), so the scores may reflect pre-Hispanic number ontologies.
135. *Faltas*: omissions in rituals are crimes punishable by the ancestors, who may withhold water or otherwise punish the entire community (Bennison 2016).
136. Not only an individual's performance at the *champería* is accounted for here: moral behavior throughout the year is a factor in determining the punishments delivered during the *champería*.
137. That is, the punishments are to be proportionate to the severity of the crime. The inclusion of "amorous encounters" here suggests that moral crimes committed outside of the *champería* are to be dealt with at this crucial point in the economic and social calendar. In 2019 (as noted earlier) elderly women in Casta described a tradition from their youth: unmarried women were subjected to physical lactation checks to determine if they had aborted babies conceived without marriage.

Then all those who have (not) been reprimanded for getting a judgment over their failings will appear as a one, two, three, or four, according to how it is to be settled.[138] For anyone who not only [?] reprimand, once that is finished, this citizen will get up and give thanks to the elders, reaching out a hand in gratitude. They receive this with the greatest attribution and respect. Once the *padrón* is halfway through, it will call all the persons present to a break.[139]

And the Secretary goes forth to the table of the esteemed nobles to continue with their offerings, which are coca and some glasses of rum provided by the outgoing Camachicos.

The chicha will be made public and available to all the citizens. Once this has finished, they will continue once again, until they reach the end in the same fashion.[140]

With it being afternoon by this point, the outgoing Camachicos will call for a definitive suspension of the proceedings, or they will announce that it has finished. And so at this point the people all leave the chosen place and call in at their home[s] to take in a little food that they prepared with some leftovers from their earlier duties. This meal will be public, for all.

Once this is finished, this luncheon will be rounded off with a glass of "Acequia" brand wine or with one or two bottles of rum.

[f. 15v] ~Saturday~ [wavy underlining]

The duties and obligations for this day. [wavy underlining]

In the morning, the Teniente Gobernador will call for the two outgoing Camachicos and will inform them of this day's obligations, which are two *chayanero* earthenware jugs [*potos*], and the Camachicos will carry these

---

138. Might these number values refer to lashes to be meted out in the future? Given that the numbers do not exceed five, perhaps the punishment system resembled the hand-based *uñancha* warnings of the Inca era.

139. Was the practice of pausing the khipu-board *padrones* halfway through a custom associated with khipu accountancy? Beyersdorff (2005: 296–297) has pointed out that Inca khipus containing annual accounts were ceremonially tied halfway through the year, in line with the importance of duality in Andean social organization.

140. Because the *padrón* account was paused halfway through, I take this section to refer to its being resumed after the break.

chayaneros to the premises. There they will approve these with a small compliance (right away, the outgoing Camachicos get ready). Right away, the outgoing Camachicos get ready, with two dictators to keep collecting the *chayanas*.[141]

Right away, the Teniente will command his functionaries to notify the *paradas* to continue with the *costumbre* at "Cuhuay," to conduct the changes of the Alfereces, Mayoralas, and [in the margin: a red ballpoint arrow] *cajeras de paradas*. The Alfereces will set off flares at each place and the Alfereces will prepare two *timbladeras*[142] or cups tied together[143] with strips of ribbons like each *parada* also has on sections of its flag, and the happiest of harmonies will continue. Once this obligation or *costumbre* is finished, the Teniente will order the suspension of the *junta* groups [*paradas*], decreeing that they must come into the office. Then each *parada* leaves with its flags, some having triumphed over the other ones. Once the Teniente arrives at the door of his premises, with his authority staff[144] in his hand, he declares the obligations and assistance requirements of that day to the public. He notifies all the parents or family guardians, telling them to come to the "Cuenta General de Señoras Originarias" [General Account of the *Originaria* Women] and lets everyone off for lunch in the *paradas*, stipulating a time limit. Once lunch is finished, he commands that the account continue in the very same way as the first day [Friday]. The functionaries carry out the meeting of all the women and for the men [*sic*]. Meanwhile, the Camachico washes the *lista* or *planilla*[145] in the same way as the first day for the approval of the numbers. Once it is approved, they bring their compliances with them to the small plaza or Cuhuay

[f. 16r] to carry on the Padrón General de los Hombres y Mujeres [General Padrón of the Men and Women], giving corrections [corrective punishments] to anyone who does not attend this *padrón*, they get given two lashes of the

---

141. In the 1980s the *chayana* was the time during the *champería* in Casta that was dedicated to rest and to alcohol (Gelles 1984b: 319). *Potos chayaneros* (earthenware jugs) are part of the ceremony, so drinking is clearly central to this aspect of the ritual. The Quechua verb *chayay* means "to arrive" and *chayana* can be translated as "arrival place." It is unclear whether monetary contributions for the drinks are being charged or whether the two volunteers are in charge of collecting and redistributing the drinking receptacles.
142. A ritual drinking vessel with handles on either side.
143. "Tied together": *engarzar* conveys the idea of linking up.
144. As before, I translate *puño* as "authority staff" or "staff of authority."
145. As explained in the introduction, the language used here strongly suggests that the *planilla* is a khipu account. While khipu accounts can be "washed" by having the knots untied, records made in paper and ink cannot be "washed" and reused.

whip. At this point, the outgoing Camachico[146] is called so that he submits the obligations of a pound of coca and a bottle of rum while the Camachico's announcer and interns and his Secretary continue with the charging of the *chayanas*, with the same *costumbres* for entering and exiting.[147]

The Teniente orders everyone to take a seat, just as on the first day, two from "Yañac" and two men from "Yacapar" as *corrigedores* [correctors] of the mentioned failings; once this is finished, the outgoing Camachico puts coca, rum, and chicha on the table of the notables and in the same pitcher, which has been made the day before, and they continue the *chaccha* publicly. The notables choose one person who is the most dedicated to join them in enjoying the *chaccha* and all the compliances.

The Teniente asks the newly elected person or electee to take a seat at his side. Once the *chaccha* has finished, the outgoing Teniente orders the married women from both *paradas* to gather together and they begin the Padrón de las Señoras [Padrón of the Married Women], counting their numbers as fulfilled or as rebels. __ Those marked down as "fulfilled" carry the no. 11 __ those marked down as "surpassed" carry the no. 15. Those marked down as "rebel" carry the no. 365.

The functionaries or Alguaciles will invite the notables to speak, then the Camachico discharges[148] [them] from their absences or failure to fulfill their duties. Then a notable person begins the council or the reprimand, making her [the woman being reprimanded] see all her failings. Once the reprimand is finished, he will let her proceed to the council, which is when all the men from the *parcialidades* get up to favor the women, as has been the custom since remote times. The women who receive the punishment will wear a *manta* folded in three sections or points and all the women will not wear any manual (monthly) items,[149] for the purpose of complying with the

---

146. At this point, and others, the singular *camachico* refers to both the *camachicos* in the plural.
147. Might the *chayana* accounts have been recorded on khipus? It is noteworthy that the *camachico* uses both a secretary and an announcer for these accounts.
148. "Discharges": *descargar* is the verb employed here, which could be interpreted as "download" if the *camachico* is involved in transferring the information relayed from the elders onto the *padrón*. However, it seems more likely that the *camachico* is involved in clearing the record, as the *teniente* and the elected person have seemingly already carried out the assigning of the numbers.
149. This section is unclear. Parentheses have been added around the word "monthly," with the word "manual," written by the same hand, replacing it above. The "monthly

reprehension in the most orderly terms, and it continues. Once the *padrón* is halfway through, it calls for rest and the Secretary [proceeds] to the table of the notables with his compliance and the [goods for?] the public *chaccha*. The chicha drinking continues with the *potos chayaneros*.[150] After the chicha is given out, he [the Secretary?] will give chicha to anyone who asks for it

[f. 16v] with the *chayanero* until he finishes with the whip in his hand. The Mr. Teniente Gobernador and notables order that the account continues and the Secretary goes to his seat and continues the account or *padrón*.[151] Once all these compliances are finished, the Teniente Gobernador announces in a loud voice the names of the nominated people from the Teniente right down to the last Alguacil Mayor, so that the community pays them due respect and attention * [in the margin: NB: go to the section below where it is marked NB]. Promptly after, the village Secretary or the *cantor* will recite the Rosary with all those present, men and women. At this point, the outgoing Camachico will lift up the [cross of] Christ and put down a lamp and a wax [candle], and they will continue the Rosary. Once the Rosary is finished, he collects the crucifix and likewise all of the ritual utensils and then all of the married women get up with their compliances and all the men acknowledge [this] with the utmost pleasure at having carried out our *costumbre* without even the slightest novelty. Giving thanks to God, they continue with their compliances.

Straight after, the Camachicos' Secretary offers out the luncheon provided by the Camachicos to all the people,[152] as during the first day.

[in the margin: NB here?-] The notables call for the outgoing Camachicos and the Camachico commands that that [sic] they tie their hands behind them and he [they] get taken to stand before the notables and receives his [their]

---

items" might refer to a waistband worn to protect the womb or some kind of menstrual item. The women who are being punished may be in a state of undress, covered only by the folded *manta* cloth. The "monthly" items which are prohibited would obstruct the punishment, so perhaps the women are obliged to be whipped with their backs bare. If the word "monthly" was simply a spelling error, perhaps the prohibited "manual" items were handicrafts such as embroidered cloths. The idea seems to be that a *manta* cloth folded in a specific way must be worn.
150. This term refers to the *putus*, *puchus*, or *mates*: the hollowed-out drinking gourds.
151. Note that *padrón* and *cuenta* are interchangeable terms. We therefore should consider the possibility that all of the *cuentas* throughout the Entablo are khipu boards, khipu devices more broadly, or other analogous mediums of accounting.
152. "People": alternatively, "men." The luncheon is offered to all the "Sres." Today food is provided to all, which presumably this was also the case at the time of writing.

punishment for having helped certain citizens or [for] having altered their mandated duties or obligations.[153] The notables order him to proceed to the council and take them to the table where the crupper[154] and whip are. Then one person comes out from among the notables' circle to give them their correction, taking the scissors and carrying out the ceremony of shaving them [cutting their hair off]. Because, as always, the women are disobedient, they create the illusion of cutting his hair and proceed to deliver the punishment with the crupper and then all the women get up to defend him and the notable heeds the pleas of the women and doesn't punish him.

All these punishments must also be done on the first day during the Padrón de los Hombres [Padrón of the Men] according to the explanations in the previous [pages].

[f. 17r] ~Sunday~

During this day, both *paradas* will proceed with their accounts of their necessary utensils and money that each of them has. The ones who will take up office[155] [should go to] the Teniente Gobernador, to the Administrator and other authorities, so they can loan them the security aids and help for the compliances of the delinquents.

Likewise, each *parada* will carry out a *relación* [payroll or enrollment] or *nómina* [list of names and corresponding roles] of the attendees or those who are present with their services, and they will carry out another one the same as this to record those who do not contribute or turn up, whether they are men and women with their *tushmac*[156] and mayorala *cargos*. This *relación* or

---

153. As previously discussed, altering duties is contrary to the logic of enforcing *camay*, which is the *camachicos*' responsibility. It is their job to ensure that people all fulfill their own respective obligations. The 2018 vice-president of the Comunidad Campesina de San Pedro de Casta explained that the Saturday *padrón* for punishments no longer exists, but punishments are still carried out on the Saturday after the functionaries have settled their accounts. "Un notable pregunta al pueblo si ha cumplido o si no ha cumplido. Si no ha cumplido, lo castigan. Es simplemente una costumbre. Cada castigo tiene que castigarle, si no ha cumplido. Ellos castigan públicamente" (He [an elder] asks the community congregation if he has fulfilled his duties or not. If he has not fulfilled them, they punish him. It's simply an obligatory custom. Each failing has to be punished, if he hasn't fulfilled it. They carry out the punishments in public).
154. *Vaticola* (baticola). The use of a horse crupper as an instrument of punishment is puzzling.
155. This means take up office as functionaries.
156. The Tushmac duties of the Alfereces and Mayoralas involve collecting meal ingredi-

nómina will be conducted in front of the gathering at "Cuhuay" in front of the authorities so that they find out or clarify the reasons for not turning up; such is the fundamental basis of the *champería* canal-cleaning fiesta.

Additionally, during this account the Alfereces will hand in the sacks of bread and crates of *chancaca*[157] to each *parada*, to each Mayordomo or Alférez from each *parada*. Once it is handed in, the Mayoralas will distribute it, each one of them pooling together their fifteen cents.

As for the men, on this day they should level up their quotas that each *parada* imposes on them. Those who collect these [sums] acting as the fee collectors will be the same Alfereces who are obliged to give a glass of champagne to each individual who pays them. At midday or later, the men will go with the Mayoralas to collect a bit of firewood from the countryside. Once they have arrived, they will proceed with their accounts.

[f. 17v] ~Monday~ [wavy underlining]

During this day, all the men from both *paradas* will finish their accounts and will get the local authorities to legalize and authorize their books.[158]

Once this is done or finished, they will wait, gathered happily awaiting nighttime. When it reaches eleven or twelve o'clock at night, everyone will get ready among themselves.

First of all, the *paradas* carry on with the harmonies in the most orderly fashion. Both *paradas* will call on the authorities to bring an end to the farewell with all the ceremonies that must be included, the old *yaravíes* and old *hualinas* and the drums. First they will come to the small plaza [Cuhuay] and then to Ursno. The Carhuayumac *parada* will go in front, followed by the Cumao

---

ents from the houses of their respective *parada* members so that this can be cooked for the *tushmada*, the meal on the Friday of the *champería* when all the *paradas* come together to eat (Llanos and Osterling 1982: 145; Ráez Retamozo 1995).

157. *Chancaca* is a solidified sugar syrup, which can be served as a liquid sauce (when heated to form syrup) or sliced straight off the block (Dargent Chamot 2017). Since the *chancaca* here is served with bread and there is no mention of it being heated, it presumably means that cold slices of *chancaca* will be eaten with the bread. Early twentieth-century sources refer to *chancaca* as being an ideal food for labor; it was recommended for workers and sportspeople (Coloma Porcari 2010: 23).

158. As explained in the introduction, the Entablo, as a form of ritual accountancy, also underwent the process of being authorized by the local authorities.

parada, accompanied by the enthusiastic playing of the *chirimías*. They will do a run of sorts, and not go about like Don Basilio Jimenez[159] and some others. The elderly men and women set off for "Gotogoto," returning from there with their flags lowered and their drums out of tune. They come back to the village, all going to their *huayronas*[160] or *paradas* with a very different sense of cheer.[161] This brings an end to this memory of our *costumbres* [a large period in blue ballpoint] since the times when it [the memory] was founded by the Indigenous [people] who began it, and to the one for which today we carry forward a memory [of] the official record of the ancestors.[162] What is written remains for what is yet to come, based on what we, the dictators [the elders dictating the regulations], remember. We have managed to make some parts be exact. Such is this memory that was dictated or directed by the elders [in the margin in red ballpoint: X] chosen to do so by the village: first, Don Vicente A. Reyes, Don Jacinto Bautista, and Félix B. Chagua, and with this we bring an end to this memory.

[f. 18r] This agreement (which has been written down [crossed out]) was discussed three years ago when officializing this book.[163] As such, we believe

---

159. Basilio Jimenez was presumably a community elder. He appears to have been a collaborator of Julio C. Tello, since Tello's notes on Casta's *champería* are preceded by the words "Basilio Jimenez—Casta" (Tello [1922] n.d.: f. 2r).
160. The word *huayronas* here appears to refer to the sites in the village where each of the four *paradas* congregate. The official respective premises of the Yañac and Yacapar *parcialidades* are also referred to as *huayronas*; these have their own respective buildings, whereas the *parada huayronas* have no demarcated territory within the village nucleus.
161. Secondary sources mention that the final Sunday of the *champería* included a sexual game played by the young people (Gelles 1984a: 88; Olivas Weston 1983: 76; Tello and Miranda 1923: 549). According to Tello and Miranda, in the 1920s this practice was an "ancestral wedding" (*matrimonio gentílico*), where the elders would select the young bachelors and maidens permitted to participate. Those who performed well at the *champería* were secretly notified that they could take part. Participation involved dressing up as the sacred ancestors and returning back along the canal toward the hills and out of sight of the other villagers. Once each of the youths had found a partner, they would stay together in the hills for a few days before returning to the village (Tello and Miranda 1923: 548–549). According to Catalina Olivares, this custom is discreetly referred to with the phrase *recoger la leña* (collecting the firewood), and the youths are expected to bring firewood with them on their return (also see Olivas Weston 1983: 76). This practice resembles aspects of a sexual courtship game carried out by the young people of Chuschi, Ayacucho, in the 1970s, where the high-altitude puna lands were "considered the appropriate place for such sexual activity, which cannot occur in the civilized village" (Isbell 1978: 119).
162. One gets the sense that *constancia del antepasado* (official record of the ancestors) could refer to a khipu. If this was the case, a select number of elders probably had the ability to retrieve and supplement any information encoded via a fiber account.
163. It is unclear whether the 1921 regulations took three years to be officially approved

that none of the citizens residing in this village since the [day of their?] birth would refuse to sign and approve it with their name.

Such was the undertaking of the present authorities, first the Síndico Don Máximo Calistro, the Señor Teniente Cristoval Jimenez, Regedor Mayor Melecio Calistro, Campo Jose M. Salinas, Regidor Campo Facundo Bautista, Alguacil Mayor Victor B. Miranda, Alguaciles Menores Cosme Obispo, Santos M. Obispo, Toribio Calistro, and Benancio Rojas, Camachicos Concepción Olivares and Simeón Calistro, Sacristán Exaltación Jimenez, Layman Yaspar Salinas, and Principal Don Justo Salinas. They were also accompanied by the Outgoing Camachicos Nicasio Salinas and Timoteo Rojas,[164] people who have obtained obligatory *cargos* of our village.

This book also goes [went] to the Alcalde Municipal [Municipal Mayor] + [+ in the margin: Don Pascual Calistro] to be checked over and authorized. The Council is also composed of Misters Pascual Gonzales Primer Regidor [in the margin: a red ballpoint arrow], Segundo Regidor Felex B. Salinas, Síndico de Rentas Don Catalino Bautista, and the Síndico de Gasto Francisco Obispo. After being checked and studied by the esteemed members of the Council, this book was passed to the Gobernador's Office, with Don Nemesio Bautista as the Gobernador, who also approved and accepted the legal regime and regulations of the duties and obligations that all the citizens of the village of Casta are subject to, and to this obligation only.

With nothing else to add nor to observe, [it] was returned to the community so that they could sign it with their own signatures.

This book will be authorized by the Justice of the Peace Don Cecilio Rojas and the Primer Axeso [Acceso] Don Jorge Obispo.

[X X X X X]

---

or whether the idea of writing this *entablo* had initially been discussed in 1918. The signatures of the community members that follow may have been added in 1924, three years after the regulations were penned. Given that the signatures are not dated, it is difficult to confirm this hypothesis, but the pencil entry objection, presumably by "Notario SC," may have impeded the approval of the Entablo as official *constancia*. This would explain a delay in approving the written regulations, as would the lengthy process involved in authorizing the regulations (as explained on the next page of the manuscript).
164. In the early 1920s Timoteo Rojas informed Tello's museum colleague artist about Casta's former human sacrifice traditions in honor of Wallallo (or Suqta Kuri?) (Tello and Miranda 1923: 522).

[f. 18v] [All signatures]

Florencio Lopez

Ysidro R. Calistro [stamped: Sindicatura del pueblo de Casta (Municipal Office of the village of Casta)]

J. B. Olivares i Yaure

J. Rojas y Salinas—Secretario de Casta [Secretary of Casta]

Silverio Miranedo [Miranda?]

Celestino Salinas

Vicente O. y Reyes

Jacinto Bautista [nearly illegible]

Jose R. Gonsalez

Cecilio Rojas

(Outgoing Camachico) Catalino Bautista

Nemesio Bautista (Alcalde Campo)[165]

Pascual Calistro

Facundo Bautista (Regidor Mayor)

Eusebio Gonzáles

Victor Perez (Alguacil Mayor)

Andrés Calistro (Alguacil Menor)

Nicolás Murrillo [?]

J. Hildiberto O. Rodriguez [with a personalized stamp: J. Hildiberto O. Rodriguez. Sastreria Casta (Casta tailor shop)]

Diósdado López (Alguacil de Campo)

Marcelino Lopez

Estanislao Calistro

Prudencio Jimenez

[f. 19r] [All signatures]

Adolfo Salinas

José M. Salinas

Concepcion Cristóstomo

Toribio Calistro

Bernardino Bautista

Santos Obispo

Vivancio Rojas

Olipio Bautista

Pedro Bautista Y.

Nazario Rojas

---

165. This signature is that of the same Nemesio Bautista identified as the *gobernador*.

THE ENTABLO 135

Claro Jiménez　　　　　　　　Pablo Olivares y Vásquez
　　　　　　　　　　　　　　　(Camachico)

Victor Bautista　　　　　　　 Juan Cl [?] Calistro

Silvestre Olivares　　　　　　Cristóbal Jímenez

Braulio Flores (aficionado)　　Tomas Perez

Doroteo Perez

[f. 19v] [in the top margin a note in pencil:] I do not agree.

Eusebio Olivares　　　　　　　Antonio Bautista
Félix Bautista Chagua　　　　　Gabino [?] Oyhorozco
Bautista Teodocio　　　　　　　Exaltación y Bautista
Félix Calistro y Bautista　　　　Emiliano S. Saliermino

This celebration or fiesta of the Walla-Walla has an attractive mythical scientific nature to it and we are losing sight of this in relationship to alcohol. In place of this [alcohol], chicha is to replace it, in order to have things coincide better with the many laws of the archaic era, and for these reasons, I hereby sign Miranda [?][166]

Vergilio Ríos y [?]

Bonifacio Salinas

I beg for my savior to have mercy
on me and I hereby sign Máximo [?]
Rojas

(Camachico Menor) M. E. Santos [?]

[f. 20r] Saturnino Bautista y.O. [?]　　　Melecio Calistro

---

166. According to Gelles (1984a), who saw the Entablo in the 1980s, this section may have been penned by Próspero Miranda, the Casteño who coauthored the 1923 paper on the *champería* with Tello. Próspero Miranda is remembered as a well-respected figure in Casta. I had hoped to find out more about him, but multiple locals stated that he has no descendants in the village. The surname "Miranda" does not feature prominently in Casta's cemetery, although a grave for a Sergeant Lazaro Obispo Miranda born in 1905 could represent Próspero's brother, cousin, son, or other relative. A "Victor B. Miranda" features in an earlier section of the Entablo as an *alguacil mayor*.

Bacilio Jimenez

Catalino Medina

Catalino Gonzales i B [?]

Pedro Echuanqui [?]

Pedro Jiménez

Lorenzo Medina y C.

Nicolas Salinas

Mario Calistro

[illegible initials] Salinas C.

R. Salinas y Yayo [?]

Félix Bautista y Salinas

Teofilo Huáman [?]

Cornelio [?] Salinas

Gerónimo Crisostomó

Genaro [?] Salinas

Wenceslao Olivares

Ferruco [?] y Calistro

Benicio[?] Salinas

[illegible, in blue pen]

Hipolito Obispo [stamped: Comunidad Indígena de San Pedro de Casta Prov. de Huarochirí. Presidencia (Indigenous Community of San Pedro de Casta, Huarochirí province. President's Office)]

[f. 20v] [all green ink] Faustino Calistro

In the village of San Pedro de Casta on day ten of the month of October of the year nineteen twenty-six, while gathered at the site of Coguay[167] on the Sunday according to *costumbre*, all the notables agreed that all the people from this point forward will give chicha according to the guidelines stated in the previous pages or alternatively a bottle of rum. Bottles of beer and wine remain banned, and to ensure adherence we hereby sign our names.[168]

Florencio Lopez
Vicente O. y Reyes

Faustino Calistro
Jose R. Gonzales

---

167. Note the alternative spelling of "Cuhuay" by this scribe.
168. This entry does not advocate for temperance but reads more like a pushback against alcohol not produced in the locality and that is not the fruit of collective labor (Bennison 2022). While bottles of beer and wines are banned, chicha and rum are permitted.

THE ENTABLO 137

J. B. Olivares i Yaure

Wenceslao Olivares

Simeón Calistro

M. O. [illegible]

Concepción Jimenez

Pascual Calistro

Jorge Obispo

Eusebio Olivares

R. Bautista

Victor Perez

Hecterio Larjo?

[f. 21 is torn out]

[f. 22r] [all black ink]

Nazario Rojas

Ynocensio Obispo

Alejandro Jimenez

Selino P mancioetta [?]

[f. 22v] [Black ink in a new hand in the main body of the page] [Note in the margin in dark-blue ballpoint: NB]

In the village of San Pedro de Casta, on the eighth day of the month of January of the year nineteen thirty-nine, while gathered in the community premises, the Commission designated by the communal assembly to organize the internal set of regulations on the date of the third of the present month. Said Commission is made up of the following undersigned: Presidente Cecilio Rojas, Secretario Pedro R. Bautista, Pro-secretario Francisco Salinas, Vocales Pascual Calixtro, Vicente Obispo, Jacinto Bautista, Concepción Olivares, Man[uel?] Obispo, Dalmacio Salinas, Diósdado López, Nemesio Bautista, and Teófilo A. Crisostomo.

After having created an interior set of regulations, which will be subject to study and approval by the Ministry for Public Health, Work, and Social Services,[169] and with it being stated in article eighteen,[170] which in addition to

---

169. The Ministerio de Salud Pública, Trabajo y Previción Social was formed in 1935.
170. There does not appear to be an article 18 in this particular law, but it is possible that this refers to legislation specifically linked to the Indigenous communities created in

the de[crees?] mentioned in it, they [the functionaries] also have secondary obligations to fulfill, and they are stipulated in the book of the "Campo"[171] and in the "Entablo." We hereby leave an official record that the book named "Entable" has been reformed by the public assembly on the thirteenth of January, nineteen twenty, that is recorded on the pages eighty-six, eighty-seven, eighty-eight, eighty-nine, and ninety of the said book.[172]

We the assembly hereby agree unanimously to leave an official record of the secondary obligations that the community functionaries have from the month of January to December, converting the literal copy from the thirteenth of January of nineteen twenty, so that this book also shows the obligations and responsibilities in order internally.

[f. 23r] Secondary obligations and responsibilities of the community functionaries during the administrative year. We hereby record that the community functionaries such as the "Campo," "Regidor Mayor," "Regidor Campo," [and] "Alguacil Mayor," who are all present, will cover the obligatory expenses during their period [of office], which correspond to them with the following exceptions.

The *comunero* who has the *cargo* of Campo will be exempt from [the *cargo* of] Regidor Mayor and the same goes for the one who is the Regidor Campo: he will not become the Alguacil Mayor. Fulfilling the obligations that correspond to each person, beginning on the first of January of each year, the outgoing functionaries have the obligation of collecting the *visitas* of the new functionaries in the company of the *comuneros*. The obligations of the outgoing functionaries are completely discharged during the village's reverences of the sowing period[173] in the puna and *maquiyal* and the farmland at Viquil so that [on] the two final days at the puna and *maquiyal*, the Síndico Tesorero will be forthcoming in covering the expenses with money from the community coffer, which he will set out in the budget.

1920 or the associated constitution. As article 12 of the Estatuto Comunal (Community Statute) explains, San Pedro de Casta was officially recognized as a *comunidad indígena* on October 27, 1936.
171. Locals confirmed the existence of the *libro del campo* in Casta, which is kept in private possession, but I was unable to locate it.
172. Thus, another manuscript called the "Entable" was in existence before 1920 and was reformed that year.
173. The sowing period is the first weeks of January during the onset of the rainy season.

The Obligations during New Year[174]

[Note in the margin in light-blue felt-tip pen: NB]

In order to fulfill the secret *costumbres* of the village, the Teniente Gobernador, Regidor Mayor, and Alguacil Mayor will contribute their corresponding obligations during the days occupied by the ceremonies. Furthermore, the Campo and Regidor Campo will contribute to these by agreeing on the arrangements for their corresponding duties for the "Carnival" fiestas and the Canal Cleaning in October. During these secret fiestas, the Camachico has the obligation [of ensuring the following duties are complied with], since the functionaries, along with their wives and families, have to assist the Alguaciles Menores, without the obligation of

[f. 23v] expenses, they present their expert works that they have a duty [to produce]. And the wives of the functionaries will present all their various kinds of expert knowledge to a specific person entitled *yachak*, who is in charge of checking these and referring those who do not fulfill their duties.[175] Afterward, they all gather together to fulfill their duties of this fiesta amidst a sense of cheer, which ends with the *curco*.[176]

Carnival Fiestas

[Note in the margin in light-blue felt-tip pen: NB]

For the Carnival fiesta, as the Yearly Calendar indicates, a canal-cleaning *faena* is carried out and is organized in the following manner:

---

174. In Casta, "New Year" refers to the first few days in January.
175. According to *yachak* Catalina Olivares, the wives must bring a *puchka*, a miniature ceremonial spinning distaff (aka a *qallapa*, a spinning tool for preparing fleece), and a *shicra* bag (a net bag made from plant fibers). As Luzmila Bautista explained, women must make their miniature *qallapa* from a *huayruro* branch and at the *pirwa* rainmaking ceremony they must *puchkar*: i.e, make their *puchkas* "dance" by spinning them around. They should also place their finest broad beans into their *shicra* bags.
176. *Termina en curco*: the *curco* or *curcucha* is a rainy dance performed in Huarochirí villages and other parts of the Andes in January during the rainy season.

Friday

The functionaries meet at the Campo's house in the company of the Teniente and the Principal to conduct the ceremony that is on the eve of the fiesta, and the Principal will remind the functionaries of their corresponding obligations for Saturday. For this [he will consider] whether the Campo and Regidor Campo have contributed to the *costumbre* in January. Those with obligations for that fiesta must make up a mesa where the obligatory expenses will be displayed: the Padrón de Comuneros [Padrón of Community Members] represented by kernels [of maize][177] is carried out from six o'clock in the evening until whenever they finish and they carry on with a nighttime vesper to the site of Hualhual, returning to the village, and they rest before the following day of the *faena*.

Saturday

First thing in the morning, the functionaries assemble in the premises where the Principal is to weigh their obligatory expenses, beginning with the two most senior ranking, "Campo" and "Regidor Mayor."

[f. 24r] Their obligations are a pound of coca, a bottle of rum, a packet of cigarettes, and two starter flares, and the two lower-ranking "Regidor Campo" and Alguacil Mayor will give half the amount, or in other words ½ a pound of coca, ½ a bottle of rum, ½ a packet of cigarettes, and a flare. The weighing scales for the coca obligations will be a traditional balance called a "Huipi."[178] After presenting their obligations inside the premises,

---

177. According to Echeandia Valladares (1981: 164–165), when the *campo* carried out this procedure (the *conteo* or Botada de Parada) during the *champería* in the 1970s, he read the names of the *comuneros* out loud from the *padrón comunal*, while his assistants categorized the kernels. Earlier in the twentieth century, this procedure likely used a khipu-board *padrón*.

178. Tello and Miranda (1923: 532) observed the use of this *huipi* (*wipe*) balance device during the *champería* in 1922. It was constructed of wood carved into a conical (gourd) shape, suspended by a weighted cord passing through the neck. Grooves carved on the wooden "arm" on its thinner end corresponding to determined weights allowed goods (presumably bagged or wrapped) to be hung by a cord or rope. They mention that the *huipi* was used to weigh the coca submissions handed over to the elders by the functionaries at the sacred site of Cuhuay before the start of the canal-cleaning work, when the coca will be shared out among the workers. A *huipi* was used in the Casta *champería* during the 1970s. All who were present observed its use, giving input on whether the weights of the coca submission matched the agreed amounts or not (Echeandia Valladares 1981: 157).

they will set off to the site of "Cohuay," from whence the Campo will call [note in the margin: a red ballpoint arrow] for the *comuneros* to gather for the assembly. Straight away, the Padrón de Hombres i Mujeres [Padrón of Men and Women] who must attend the *faena* will be carried out. Once the *comuneros* are gathered together, the functionaries return to weigh their obligations [once again] so that they know if each person has complied. Promptly afterward, the two Camachicos present the chicha obligations according to the *relación*, for the married *comuneras*, the widows, and the single women as well as widowers or single men who have a turn [ration] of [irrigation] water by sharing this pitcher consisting of [chicha to the value of] one *peseta* or (twenty cents) on that day and on Monday. During this event, the Síndico <u>Tesorero will give a kilo of coca</u> for the two *faena* days, as will the inspector of the balance[?]. Having finished the demonstration of the obligations, the Campo repeats to the young people once again whether they are listed in the Padrón Comunal [Padrón of Community Members] or not as being on cross duty for the places where the *costumbre* will be carried out, so that they comply. Then straight away he names the four Mayordomos, two for the men and two for the women. Once this has been designated, the four functionaries begin their goodwill toasts, a so-called Fiambre. The *comuneros* all leave in no particular order to Hualhual, where they begin the *faena* under the supervision

[f. 24v] of the Mayordomos. Following a brief *chaccha*, another group sets to work at another spot, at Huascuila. In the same manner, they clean the [canal] trajectory of the *comuneros*. The functionaries who are at Cohuay accompanied by the elderly *comuneros* take charge of carrying out the repairs on the animal enclosures, the pastures, or the track from the village to the site of Huayacocha. From Cohuay, they set off, the functionaries releasing a flare after having left behind the minor functionary's obligation, some chicha

---

If the *huipi* sat horizontally, this indicated that the coca weighed ¼ pound (Llanos and Osterling 1982: 127). The *principal* still uses a *huipi* today: each bag of coca suspended from the *huipi* is lifted up for all to see. Although the *huipi* used today appears to be very old (multiple locals put it at over a century old, if not considerably more), it does not appear to be the same one depicted in Tello and Miranda (1923). The use of balance scales to measure tributes and obligations points toward a level of standardization that, in addition to checking ritual submissions, would also have facilitated trade with other groups, perhaps on an imperial scale. For Dalton (2020: 296), *wipes* [*huipis*] made from gourds and pre-Hispanic balances made from bone functioned alongside *khipu* records and *yupanas* [counting devices, usually a tabular abacus with loose counting units] to support more bureaucratic organizations.

and the commission's expenses from the *chicra*[?] inspector.[179] They go to the site of Hualhual, stopping off at Pampacocha with their respective compliances to be carried out where required. Arriving at the canal intake that goes toward Maiguai,[180] they oversee a brief ceremony and continue, going along the canal, checking the condition that the *comuneros* have left it in until they run out of their compliances. After the drinks from their "Fiambres," the four functionaries and the Camachicos bringing the chicha proceed to the site of Huayacocha, giving a signal by means of a flare at Oclu-guiron[?]. Hearing that, those who went to do the cleaning at Huascuila carry on at Huayacocha Lake, where the functionaries will go in [to the reservoir] to the cheerful tune of the *chirimía* enthusiasts to give [out?] drinks from their provisions. Straight away, they all set off together to the *costumbre* site to continue with the inspections of the "Huallquis," "Eshkupuros," and bells. Once the young enthusiasts finish, they [all?] get a break, partaking of a light snack. Directly afterward, they continue to take part in the obligations that are displayed at Cohuay[181] and carry on the work once again until they finish. Then they gather together once again along with

[f. 25r] the elders and the Teniente, who arrive when it is time for the *padrón*. This is when the Campo calls them all to attend their *padrón*, and it begins with the Secretary carrying a list of all the nonattendees. Once the Padrón de Comuneros [Padrón of Community Members] has finished, he starts the one for chicha or pitchers, for which the "Camachicos" give accounts. At this moment, the Campo, accompanied by one of the functionaries, takes the crosses out to the sites where the *costumbres* will be carried out on Monday. [This is done by] the young people, by tradition. After finishing, they will return to the village cheerfully, drinking the chichas at the *costumbre* sites Ocluguirron [?], Paxxaguirma[?][182] [this section is unclear] full and the Cabildo[183] sends everyone back to their homes. The functionaries try to convene right away in the Campo's house to organize Sunday's fiesta.

---

179. If the functionaries have been required to wear their *shicra* bags so that they can be inspected, this has not been pointed out in the regulations. Perhaps this inspector is the same person who inspected the weights of the coca using the *huipi* balance.
180. This is an alternative spelling of the toponym "Mayguay."
181. Presumably, this means that all the workers are expected to make sure they fulfill their obligations listed on the *padrón* accounts.
182. This may refer to the same site called "Pacsagumo" below, where a rain divination game is apparently played.
183. Cabildo: "village council" (Salomon and Niño-Murcia 2011: 6).

Sunday

On this day, the functionaries meet as early as possible in the Campo's house to carry on curiously[184] with the *costumbres* that they are obliged to carry out. They continue setting up the table in the best way they see fit. For this, their wives and families are gathered together for the cooking duties and they get an extra committee ready, through which the Camachicos collect the chichas for Monday and also get the *toros*[185] and an Inca menu ready for the lunch on Monday for all the *comuneros*. After this, everyone sets out for the journey to Maiguai, with one Camachico staying behind to get the cooking equipment ready and asking for the widows and single women to help him in the kitchen at nighttime. On the route to Maiguai they practice everything they must do on Monday, stopping off at the site of "Cueca" [for] a brief rest.

[f. 25v] [in the margin in blue ballpoint: an arrow] Right away, the "Campo" performs the *costumbre* for the road from that point to Bailana Pastos [with?] three Alguaciles Menores and one Camachico announcing the group's departure immediately afterward by using a flare. They continue with everyone behind them in almost complete silence to the site where the road group awaits them. After they all share a drink, they continue to the canal intake, where they also carry out secret ceremonies. They proceed, stopping at Chacchadera to fulfill the observations of the *huallqui* items, *eschcupurus*, etc.,[186] and to play carnival[187] with natural dyes that are [illegible] at this place. They carry on to Maiguay for the *visita* of this hamlet. They call in an Alguacil so that those who live in this [illegible] for a moment. Right away they stop off at "Ñamuc"[188]

---

184. As noted, expertise and skills are described as *curioso* in Huarochirí if they are local, ancestral forms of knowledge.
185. *Toros*: literally, "bulls"; however, the term also refers to guinea pigs in Casta. It is unclear if these *toros* are guinea pigs to be cooked. In the 1980s, the *toros* in this part of the ceremony were ingredients for a maize broth (Gelles 1984a: 169).
186. As collaborator Doña Anselma Bautista Pérez explained, today men must wear their *huallques* containing the necessary items during the Carnival traditions as well as at the *champería*. We should assume that these Carnival "observations" are made on the khipu-board Padrón de Huallque.
187. To "play carnival" [*jugar carnavales*] means to playfully throw powders, liquids, or paper ribbons over each other. The physical characteristics of this site lend themselves to playing carnival.
188. This site may not relate directly to the huaca Chaupi Ñamca of the Huarochirí Manuscript; chapter 10 explains that a male huaca satisfied Chaupi Ñamca sexually, after which she turned into stone (Salomon and Urioste 1991: 78). In Collata (near Casta), a stone shaped like female genitalia was visited by men who would interact with the stone.

before proceeding to Lecas [?] Lake,[189] where they carry out the ceremonies with great respect and morality, where they hand in the *curiosidades* of the Alguaciles Menores, which are *tacllas*,[190] and they go back to Ñamuc to continue with the *costumbres*. Straight away, the Campo, accompanied by one Alguacil, is designated to go to the houses of those who live there to notify them about the "Piso" quota that they are obliged to satisfy according to the area of land that they own.[191] Right away, they return to the village with the cheer of the *chirimía*; and when they arrive, they collect their things to take to the ceremony before going back to their homes. At this moment, the Camachicos oversee the cooking in the kitchen, surrounded by enthusiasts playing all manner of musical instruments.

[f. 26r] they continue in the kitchen all night ahead of Monday morning.

Monday

In the early hours of Monday they will do the same as on Saturday and after lunch in [the house of?] the Camachico and the respective breakfast in the house of the Campo they all will set off together with the same *costumbre* obligations until they arrive at the site of "queca,"[192] carrying out inspections of those in charge of the cross, checking if they put the crosses in place and

---

This practice, described by poet Zoila Forss Crespo Morayra, reportedly no longer persists (Zoila Forss Crespo Morayra, in a presentation at the Centre for Amerindian, Latin American and Caribbean Studies, University of St. Andrews, April 24, 2018). Despite this intriguing parallel, the term *ñamoc* (and the synonymous variant *ñamca*) features in the names of various huacas of the Huarochiri Manuscript: Tantañamoc, Chaupiñamca, Mamañamca, Manañamca, Yanañamca, Tutañamca. These huacas may have formed part of a Huarochirí-wide ancient llacuaz lighting cult (Taylor 1987: 235), just as the *ñamoc* of Casta may have, too.

189. Might this site be "Lacsa"? According to an oral narrative recorded by Gelles, there appears to be a spring or well at Lacsa (Gelles 1984a: 172).

190. The Quechua word *taclla* (*taqlla*) refers to a plow, including the hand-held plow and the *chakitaqlla*, the Andean foot plow. For an in-depth discussion of the *tacllas* used in Casta, see Echeandia Valladares (1981: 40–48). The *tacllas* submitted by the *alguaciles menores* here are "curiosities" because they are miniature in size and are said to bring good luck. When describing these "small foot plows" (*chakitaqllas chiquitas*), the ritual expert Doña Catalina Olivares gestured with her hands, indicating an item around the size of a hand. Apparently, the items are buried in the earth once submitted and approved, although I was also told that the mini foot plows are left there overnight. Perhaps they are buried and then later retrieved?

191. "Cupo de Piso" appears to refer to a land taxation system.

192. This is an alternative spelling of the toponym "Cueca."

got the *peanas* [bases] ready at all the *costumbre* sites and at all the altars. They make a note of what their respective punishment is, or they do it when they arrive to the Cabildo in the afternoon [written above, by the same hand: in the event of not fulfilling the work]. After a brief rest, the Campo will get the attention of the devotees who are on the route, carrying it out in the same way the functionaries did the day before, until they reach the canal intake at Mayhuay, where the *faeneros*[193] sit down in order of age, ready to present their corresponding obligations. One functionary will have left his obligations for the elders, which they will set out. Straight away, the Campo will give out a signal to leave the work after giving out his obligations and submitting the women's proportional expenses to the Mayordomos. They leave the work [site], setting off a flare signal [in the margin in dark ballpoint: NB]. They stay for a moment until the *faeneros* advance, reaching the site of Chacchadera for a new gathering where they partake of the functionaries' obligations and provisions. Straight afterward, the inspections of the *faeneros* are carried out, for which all the *faeneros* present the *huallques, escopuros*,[194] and *cascabeles*. All the *faeneros* must do this and the same goes for the Mayordomo overseeing the work. For the functionaries, the same goes for the Camachicos with their chicha for sharing out, collected from the *comuneras* and wives of the *comuneros*. After a cheerful dance, they set off a flare signal and head back, leaving the *faeneros* right there at Chacchadera. All the functionaries set off together for the site of "Pacsa" and after receiving the

[f. 26v] work, and once the [married] *faeneras* are gathered, each functionary, the said women, and the Mayordomo toast a drink. In the same manner, the Camachicos will share out the chicha and provisions, coming back to "Lecas" Lake straight away [in the margin in blue ballpoint: NB and an arrow], where they find the *faeneros* who were left at "Chachadera" already at work. After a brief sharing out of the provisions of the functionaries' and Camachicos, they set off for the site of "Ñamuc," calling the Mayordomos of both the men and women via an Alg[uacil?], to the *padrón*. They [the Mayordomos] get their people gathered at this place. With all the functionaries gathered, they give out the final drinks from their obligations, showing the last drop of rum and the last coca leaf so that the *faeneros* can certify that they have finished the work obligations. They take stock of the obligatory levels of their compliances,[195]

---

193. *Faeneros* are collective laborers.
194. Also *eshcupuros*: small gourd containers for storing lime powder for coca-chewing.
195. The phrase "toman cuenta de los pisos obligados su complimiento" is unclear. It could mean that the work will be checked to ensure that the workers have reached the

which is for those same people. The ones who did not fulfill their duties are made to fulfill them. After all this, the Campo will carry out the respective *padrón* to check the attendees and nonattendees.

In the same manner, he will get everyone to set off and play carnival, making sure this does not compromise anyone's health, bringing everyone together to the site of Shamashama. Here the Camachico consumes a pitcher of chicha or a quantity according to the amount of people,[196] continuing to "Taloc." From there to "Puntangal," the Camachicos carry out the same obligations as on the previous [day?], with the functionaries sharing out their provisions, if there are any. This is where a lovely game carried out by the *faeneros*[197] gets underway. They set off for the site of "Pacsagumo," where the community elders and authorities wait, passing by the black place, which is noteworthy for its history of carnival games, and they arrive at Pacsagumo. The elders anxiously wait to learn of the good or bad news from the functionaries and the *faeneros*. Right after the news, the Camachico functionaries make a toast [and give a drink] to the elders and likewise the *faeneros*, handing out

[f. 27r] bunches of wild flowers from the Campo as a token to signify the memory of the day's work, reverence, and respect. Right after, they get everyone to set off toward the site of "Uhsno," where they hold back for a moment. The Camachico once again serves out the chicha, and they proceed with the Cabildo in front in the midst of happy games and *chirimía* music, in order of the functionaries, the authorities, and the elders. The triumphant party of enthusiasts are free to enter the Cabildo during their game, so they can flank

---

level that they are obliged to work on or that there will be a check to see if they have fulfilled all the steps required of them during the work.

196. Although the text says the Camachico consumes the chicha, it seems more likely that he doles it out, as the amount to be consumed is proportionate to the amount of people present.

197. It is unclear what the game consists of. Carnival games in Huarochirí tend to include *yunsa* (also *cortamonte*), which is a game where participants take turns to try to fell a tree whose branches have been decorated with prizes. The game appears to have an element of augury. Gelles (1984a: 88) interprets the carnival "game" as a sexual one, but there appears to be a divinatory aspect to it. Perhaps this section refers to the oracular dice game of *pishca* (*pichca*) played in the Tupicocha annex of Pacota. The Pacota authorities play *pishca* in January to foretell the rains in the coming year (Salomon 2002a). Workers in Casta also played oracular games, including a rain divination game involving throwing coca leaves at the base of Cumau Waterfall. This is another possibility: the toponym "Pacsagumo" is suggestive of a waterfall or other fast-flowing source of water. Alternatively, this may be a vague reference to "playing carnival," which is described more explicitly in other sections of the February traditions.

[them as they carry] their victory banner. After a little entertainment, the Teniente Gobernador gets the noise to stop for a moment and carries out a check to see if the functionaries have correctly fulfilled their obligations and to check the *faeneros* and their work, both in the canal and in said lake [the reservoir]. This is when the Camachicos finish off by serving out the chicha. Right afterward, in order to set to rest the *costumbres* that we are noting down, the authorities and elders come out in hierarchical order in a parade including each one of the noted functionaries. The Teniente Gobernador orders everyone to go home afterward so as not to upset the public order.

Obligations of the ecclesiastical employees.

If there is to be a Mass on the following days: matins,[198] doctrines, Santo Rosario, and Sunday, each Church Mayordomo has the obligation to provide half a pound of wax candles, accounting for the fact that this is from Ash Wednesday to the Day of the Resurrection[199] on Sunday. Furthermore, they must provide incense for the Masses and matins if it should be necessary during Holy Week on the day of Palm Sunday. They provide two palm branches, providing one each. With the cooperation of the Regidor Mayor, who gives errands to the youths, they provide olives[200] for the necessary celebration. On Monday, they wash the cloths and tablecloths from the church alongside the single women, with the Mayordomo providing everything that is necessary for the washing. Holy Tuesday: X. Holy Wednesday: submit all the total number of wax candles according to the amount dictated in the book of the

[f. 27v] church, all adorned with flowers, and have burning half a pound of candles that they contribute as part of their obligation. Holy Tuesday.

From Mass time onward, have a pound of candles burning constantly, each of them burning until the Day of the Resurrection on Sunday, ensuring that the candles that are fizzling out and the *centella* candles[201] under their care keep burning in the right proportion, from this day to the Day of Resurrection on Sunday. Good Friday. They will provide a sufficient amount of cotton[202]

---

198. Matins are church services held in the morning.
199. Easter Sunday.
200. Olive branches. These would have been used in the Palm Sunday processions.
201. *Centellas* are thick church candles that are kept burning during Easter celebrations, starting on the Day of the Resurrection.
202. Cotton wool. It is unclear what the cotton was used for, but a later entry in the Entablo describes the use of cotton wool for divining rain. According to Sandamianinos,

148 THE ENTABLO MANUSCRIPT

so it can be handed out and in the same [way] the Regidor Mayor will bring Florida water,[203] one or two vases, as necessary. This will come out of the coffer or the expense will be noted in his account. We also hereby record that on Ash Wednesday, when there is Mass,[204] they will prepare the palm and olive ash. During the matins, they will un[?][205] an oil lamp with two pounds each between the Mayordomos, accounting for the fact that the Camachicos will contribute the altar, which is to consist of the best fruits as a tribute to the Lord. On Holy Thursday, [after?] collecting potatoes from each *comunero*, they will change the flowers of the deceased so that they can then bring more rosemary branches of their own to decorate the holy tomb and chapels in preparation for the Lord being placed [there].

Responsibilities of the layman.

During Lent, he leads the prayers on Wednesday, Friday, and Sunday, when there is no priest during doctrine hours. He must get the single women to make an arch of natural flowers for the Holy Rosary, and he must also get these same women to collect flowers with the petals taken off,[206] for the days when there are matins and the Holy Rosary, in case there is a procession. He must get the young unmarried men to bring flowerpots filled with flowers for the crucified Lord on the same days. On Holy Saturday, he is in charge of decorating the choir and altar with flowers with the single women. It is the sacristan's obligation to have the candles in the vestry burn on matin days,

---

Easter is supposed to align with the end of the rainy season, so it is possible that Casteños used the cotton for the management of rain. At the beginning of the rainy season, two different kinds of cloud-like aerated, fluffy substances are used to bring on the rains. As explained earlier, seafoam is used to generate rain clouds. Casteños also explained their use of the cotton wool that features in the inventory of ritual items at the end of the Entablo: at the January *pirwa* rainmaking ceremony. It is placed atop the ritual *mesa* (table: a set of sacred objects laid out for ritual activity, usually on a cloth placed on the ground) to divine rainfall in the year ahead. If the cotton becomes wet, it will be a good year with sufficient water. Cotton wool is used in rainmaking rituals throughout the Andes. An account by Vera Delgado (2011: 148) on the canal-cleaning ceremony (Yarqa Haspiy) in Coparaque in the Colca Valley mentions that cotton features in offerings to the water deities, as does an account of a Kayawalla rainmaking ritual in studies by Rösing (1995) in Bolivia.
203. Florida water is a scented cologne used in Andean rituals and healing practices (see, for example, Polia 1989).
204. The Spanish text indicates uncertainty as to whether Mass will happen or not, expressed through the use of the subjunctive of the verb *haber*: "cuando haya misa."
205. The Spanish reads *des-visarán un belón* [*velón*].
206. This refers to the preparation of confetti.

Holy Rosary days, and doctrine days, as well as being available for the funeral, doctrine and other fiestas for the bell-ringing.

[f. 28r] He must also be available to help the priest whenever he asks for it and he must ring the call to prayer every afternoon from the first of January onward.

The Community Cantor.

Has the obligation to attend church to carry out the Holy Rosary on the *costumbre*[207] days during Lent and to accompany the deceased from the moment they cease to exist until their funerals on a flat area. During Holy Week, vespers and *oficios*[208] alongside the priest, should there be one [available], and if not, alongside his *compañeros*, must organize it well and in agreement with the Principal or community council and other ecclesiastical staff. Additionally, we hereby make an official record that on the 31st of December in the afternoon the outgoing functionaries from the community assembly make a visit to [inaugurate] the new ones, or the incoming ones, leaving behind a small offering.

[In the margin in red ink: Viene de la F6. Reforma—]

—Reform—

Based on the observation of the Alcalde Campo Don J. Hildiberto Obispo:[209] taking into consideration the fact that the Menores Alguaciles [Alguaciles Menores] who are appointed for the *costumbres* in October and at Carnival are obliged to carry their own provisions with them; a quarter of pisco, coca, and cigarettes, so that there is enough to benefit the community. This regulation is officially approved and applies henceforth.

We also hereby leave an official record that since remote times, during the month of December from the 26th until the 30th, the functionaries such as the Campo, the Regidor, the Regidor Campo, and the Alguacil Mayor will

---

207. The word *costumbre* is used here to relate to specific days during Lent. Thus, it is not just syncretistic irrigation rituals with pre-Hispanic roots that are *costumbres*: Christian customs are also referred to with this term.
208. An *oficio divino* is a Catholic liturgical prayer.
209. A personalized stamp earlier in the Entablo identifies J. "Hildiberto O. Rodriguez" as the village tailor.

organize *faenas* so that the roads are cleaned by the *comuneros* from the village to Chauca and from the village to San Antonio, with the Campo overseeing

[f. 28v] from the village to Huachupampa. The Regidor Campo and the Regidor Mayor will oversee the work to clean the village, at the entrances and exits. This will be done by the single women, who will be accompanied by the Alguacil Mayor.

For the village maintenance work[210] at New Year, the Regidor Mayor will submit the [?] to the residents and with their respective cross, which they are obliged to provide, so that it can be handed over to the new functionary. The same goes for the *papal*; [potato field checks?]. Straight after, on the 4th of January, the Campo along with the Regidor Campo will go to Rairay hill to hand over the [illegible] to the new functionaries: the Campo oversees Rairay, Chacc-saygua, Moya, Shirapamku, and Pitic with the respective crosses and demarcations and legalities.

In the same way, the Regidor Campo oversees Racray to Racraquiron, the Punta de Bitama, Carhuachayco, Namanlilpa, from there to Zambo and Carema. All the workers will return to the village with the utmost cheer, and the Regidor will get the single women to prepare a feast.

On the 5th of January, the maintenance work will continue at [or from?] Pitic Santa María, Tomesilla to Tandari [carried out] by the comuneros. The Campo will go along the length of the Mayg[uay?] canal, certifying that the[re are no] sticks from trees such as the willow [?] inside the canal.[211] He will check this from the intake to Matoca. When he arrives at the village, the Campo will elect an expert witness for the necessary work at the village of "Mayguay," in the event that it is in a state of disarray or they are not [compliant] with their duties.[212] The Campo will proceed to punish them at the site

---

210. The term used here to refer to the New Year work is "reserencias." This term appears to be idiosyncratic; Gelles also reports the use of this word in Casta to refer to the collective work carried out around New Year (Gelles 1984a: 164).
211. According to Casta's "Auto redondo" manuscript (CCSPC 1711–1808: f. 62v), which is concerned with the delineation and jurisdiction of Casta's boundary lines, Casta had cornfields located in Mayguay (Mayhuay) in the early nineteenth century.
212. In the 1980s, the work at Mayguay (also Mayhuay) included cleaning a large dam (Gelles 1984a: 170). Since the tract of canal between Mayguay and Santil is so far from Casta village, in the 1980s only a small group of youths cleaned it and were the last to return to Casta when it was becoming dark (Gelles 1984a: 170).

of "Ñamoc[i.e., Ñamuc]." From there, they will all set off together to Santil and to the estate of Santo Domingo, where the lease

[f. 29r] holders and neighbors from Callahuanca will be gathered together at the site of the border limit. There the Campo, along with his Alguacil, will have a cross erected and [he or they will] elect expert witnesses to check the *chirimoya* orchard and the state of the estate. After a brief moment, the Síndico Personero, the Treasurer, and the rest of the *comuneros* briefly drink a glass of beer in the manner of someone livening things up with the Chirimía. Promptly after, they continue with the expert witnesses, stopping at Huamanshanca, Viquil, where they will gather at the cross for the accounts of the commissions.[213] After this is finished, they will come to the hamlet of Cumpe, meeting with the authorities. The new Campo will proceed with the *visitas* for the hamlet, and if there should be any disrepair, he will proceed with the corrections; afterward, he proceeds to the hamlet of "Huinco," and the same observances will be carried out. After a moment with the hamlet's authorities, he returns to the village carrying branches of plants for the baby Jesus and checking the cross altars, to make sure the outgoing Campo has left the cross that he will hand over to the new one. When they arrive at the stone site trail, the village will receive [them] with some Doctor Dances[214] and the maintenance workers[215] will hand in *amancaes*[216] flowers to the authorities and elders. Straight away, the village will be refreshed with the ringing of bells along to the Cabildo, where a full account of all matters relating to the

---

213. If the accounts of the "commissions" are kept on *padrones*, could there have been separate *padrones* for the account-keeping practices focused on the boundary limits and the annexes?
214. During the New Year "baile de los doctores" on January 2, 2019: men dressed in waterproof ponchos were accompanied by a young boy dressed up in medical garb, all of whom danced a series of heavy-footed steps from the evening through to the morning to the sound of the *chirisuya*. The "doctors" repeatedly grunted and babbled unintelligibly as they danced, while one dancer asked for the huaca Suqta Kuri to carry him away. The dancers in the "baile de los doctores" lead a procession, followed by their wives and other functionaries through the streets of Casta, stopping at the premises of the Comunidad Campesina, the sacred site of Urquwasi (Mountain House), the premises of Yañac, Yacapar, and the church, ending at the judiciary premises in the main square. The dance and associated ritual offerings made at the various locations are intended to bring the rains.
215. The term used to refer to these workers is 'reserencieros'.
216. *Hymenocallis amancaes*, a bulbous plant with a daffodil-like yellow flower, which grows in the Lima-facing lomas. Large areas there were occupied by migrants to Lima from the early twentieth century onward. As such, the flower is at risk and has recently become the subject of conservation campaigns (*El Comercio*, June 24, 2019: https://elcomercio.pe/vamos/peru/flor-amancaes-descubre-simbolo-lima-florece-noticia-648682-noticia).

[functionaries' performance in leading the] maintenance work will be given and punishments given to the outgoing functionaries, such as the Campo and the Regidor Campo, who covers the route from Caracoma to Toro Puche and the *visitas* for the "Opica" estate.

We also hereby leave an official record that the expenses from the breakfasts down to the final [item] will be contributed by the Síndico Tesorero according to the *entablos* for budgeting.

We the community authorities hereby leave behind

[f. 29v] an official record with all the *comuneros* so that for all time, until the final generations, it is respected as an immortal memory.[217] We hereby sign today, in San Pedro de Casta on the 15th of November of the year 1947. Also, during the accounts, the Campo will bring the cheer of the village to Carhuayumac and the Regidor Campo will do so from Pampacocha to Huayacocha. Each of the new and outgoing functionaries will bring their expenses and the cheer of the Chirimía.

All these are recorded here because they were missed out in this honorable book. And we hereby sign:

Benito Flores

Diosdado Lopez

[stamped: Comunidad Indígena de San Pedro de Casta Prov. de Huarochirí. Presidencia (Indigenous Community of San Pedro de Casta, Huarochirí province. President's Office)]

Cecilio Rojas

Tiburcio Rojas
Antonio Bautista [stamped: Comunidad Indígena San Pedro de Casta. 1er Vice-Presidente (Indigenous Community of San Pedro de Casta, Huarochirí province. 1st Vice President)]

---

217. "Se respeta como recuerdo imperecedero."

M. Agapito Medina   Campo C [illegible]
Catalino Gonzales i R [illegible]   Campo Juan H Obispo
Juan Jimenez
Gabino Rojas

                             Vivancio O.[?]

[f. 30r] Repairs to the "Carhuayumac" canal

At the community premises on the fifth day of the month of May of the year 1947, with all the community authorities gathered together and present, we hereby leave an official record of the earlier project by the functionary Alcalde Campo Don Juan Hildiberto Obispo and his *compañeros*, given the many years that the canal from Carhuayumac to Pampacocha has gone without being repaired. This gave rise to the interest in carrying it out with the [allocated work days?][218] from the months that he is in charge of, with the *cargo* of providing tools. The augers, drills, and explosives expenses for the workers were complied with.

And with this, we the authorities hereby leave a record in agreement with the *comuneros*, and we hereby sign:

Benito Flores   Diosdado Lopes

[stamped: Comunidad Indígena de San Pedro de Casta Prov. de Huarochirí. Presidencia (Indigenous Community of San Pedro de Casta, Huarochirí province. President's Office)]

                             Tiburcio Rojas

Cecilio Rojas
                             M. Agapito Medina

Catalino Gonzales R. [illegible]
                             Juan Jimenez

Campo Juan H Obispo   Gabino Rojas

---

218. The unclear word is *corralajes*.

[f. 30v] 1952

[In the top margin in blue ballpoint: 27 pages in the book of the Entablo][219]

On the date the seventh of January of the year nineteen fifty-two, having taken account into the ancient and superstitious *costumbres*, we have decided to make an inventory of the secret objects that serve as folklore.[220] These are a round stone that used to represent the village[221] and its inhabitants en masse, a small brown triangular stone that represented Sami Dios,[222] a metal object that represented the wealth of the village,[223] and a long stone figure that represented the *curador* [healer] or witch, a piece of cotton or white wool that represented the clouds to foresee if there would be rain or not, unsweetened chicha, which functioned as liquor for the works carried out between the

---

219. This marginal note indicates that the pages of the Entablo were subject to an inventory in recent decades. Salomon and Niño-Murcia (2011: 55) note that the community in Tupicocha annually inspects its entire archive at a General Audit.
220. At least two of the stones and the metal object described here as "folklore" were still in use in 2021. They are used to divine the conditions for the coming year during the *pirwa* ritual in January. The inventoried items are associated with the singing of Quechua songs. Although they have been inventoried in a manuscript written largely in Spanish, it is possible that ritual items such as this were previously inventoried on khipu devices. The items are considered crucial to community well-being. The manual passing of the objects from one functionary to another (see figure 1.16) is indicative of the individual responsibility of each functionary for the well-being of the community.
221. Carlos Alberto Olivares Bautista mentioned during a video call in 2021 that this stone weighs between three and four kilos. Echeandia Valladares (1981: 36–37) explains that the Regidor takes custody of a circular highly polished stone representing the village, which he passes onto the incoming Regidor during the January *pirwa* ritual. Likewise, Gelles (1984b: 329) explains that the functionaries hold secret rituals where the outgoing ones transfer ritual paraphernalia to the incoming ones. Through the transferring of these objects, the functionaries reaffirm social bonds with one another and with their ancestors; according to Kemper Columbus (1998: 442), stones represent kinship and affiliation.
222. In other words, "Sami God." This is the only known reference to a "Sami Dios" in the Andeanist literature that I am aware of. A collaborator in Casta stated that Suqta Kuri is associated with Sami Dios. The Sami Dios stone appears to be the same stone that locals today call the *indio* (Indian), which represents the *comuneros* and their hard work on the land. Allen (2002: 33–36) defines *sami* as an "enlivening force." It is fitting that a being named the Sami Dios features in this account of water customs, given that *sami* is transmitted from one living thing to another. *Sami* is said to permeate musical instruments (Allen 2002), and a lack of it can affect musical ability in the player. In this respect, *sami* appears to assist in the fulfillment of personal ability, skill, and work. As we have already seen, this is assessed by the ancestors during water rituals. For further information on the kinds of power that these objects, known as *illas* and *conopas*, are said to transmit, see Allen 2016.
223. President Carlos Alberto Olivares Bautista described this item in 2021 as a square shaped "stone" "que representa al caja, al tesoro, al ahorro del trabajo" (that represents the coffer, the treasure, the savings amassed from work).

cura and the *yachak*.[224] We hereby leave an official record submitted by Mr. Gabino Obispo and Mr. Juan Obispo as presidents.

Juan Ho. Judge   Gabino Obispo

[ff. 51–52 have been torn out]

[f. 53r] [a note in pencil:] As the owner of this book, which, having given it, I am.

[signature, with flourish below:] Notario S C

[f. 103r] [in black ink script, a sheet of plain paper attached with tape at the back of the notebook reads:][225]

List of the animals and owners who will pay a penning fee that goes into the community coffer. As follows:

Owners	Day	February	Cows	ox	*Bulero*[226]	llamas	mules[227]	Pig	Price
Nemecio B	2	"	"	1	"	"	"	"	010
Juan O.V.	3	"	2	"	"	"	"	"	080
Mario C	4	"	1	"	"	"	"	"	050
Marcelino L.	6	"	1	"	"	"	"	"	030
Estanceslao C.	6	"	1	"	"	"	"	"	040

---

224. Echeandia Valladares (1981: 154) was told in the 1970s that the *yachak*'s work on the eve of the *champería* (Sunday) involved setting out small figurines representing different kinds of tools for farm work. All the workers had to approach the *yachak* with their papers and do so with a sense of seriousness; otherwise she would punish them. As explained earlier, the men must submit miniature *chakitaqllas* (foot plows) to the *yachak* today. Catalina only mentioned foot plows so it is unclear whether other kinds of miniature tools continue to be submitted.
225. The handwriting matches that of the 1921 scribe Máximo Calistro, who penned the first part of the original set of regulations, but the use of tape may mean that this sheet was previously unattached or stored elsewhere and was fixed to the notebook at a later point.
226. A *bulero* is a "pardoner." This category may refer to a fee exemption. The inconsistent capitalization in the headings reflects the original manuscript.
227. This category is listed as *bestias* in the Spanish table, which can be translated as "beasts of burden."

Hipolito O.	6	"	"	"	"	"	"	2	040
Catalino B.	7	"	1	"	"	"	"	"	040
José M.S.	7	"	1	"	"	"	"	"	020
Paula G.	8	"	1	"	"	"	"	"	050
Rafaela S.	8	"	"	"	1	"	"	"	050
Nemecio B.	9	"	3	1	"	"	"	"	140
Santas G.	14	"	1	"	"	"	"	"	030
Santas S.	14	"	"	"	"	1	"	"	040
Petronela P.	14	"	2	"	"	"	"	"	080
Eucebia Ch.	15	"	1	"	"	"	"	"	030
Gabina B.	17	"	1	"	"	"	"	"	050
Paula S.	18	"	1	"	"	"	"	"	040
Cecilio	"	"	1	"	3	"	"	"	140
Paula G.	17	"	1	"	"	"	"	"	040

[In the bottom margin of the animal inventory grid, Jesús Salinas Rojas, the 1990–1993 secretary, has written in blue ballpoint:]

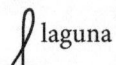

laguna

Secretario de 1990–1993

Jesús Salinas Rojas

[in black ink script matching the handwriting of the 1939 scribe:]

Expenses on the 2nd of February: 1,50 [1.50 *soles de oro*?] and two more *soles* for the [???]. For the date the 7th of the present month and in the *faena*, the expenditure is 1,75 [1.75 *soles de oro*?] and *peones* [substitute workers]—20 coca 40 cigarettes 80 expenses on the road.[228] Expenses for the 19th of February for the *faena* at Huayacocha lake.

---

228. This apparently refers to expenses incurred for the work on the roads described in the regulations for the Carnival period.

3
EL ENTABLO

[Cover:] ENTABLO

78
ENTABLO COMUNAL

[Inside cover—in black ballpoint:] 92

[f. 1r] [in pencil:] Libro No. 8

9

[written upside down:] Severino Crisós[tomo?]

[in red ink quill script:] Advertencias

Este libro tan legendario de todos los[1] costumbres ynteriores[2] de nuestra comunidad desde el Teniente & hasta el último eclesiastico,[3] debe hacerse academia en los primeros dias[4] del mes de Enero; por el "Campo" o el Sr. Principal. para saber las obligaciones. Casta. 10.-15.-de 1947.

El A. Campo

[A flourish beneath the signature covers a section of the note in pencil below.]

---
1. "todas las." Hereafter, all other unusual spellings, grammar, and punctuation are footnoted only at the first occurrence.
2. "interiores." Sometimes spelled "ynteriores" in the text.
3. "eclesiástico." Sometimes spelled without an accent in the text.
4. "días." Sometimes spelled without an accent in the text.

[in pencil:] Hago saber que no estoy de acuerdo en este entablo porque es de pocos todavía.

[f. 1v] [in blue ballpoint on a fresh white sheet adhered to the back of f. 1r:]

#92 Por haberse perdido y apareció con su copia fotográfica

[f. 2r] CHAMPERIA 1921

[in blue ballpoint:] ENTABLO

92

Champeria[5]

[f. 3r] [a flourish in pencil in the top margin may have been made by Notario SC] "Reglamento interior para los (*ciudadanos*) [underlined and put in parentheses, with "comuneros" written above in red] durante la faena en el primero de octubre de todos los años para la limpia de acequia de este pueblo à[6] la toma de Carhuayumac que principia de lunes a lunes."

"Los ciudadanos de Casta_____"

En vista de muchos controles y desacuerdos en las obligaciones comensando[7] desde el teniente asta[8] el ultimo[9] que es el camachico no cumplen con sus obligaciones y deberes acordaron hacer constar popularmente bajo nuestras firmas afin[10] de hacer cumplir y cumplan puntualmente y no aleguen motivo titulandose[11] de no haber constancia y menos fuerza de ley. Como todos nos sometimos a este regim[12] por ser la base fundamental por el caño de donde vivimos y saciamos nuestra sed desde que nace hasta que llegua[13] la última hora de nuestra muerte nos sometimos a firmar en el presente libro a fin que

---

5. "champería." Sometimes spelled without an accent in the text.
6. "a." The text often uses the spelling "à" or "á."
7. "comenzando."
8. "hasta."
9. "último." Sometimes spelled without an accent in the text.
10. "a fin." Often spelled "afin" in the text.
11. "titulándose."
12. "regimen"? The use of the term *regim* may reflect linguistic influences from European liturgical or philosophical texts.
13. "llegue."

quede constancia para los futuros los dictamines dictadas por la comunidad y tres ancianos notables que al fin se hallara grabado sus nombres.

Dada en la [torn] gobernacion[14] bajo la presid[encia? [torn] . . .

[f. 3v] [Three lines in pencil have been drawn here:] ///co personero Don Maximo Calistro [signature]

―――――――

―――――――

Casta, diez y ocho de octubre de mil novecientos veinte uno.
Nemesio Bautista [signature with flourish]

Tambien[15] anotamos que la faena debe ser el primero del mes de octubre y el turno se juntara en caso no haya terminado, afin de no tropesar[16] con dificultades en dicho trabajo.

       Maximo Calistro [signature with flourish]

[f. 4r] Domingo en la Tarde

Obligaciones de los funcionarios y sus deberes en dicha faena.

[Note in the margin: Primero 1] Para dar principio a la faena de la limpia acequia el día anterior que sera[17] el Domingo víspera de los trabajos: la corporación política compuesta de todos los funcionarios precedido[18] por el Señor Teniente Gobernador del pueblo, se reuniran[19] en una convocatoria privada ò[20] secreta en la casa del Alcalde Campo como el Rejidor[21] mayor, Rejedor Campo, alguacil mayor, los cuatro menores y finalmente los dos camachicos, con el fin de obcerbar[22] todo[23] los procedimientos pertene-

---

14. "gobernación."
15. "también." The accent is often omitted in the text.
16. "tropezar."
17. "será." The accent is often omitted in the text.
18. "presidido."
19. "reunirán." The accent is often omitted in the future tense in the text.
20. "o." Often spelled "ò" or "ó" in the text.
21. "Regidor." This word is spelled variously throughout the manuscript.
22. "observar."
23. "todos."

cientes á los trabajos a siguiente día lunes, en esta, en esta reunion[24] privada dictara[25] toda[26] las medidas precautorias y trasan[27] planes sobre todo[28] los cumplimiento de las obligaciones en formula[29] preparada y sabida. Para lo que los camachicos estaran[30] presentes anticipadamente con toda[31] sus obligaciones que le corresponda; por ejemplo, los camachicos, entregara[32] tres toritos que nosotros acostumbramos decirlos que estos los ciudadanos les proporcionaran[33] y estos los utilizaran[34] en los lugares donde convenga. primero, donde han de dar principio al trabajo los hombres que es àtras[35] de la (Yglecia[36] y el Colegio) otro en Quinituca otro en Mashca, y los funcionarios a conjuntamente daran[37] una inspeccion[38] todo[39] reunidos à los sitios de los que han de trabajar en la acequia, saliendo reunidos en el sitio de la plaza chica llamado [torn: Cu-?]

[f. 4v] -huay hasta llauli de donde se regresaran[40] a la casa del Campo, este biaje[41] sera por la acequia, cumpliendo con los deberes en el lugar de huanca acequia, también pampacocha y otros puntos que sera dirijido,[42] por el quien sabe y representa.

[The writing continues in faint, possibly diluted, ink.]

[In the margin: Segundo =] Día Lunes: El día lunes en la mañana de hora temprano, todos unanimamente[43] los funcionarios políticos, como el Campo,

---

24. "reunión."
25. "dictará."
26. "las."
27. "trazan."
28. "todos."
29. "fórmula."
30. "estarán."
31. "todas."
32. "entregarán."
33. "proporcionarán."
34. "utilizarán."
35. "atrás."
36. "iglesia." Sometimes spelled "yglesia" in the text.
37. "darán."
38. "inspección."
39. "todos."
40. "regresarán."
41. "viaje."
42. "dirigido."
43. "unánimemente." Sometimes spelled "unanimamente" in the text.

Regidor, Regidor Campo, Aguacil Mayor, dos Camachicos y los Alguaciles Menores se reunirán en la casa del Teniente Gobernador, todos dividamente[44] bien organizados y preparados para salir al trabajo de la Champeria, en esta reunión los funcionarios confrontarán sus obligaciones para este día el Sr. Campo dará, una libra de coca, una botella de ron, Dos cajetillas de cigarros de cualquier número, dos cohetes de arranque; la misma obligación dará el Regidor Mayor, El Regidor Campo dará media libra de coca, media botella de ron, una cajetilla de cigarros de cualquier número, y un cohete, y el Alguacil Mayor dará lo mismo que el Regidor Campo. Los camachicos recaberán[45] de las Señoras mujeres de estado, ya sea viuda ò viudo, ò mejor dicho de todas las que no tengan turno de agua; unos veinte cántaros de chicha de jora, ó de maíz negra, calculado en cantidad de una arroba cada cántaro. Y con este objeto reunidas [in the margin in blue ballpoint: X] ya en el lugar Cohuay, colectados sus obligaciones cada una en sus ramos, pues los referidos funcionarios así como los camachicos mostrarán sus obligaciones a los trabajantes en pesos legales, y medidas convecidas[46] para lo que estarán todos los hombres y mugeres[47] recibidos en este referido lugar, por llamada de los funcionarios a [faded: . . . ando] verbal. En seguida el Campo . . . [faded] entre los trabajantes nombrará

[f. 5r] tres mayordomos para los trabajos, y estos mayordomos serán uno para los hombres, y dos para las mujeres.

[The handwriting and ink differ from this point.] En seguida todos los funcionarios proceden a dar a todos los trabajantes de sus obligaciones cocas en proporciones necesarias, menos la botella de rón[48] y los sigarros[49] que lo reserbarán[50] para la chaccha de Huanca=Acequia,[51] Esto era o es al tiempo que salen los funcionarios; luego de las obligaciones que llevan.

Uno de los siguientes ya sea el Rejidor-Campo o Alguacil Mayor uno de ellos dejarán para el trabajo de los mayores, ½ libra de coca, ½ botella de rón y

---

44. "debidamente." Sometimes spelled "dividamente" in the text.
45. "recabarán."
46. "convencidas."
47. "mujeres."
48. "ron." Often spelled with an accent in the text.
49. "cigarros." Sometimes spelled "sigarros" in the text.
50. "reservarán."
51. On compound toponyms such as this one, equals signs are sometimes used in place of a hyphen.

una cajetilla de cigarrillos y un cuhete,[52] al camachico un cántaro de chicha dejará, y con esto estando ya expedito todos pues el Campo sonará un cuhete y saldrán al trabajo los hombres. [tick mark in blue ink.]

Una[53] vez en el lugar del trabajo que es tras de la Yglesia pues el mayordomo nombrará un medidor de tareas que procederá à medir en toda la distancia del trabajo del día, en los que se hiran[54] colocando todos los hombres en sus respectivas tareas en orden numérico; principiando los hombres de trás[55] de la Yglesia y las Srs. mujeres una parte de Lalancaria y otra parte de Simancaria del sitio que sus respectivas mayordomos figen[56] el trabajo.

Mientras tanto los trabajantes hacen la limpieza de la acequia de tras de la Yglesia a Huanca-Acequia: pues los funcionarios saldrán de cuhuay[57] todos juntos en dirección a Huanca-Acequia, por el sitio donde han principiado las [in the margin in blue ballpoint: an arrow] tareas los hombres, para lo que los funcionarios sonarán otro cuhete, y en esto quedarán con los mayores un camachico y un Alguacil menor. Y así armonizado[58] por medio de una Cheremía[59] que será una persona alicionada[60] él que toca, luego llegando al sitio de Huanca=Acequia, los funcionarios se derijerán[61] con los tres mayordomos y al intrevistarse[62] sera ofertado a los mayordomos con una copa de licor por los funcionarios de sus fiambres y los Camachicos un vaso de chicha.

En seguida el Campo se derijerá con los mayordomos a que se[63] reunen[64] la gente en el sitio ya fijado "Huanca-Acequia" a tomar unas hojas de cocas y vasos de chichas, en este lugar se fijará una cruz sobre la peana que existe desde tiempos muy antiguos; que esto será mandado por . . . [illegible, dark-

---

52. "cohete." Frequently spelled "cuhete" in the text.
53. The "u" has been underlined in blue ballpoint.
54. "irán." The accent is frequently omitted in the text.
55. "detrás."
56. "fijen." Often spelled "figen" in the text.
57. The faded toponym "cuhuay" has been refreshed in blue ballpoint.
58. This was originally spelled "amonizado," but another scribe or reader has corrected the spelling, entering the missing "r."
59. "chirimía."
60. "aleccionada."
61. "dirigirán." Conjugated forms of "dirigir" are sometimes spelled "derigirar" or "dirijerar" in the text.
62. "entrevistarse."
63. Another scribe or reader has corrected the grammar, entering the reflexive "se" in black ink; originally it was absent.
64. "se reunen a la gente."

ened paper] Una vez reunido[65] la gente ó los lamperos en este . . . [illegible, darkened paper]

[f. 5v] mujeres se pasarán a los sitios Laco, los de Semangaria y los de Lalangaria a Olacocha en dichos sitios esperarán á los mayordomos.

Con este motivo con los hombres que están en Huanca-Acequia, los funcionarios procederán a repetir las cocas licores y cigarrillos de sus obligaciones que serán distribuyidos[66] por los alguaciles de cada cual, principiando por el campo.

En este lugar mientras están en ese descanso y tranquilidad de los trabajantes, principiarán el padrón de Huallque y poronguitos labrados, que esto debe ser unas curiosidades que demuestra el trabajo manual de cada persona de su casa, esto consiste una taleguita dividamente bien labrada de hilo de diferentes colores y el poronguito tambien bien labrado según el[67] afición de cada persona, y así mismo el estrumento[68] de la *chirisuya* o Chirimía se le obligarán a los que sepan tocar y a todos bajo la pena de ser reprendido y castigado en el mismo sitio.

[in the margin, a note in the same red ink as the 1947 entry: Reformado en 1947—pasa a la pagina[69] = 51. The note alerting the reader to the reform was written in response to the following section:]

Y asimismo el mayordomo de los hombres harán[70] el padrón con los funcionarios desde el Campo hasta el último alguacil.

En seguida el camachico procederá a dar chicha a todo[71] los trabajantes en proborción[72] satisfatoria y así[73] al mismo tiempo dos alguaciles del campo y el Rigedor, invitarán en licor sus fiambres a todos, que esto lo costea el[74] Campo y Rejidor Mayor, que costará de una tercia de una botella corriente

---

65. "reunida."
66. "distribuidos."
67. "la."
68. "instrumento."
69. "página."
70. "hará."
71. "todos."
72. "proporción."
73. "así." The accent is often omitted in the text.
74. "al"?

en líquido y despues[75] de un momento repite otra vez el Camachico con repartir la chicha esto es para la salida al trabajo: durante esta reunión el campo a voz popular nombrará sacsaneros o revisadores de la acequia para los dos grupos de las Srs mujeres que iran a disposición de sus respectivos mayordomos de las Srs mujeres para que toman entra ellas; en seguida se levantarán los mayordomos con sus gentes al trabajo, cada cual a los sitios donde han dejado el trabajo o mejor dicho los mayordomos a Laco uno de ellos; a Olacocha el otro, quedándose en este sitio Huanca-Acequia todo[76] los funcionarios por algun[77] rato hasta que los trabajantes boltean[78] el cerro Otagaca, en esto se dirijeran todos a dirección a Pampacocha y que en el sitio de Quinial al verse con los mayordomos el Campo y todo los funcionarios de sus fiambres invitarán una copa de licor, y al mayordomo el camachico una [obscured by tape residue]

[f. 6r] chicha, y los funcionarios se dirijeran directamente a encontrarse a las señoras mujeres y mayordomos de dichas Señoras y el trabajo está dispuesto de la primera parte de Señoras mujeres, los funcionarios invitarán de sus fiambres a los que a los que les sempatiza[79] y los mayordomos y al camachico la chicha que lleva. [dark-blue ballpoint tick]

De este sitio de Huanca-Shilca y biendose[80] con los[81] Srs. mujeres, los funcionarios invitaran[82] de sus fiambres y de este sitio se regresarán todos los funcionarios unidos con todas las mujeres hasta el sitio Chushgua que en este lugar esperan los Srs. mayores; en este caso los hombres lamperos biendo[83] que los funcionarios ya vienen pues dejaran[84] el trabajo donde quede; pero que no exeda del lugar "Oculi" que también se reuniran[85] en el sitio Chushgua, en este sitio[86] ya reunido[87] todos hombres y mujeres, procederán con el

---

75. "después." The accent is often omitted in the text.
76. "todos."
77. "algún."
78. "voltean."
79. "simpatiza."
80. "viéndose."
81. "las."
82. "invitirán."
83. "viendo." Conjugated forms of "venir" sometimes spelled with "b" instead of "v" in the text.
84. "dejarán."
85. "reunirán."
86. "sitio."
87. "reunidos."

padrón general de los asistentes a la faena cobrando o fijando multa de un sol a los hombres al momento 50 cts a las mujeres para lo que los mayordomos darán cuenta de las personas que han estado a su cargo: durante esta reunión los funcionarios procederán a repartir los gastos que han sobrado de sus obligaciones y fiambres y terminarán con todo[88] los sobrámenes[89] hasta dejar sacudido los mantos de coca y los cántaros de chichas vacíos.

En seguida el Campo prosederá[90] a mandar que figen cruces en el siguiente día, en todo[91] los sitios que hayan pianas,[92] como son desde la toma o desde Casta-Cuhuay por los sitios de la acequia y [faded] mino hasta la toma de "Carguayumac," para esto serán todo[93] los jovenes[94] solteros de dos en dos bajo relación y responsabilidad y asi[95] mismo los mayordomos mandarán, a bajar la cruz de "Lacsa" con las personas que les halle por conveniente y una vez todo listo. [tick in black ink]

Uno de los mayores principales proclamarán[96] a los nuevos elegidos funcionarios políticos que representarán en el año próximo entrante desde el Teniente Gobernador hasta el Alguacil mayor.

Y luego enterado de todo y terminado, ordena se desplaguen[97] todo[98] la gente al pueblo, en trayecto limpiando el camino en toda sus partes desde Chushgua a Casta.

[f. 6v] <u>Día Martes sus deberes</u>

Día Martes: En este día todo[99] los funcionarios lo mas[100] temprano que sea se reunirán en la casa del Sr. Teniente Gobernador desde el campo hasta el

---

88. "todos."
89. "sobrámenes": an apparently idiosyncratic term ("sobrantes"?). The accent is marked in blue ballpoint.
90. "procederá."
91. "todos."
92. "peanas."
93. "todos."
94. "jóvenes." Sometimes spelled without an accent in the text.
95. "así." The accent is often omitted in the text.
96. "proclamará."
97. "desplieguen."
98. "toda."
99. "todos."
100. "más." The accent is frequently omitted in the text.

último alguacil y los dos camachicos, todos con sus respectivas obligaciones que han llevado en[101] día anterior y así mismo confrontarán sus gastos obligatorios, una libra de coca, una botella de rón, dos cajetillas cigarrillos y dos cuhetes el Campo y Regidor mayor ½ libra coca, ½ botella rón, una cajetilla[102] cigarrillos, y un cuhete Rejidor Campo y Alguacil mayor repectivamente.[103] [tick in dark ink]

De acá todos reunidos conjuntamente desde el campo hasta el último alguacil y camachico, se hiran a la reunión de "Mashca,"[104] para lo que darán una señal de aviso de salida a la gente del lugar o Serro[105] de Otagaca con un cuhete, a èsta[106] señal la gente se iran[107] a reunirse todos hombres y mujeres en el sitio ya indicado "Mashca." [note in black ballpoint: 2]

En este sitio una vez todos reunidos, seguirá el padrón general de los asistentes al trabajo, en seguida demostrará las obligaciones que se indica arriba según peso y medida legal, así mismo los camachicos entregarán de sus colectivas veinte cántaros de chicha de jora de arroba cada cántaro.

[In the margin in blue ballpoint: X] Acto continuo las Srs. mujeres salen a dirección a Huanca-Shilca donde ha quedado el trabajo del día anterior mientras tanto caminan los Srs. los hombres toman o mastican y chacchan coca, y advierten a los mayordomos a que procedan en forman[108] legal con los trabajantes en cuanto a sus tareas y dando sus gastos para el trabajo como el día anterior y los sacsaneros o revisores de la acequia así mismo como el día anterior.

Y dejando gastos para los mayores como el día anterior saldran[109] todos los trabajantes bajo sus mayordomas, quedando en este sitio los funcionarios hasta un rato charlando con los mayores.

Asi los hombres principiarán el[110] trabajo de "Oculi" sitio donde debe quedar el anterior trabajo y las Srs. mujeres los que dejaron el trabajo en "Olacocha"

---

101. "el."
102. "una cajetilla de cigarrillos."
103. "respectivamente."
104. The faded "M" of the toponym has been refreshed with a blue ballpoint pen.
105. "Cerro."
106. "esta."
107. "la gente se irá."
108. "en forma"?
109. "saldrán."
110. "principiarán al trabajo."

en la quebrada, pasara de Huanca-Shilca [in the margin in blue ballpoint: an arrow] a Socalun dentro; y los que dejaron el trabajo en Huanca-Shilca pasarán a la toma y de la Toma vendra[111] limpiando hasta encontrar con los que suben de Huanca-Shilca.

[f. 7r] Asi es que los funcionarios de "Mashca" se van al sitio Chacchadera a la salida sonando un cuhete, y se dirijerán por el camino tomando la acequia desde "Oculi" y una vez en la "Chacchadera" los funcionarios entrevistarán con los mayordomos en la misma forma que el día anterior y ordenará a que dejen sus tareas y se reunan[112] en el sitio ya mensionado[113] y procederan[114] con todas las obligaciones y padrón lo mismo que el día anterior y una vez terminado se iran los funcionarios, se iran por la acequia hasta el pie del Chorro de "Comau" para esto el camachico dejarán[115] como el día anterior los cántaros de chicha que el camachico le halle por conveniente y según el número de trabajantes que hubieren o hayan consumido.

Los funcionarios al salir sonorán[116] un cuhete esto es de "Chacchadera" y dejará un cuhete para los trabajantes. [note in dark ink: 2]

En seguida despues que los funcionarios se ván,[117] pues los trabajantes procederán en terminar sus tareas que como de* [in margin: *costumbre] se los tocan hasta "Laco."

En este lugar de "Laco" una vez terminado la faena de champeria toda la gente lamperos[118] salen al lugar donde se verifica la merienda de el[119] día miércoles en este día martes se hará la limpieza del sitio acostumbrado, en forma legal dividamente higiénica, arreglado los asientos como para todo los concurrentes, y en seguida terminada la limpieza procederan[120] a tomar sus alimentos o fiambres, esto mientras los funcionarios [in the margin: *regresan] del[121] lugar de "Comau" juntamente con las Sras. mujeres.

---

111. "vendrán."
112. "reúnan."
113. "mencionado."
114. "procederán."
115. "dejará."
116. "sonarán."
117. "se vayan/se van."
118. "lampera."
119. "del."
120. "procederán."
121. Another scribe or reader has corrected the text: "del" has replaced the original "al."

Para tal los mayores llegarán a éste sitio y una vez que lleguen[122] toda la gente en éste lugar de "Laco" procederan al padrón tal como en el día anterior y una vez terminado se regresarán limpiando en el trayecto el camino que este sucio hasta éste[123] pueblo de Casta.

[Note in the margin in blue ballpoint: ojo, meaning NB] Y una vez que están[124] en este pueblo los funcionarios vendrán todos juntos hasta este pueblo a la casa del Teniente Gobernador a efectuar la cuenta en la forma establecida desde tiempo muy antiguo.

[f. 7v] Para tal el Sr. Teniente de obligaciones pondrá para la cuenta un cántaro de chicha de jora de arroba que se dice un cántaro de a cuatro, una botella de rón y una libra de coca; en esta cuenta se tomaran[125] razón de los camachicos el número de cantaro[126] que se han envertido[127] en los días que se vencen y ver cuanto sobra para distribuyir[128] en los días que preceden.[129]

En esta relacionará de una manera verbal a todas las Srs. mujeres tantos viudas[130] casadas y solteras a todas los que tienen turno de agua hasta los hombres viudos o solos, en esta relacion[131] que sigue de viva voz irán distinguiendose[132] a las Srs. por parcialidades o por cofradía para esto lo separarán verbalmente [note in the margin: X] dos personas muy juiciosos,[133] que a la llamada el[134] Rejidor mayor contestarán los nombrados espisificando[135] o clasificando de que cofradía pertenese[136] y al mismo tiempo llevarán el cómputos de los cántaros de chichas que resulten en números de granos para lo que el Regidor mayor pondrá en el suelo una sobre mesa y los granos, despues en seguida procederá con las clasificaciones y distribuciones de los habitantes por

---

122. "llegue."
123. "este."
124. This was previously written in the subjunctive: "esten." An "a" has been written over the "e" in blue ballpoint and the accent was entered by the same hand.
125. "tomarán."
126. "cántaros." The accent is sometimes omitted in the text.
127. "invertido."
128. "distribuir."
129. "proceden"?
130. This was previously spelled "vuidas," but the spelling has been corrected.
131. "relación."
132. "distinguiéndose."
133. "juiciosas."
134. "del." The "el" has been added by another hand, squeezed into the line.
135. "especificando."
136. "pertenece."

paradas y para ésto[137] se nombrará dos personas mas para que lo enumeren en granos fijándoles a las paradas "Carguayumac" "Cumau" "Yanapaccha" y Ucusha para éstos actos ya estarán los alferes[138] de las paradas presentes con sus cumplimientos de obligación y así mismo los Michcos que llamamos a los que van a remplasar[139] como son Campo, Rejidor Mayor, Rejidor campo y Alguacil mayor que son cuatro los Michcos.

Lo que en esto mismo día todos los funcionarios reunidos despues del padrón tiene de obligacion[140] el Alcalde Campo entre todos andar por las calles anunciandos[141] a todos las personas a que parada corresponde (corresponden)[142] "Carguayumac," "Cumau," o "Yanapaccha"[143] una vez terminado el paseo buelben[144] a reunirse todos dando cuanta[145] de sus cumplimientos.

En seguida el Alcalde Campo nombrará[146] un cantor dando por cumplimiento ½ botella de ron y el Rijedor pondrá su cascabel. El Rigedor Campo pondrá un palo de chonta y luego [torn].

[f. 8r] [re-?]-unión saldran[147] al paseo dando principio del Campo dando por cumplimiento rón, coca y sigarros y asi susecivamente[148] el Rejidor mayor el Rejedor campo y el Alguacil Mayor dado termino todos[149] estas obligaciones y reunidos iran a casa[150] del Teniente Gobernador los aficionados y jóvenes jugadores de caballos pediran[151] manifestación a los mayores una vez aceptado ocurirían[152] a la sala del H.[153] Concejo[154] en el instante o sea en el día siguiente

---

137. "esto." Sometimes spelled with an accent in the text.
138. "alfereces." Variously spelled in the text.
139. "remplazar."
140. "obligación." Sometimes spelled without an accent in the text.
141. "anunciando."
142. The grammar has been corrected in parentheses by the same hand.
143. Note the irregular spelling of "Yanapacha" here as "Yanapaccha."
144. "vuelven."
145. "cuenta"?
146. This word has been refreshed in blue ballpoint.
147. "saldrán."
148. "sucesivamente."
149. "todas."
150. "a la casa."
151. "pedirán."
152. "ocurrirían/ocurrirán."
153. The elaborate "H" probably signifies "Honorable"; the respectful term "honorable consejo" means "honorable council."
154. "Consejo."

sacar sus respectivas licsencias[155] luego los jóvenes encontrándose alegres ará[156] compañía con los Srs. mayores à un paseo con su entonación o canto de Hualina y cascabeles.

~Día miércoles~ [wavy underlining]

Sus deberes y obligaciones

El miercoles[157] en la mañana el sr. Alcalde Campo pondrá un desayuno para toda la comunidad una vez que esté listo o preparado dará un avizo[158] cuya señal será la llamada con un cuhete.

Y la misma[159] ará el Rijidor mayor tambien anunciando con un cuhete la llamada.

Lo mismo el Rijedor campo y tambien el Alguacil mayor.

Terminado estos deberes de obligaciones el Sr. Alcalde Campo proporcionará para sus relebos[160] una manta Tarmeña un broche o prendador y un bastón y corredor[?].

Lo mismo ará el Rijedor mayor el Rejidor campo y Alguacil mayor terminado ésto los entregará a los Michcos éstos nombrados Michcos proporcionarán una medida de mate para recoger o recibir las cocas de los funcionarios y éstos mismos Michcos proporcionaran[161] una manta cada uno para recibir la coca en seguida pasarán a la tenencia los Michcos llevando la medida para que [darkened paper: las aprueban?] los mayores en seguida principiaran[162] a recojer[163] la coca de los funcionarios primero del Campo segundo del Rejidor Mayor

---

155. "licencias."
156. "hará." Sometimes spelled "ará" in the text.
157. "miércoles." Often spelled without an accent in the text.
158. "aviso."
159. "lo mismo."
160. "relevos." Sometimes spelled "relebos" in the text.
161. "proporcionarán."
162. "principiarán."
163. "recoger."

[f. 8v] daran[164] una medida completa a sus relebos cada uno.

El Rijedor campo y el Alguacil mayor dará a medias cada uno sus obligaciones a cada uno de sus relebos.

Terminado ésto pasarán los Michcos al lugar de costumbre de "Cuhuay" y daran la voz al Campo y a los demas funcionarios al mismo tiempo preparán[165] sus caballos los funcionarios desde el Campo hasta el último que son los camachicos en buen órden y bien encillados[166] y adornados los caballos con cintas y flores tambien cascabeles y sus varas también bien adornados[167] a todo gusto de cada cual una vez reunidos todos los funcionarios a caballos en la casa del Alcalde campo pasarán a la tenencia en órden todos con su bastón de chonta con piezas de plata en la mano derecha tras de ellos irán o siguirán los aficionados de caballo después del permiso del Sr. Teniente pasa al lugar de costumbre de "Cuhuay" todos a caballos y en éste lugar todos se apiarán y pasarán a donde se conserva el orden y dará un saludo al público que se encuentran en dicho lugar. [Note in dark ink: 2]

El Sr. Alcalde campo despues de cumplir con sus moralidades y prudencias pondrá su cantor en seguida los alferes de ambas paradas pondrá una bandera de bicolor cada uno bien adornado de cascabeles y plumas y continuarán el canto de Hualina en este acto los alferes de ambas paradas dará[168] sus complimientos a los mayores de el[169] mismo modo dará los Michcos una invitación de [in the margin: a tick in blue ballpoint] coca a los mayores. [two lines have been added in the same blue ballpoint: //][170]

Una vez terminado éste[171] partirán su marcha al lugar de "Otagaca" y de ahí dará la voz con un "Huajay"[172] que alertará a los expectadores[173] y luego los

---

164. "darán." The accent is sometimes omitted in the text.
165. "prepararán."
166. "ensillados."
167. "adornadas."
168. "darán."
169. "del."
170. A reader has flagged the section that reads *coca a los mayores*. The tick is located in the margin, and two parallel lines close off the highlighted section.
171. "esto."
172. "waqay." *Huajay* is a hispanicized spelling of the Quechua word *waqay* (to weep, wail, cry out).
173. "espectadores."

funcionarios en unión de los aficionados suspenderán la hualina y procederán a poner el órden[174] una vez que se encuentran ya expeditos se pondran[175] de rodillas y daran[176] reso[177] varias oraciones para que le lleven con bién[178] y encomendándose con todo corazón la fe que acaban de rezar para con Dios. Despues de cumplir todos sus deberes todos los funcionarios y aficionados acabalgarán sus caballos y ent—[torn page]

[f. 9r] á la formación formando en primer órden el Alcalde campo en seguida el Rijedor mayor y asi susecivamente[179] los demás hasta el mas ultísimo aficionado.

El Sr. Teniente hará uso de su palabra encargándole y encarisiendolos[180] los deberes que deben cumplir y vijilar[181] la paz y tranquilidad del trayecto y encargando que las personas que cometieren cualquier desorden será capturado como conspirador y trastornador del órden público una vez puesto a mi disposición pasaré al Fuero Judicial y que sigan los tramites de ley. [Note in black ballpoint: X]

Despues de ésta manifistación[182] el Sr. Teniente contará en orden el número de una, dos, y tres al terminar el último número partirán[183] los de acaballos hasta el lugar de "Taquina" [note in black ink: +ojo] [corresponding note in the margin in black ink: +Aqui El Rejedor Mayor sonará un cuhete que a él le pertenece la parada.] donde esperarán los Michcos llegado al sitio se reunen en primer lugar los funcionarios y despues los aficionados y continúan la alegría de Hualina generalmente todos midiante[184] ésto despues de entrevistar los Michcos con los funcionarios partirán al lugar de "Mashca" de ahí alertará a los funcionarios y aficionados con una voz de Huajay y al mismo tiempo partirán el Campo con todos y el Alguacil Mayor de su cuenta sonará un cuhete para la salida hasta el lugar de Laco donde donde ahi[185] descansarán

---

174. "orden." Sometimes spelled with an accent ("órden") in the text.
175. "pondrán."
176. "darán."
177. "rezo."
178. "bien."
179. "sucesivamente."
180. "encariciéndolos."
181. "vigilar."
182. "manifestación."
183. The accent on the "a" has been added by another hand.
184. "mediante."
185. "ahí." Sometimes spelled without an accent in the text.

EL ENTABLO   173

o se reunirán otra vez y siguiran[186] con la misma alegría los funcionarios y aficionados con las banderas de ambas paradas y los Michcos exijerán[187] a los camachicos la entrega de los veinte cántaros o mas que haya cántaros de chicha recabada[188] de las Srs. mujeres de "Yacapar." [note in blue ballpoint: X over scribbles in red ballpoint]

Completado todos estos veinte cántaros o mas dividiran[189] el Michco de "Carguayumac," seis cántaros o mas lo que le toca para Carguayumac, y seis cantaros o mas para "Cumau."[190]

Cuatro cántaros o mas para "Yanapaccha" y ultimamente[191] cuatro cántaros ó mas para "Ocshayco o Ocusha."

Estando terminado esto partirán la marcha lo[192] Michcos y los funcionarios continuará la alegría hasta ciertos momentos y partiran[193] a caballos los funcionarios y aficionados en éste lugar o salida sonará un cuhete el Regidor Campo hasta el lugar de "Huanca-Shilca" en dicho lugar [faded]

[f. 9v] y parada de "Cumau" con la caja o tinya y con las entonaciones de yaravíes cantadas por las mayoralas de dicha parada una vez reunido[194] todos hará[195] una pequeña envitación[196] de un exelente[197] almuerzo a todo aire en primer lugar a las autoridades y funcionarios y mas personas que se encuentran en éste mismo [momento?]-evento los alferes de dicha parada dictara[198] una copita de Chacpacne.[199]

En seguida pasa los funcionarios al lugar de Soculún donde los esperan la parada de "Carguayumac" con las mismas intonaciones[200] de tinyas y yaravíes

---

186. "seguirán."
187. "exigirán." The "n" has been added in black ink.
188. "recabadas."
189. "dividirán."
190. The toponym has been emboldened in black ink.
191. "últimamente."
192. "los."
193. "partirán."
194. "reunidos."
195. "harán/se hará."
196. "invitación." Sometimes spelled without an accent in the text.
197. "excelente."
198. "dictará."
199. "champaña."
200. "entonaciones."

entonadas los cantos por las simpaticas[201] mayoralas[202] estando reunidos todos de la invitacion de un pequeño almuerzo que contiene de diferentes clases de comida[203] incaicas.

Terminado esto parte el Michco a la toma adjunto con sus trabajadores llegado à la toma donde se levanta el agua el Michco envita[204] a los trabajantes un poco de coca y chacchan.[205] Terminado este acto sigue[206] los trabajadores al trabajo en éste ácto[207] que se encuentran el Michco y sus trabajantes salen los funcionarios a pié[208] hasta la toma al recibir el trabajo llevando sus fiambres dichos funcionarios como coca, ron, cigarros y sus cuhetes que ésto empleará en los lugares de custumbre[209] principiando del lugar de "Pariapungo" despues de esta seremonia[210] secreta pasa[211] los funcionarios a la toma donde se encuentra con el Michco y los funcionarios brinda[212] sus fiambres algunas cupitas[213] desde el Campo hasta el último que es el camachico.

Y en seguida los funcionarios emprenden sus regresos por la acequia revisando el trabajo hasta el lugar de "Silguerito" á donde le espera la parada con la alegria[214] de tinya y yaravíes.

Despues de pocos momentos bajan a la acequia a hacer una ceremonia secreta en la Paccha o Chorro (q) y despues [torn]—partó los funcionarios soñando un cuhete hasta el lugar [torn] "Cumau" a donde continúa una ceremonia secreta y sus [torn]

[f. 10r] ... un cuhete esto es al pie de chorro grande de "Cumau" al mismo tiempo parte por la misma acequia hasta el lugar de "Huancaquirma" llegando al lugar salen los funcionarios a entrevistarse y saludar a la parada de "Cumau"

---

201. "simpáticas."
202. The original spelling "mayolalas" has been corrected by another hand: first "l" has been crossed out and replaced with an "r."
203. "comidas."
204. "invita."
205. Originally spelled "chachan": another "c" has been added above by the same hand.
206. "siguen."
207. "acto."
208. "pie."
209. "costumbre."
210. "ceremonia." Sometimes spelled "seremonia" in the text.
211. "pasan."
212. "brindan."
213. "copitas." Sometimes spelled "cupitas" in the text.
214. "alegría." Accent sometimes omitted in the text.

con sus entonaciones correctas como són[215] hualinas tono de Chirimías que cantan al son de los cascabeles despues de cumplir con todos estos deberes espera a recibir el agua que el Michco de Carguayumac lo entrega al Michco de "Cumau" (recibida el) una[216] vez cumplido esto las dos paradas y Michcos reciben el agua con muchos tiruteos[217] de dinamita cuhetes cuheterillos[218] y mas explosivos que adornen[219] el recibimiento cumpliendo todo[220] estos deberes los funcionarios parten por la misma acequia hasta "Yanapaccha" a donde hace una ceremonia secreta y siguen hasta la loma de Huanca-Shilca a donde se encuentran con los dos Michcos "Yanapaccha" y "Ocusha" a donde partecipan[221] de sus ricos fiambres algunas cupitas de Carapongos Lunaguaná y Expor[222] Malta Callao y Lima.

[a blue ballpoint place mark: —] En seguida parte por la misma acequia sonando un cuhete con las mismas alegrías hasta el lugar de "Ocshayco" punto de donde salen de la acequia al camino esto es antes de llegar a la loma de "Ocshayco" y ahí toman sus caballos los funcionarios palanganas y (pa) espera á los aficionados para partir en la cabeza con mucha òrden hasta el lugar de costumbre que es "Ocshayco" la pampa donde se encuentra una cruz.

En este punto lo esperan ambas paradas y siguen[223] con sus cumplimientos, las paradas; una vez terminado parten las paradas hasta el lugar de "Pisca-tambo" punto donde lo esperan con las entonaciones de yaravies[224] y tinyas mientras esta[225] venida quedan los funcionarios con la alegría de los ricos tonos de hualina despues de pocos momentos parten los funcionarios hasta el lugar de "Laco" (h) antes de partir deja advertido que los aficionados sigan de dos en dos con buen cuidado a sus caballos para conocer la prueba de ellos.

---

215. "son." Sometimes spelled with an accent in the text.
216. "Una" and the parentheses preceding it have been emboldened in black ink.
217. "tiroteos."
218. "coheterillos."
219. "adornan."
220. "todos."
221. "participan."
222. The "E" in "Expor" was originally lowercased and has been capitalized by the same hand.
223. Originally spelled "siguien," this has been edited by another hand.
224. "yaravíes."
225. "está."

Reunidos todos en el lugar de "Laco," el Sr Alcalde Campo (y el)[226] dara[227] la voz para la invitación general aun[228] banquete tan exelente[229] y decsente[230] en sus sirvicios.[231] [faded]

[f. 10v][232] de estar en toda voda[233] los camachicos en la mitad del banquete lebantará[234] con sus complimientos y una bolza[235] de shicra puesto en el pecho procederá a invitar a todos lo que se encuentra sentados en la voda y éstos[236] que reciben retornará con otra igual y mas un viscocho[237] pondrá en la bolza que mantiene y darán principio por cada extremos[238] de los asientos y cruzarán al medio alegre y descentemente.[239]

Despues de la invitación resarà[240] una oración y en seguida ordenará[241] el Sr. Campo las mesas o banquetes que se encuentra servido[242] terminado estos actos los cuatro Michcos llaman a la colecta de[243] los veinte cántaros o mas que han distribuydo[244] en la mañana y entrega a los camachicos los que han llevado en seguida del[245] padrón el Sr. Rejedor en precencia[246] de los camachicos una vez terminado recoje[247] sus cántaros las Srs. mujeres

---

226. In an apparent error of omission, the functionary who must collaborate with the *alcalde campo* here is not specified.
227. "dará."
228. "a un."
229. "excelente."
230. "decente."
231. "servicios."
232. Much of the punctuation on this page appears to have been added or emboldened in black ink.
233. "boda."
234. "levantará." Conjugated forms of "levantar" are sometimes spelled in the text with a "b" instead of "v."
235. "bolsa." Sometimes spelled "bolza" in the text.
236. The "e" has been emboldened in black ink and an accent was also added.
237. "bizcocho." Sometimes spelled "viscocho" or "biscocho" in the text.
238. "extrema."
239. "decentemente." The period has been added in black ink.
240. "rezará."
241. The accent has been added in black ink.
242. "que se encuentren servidos."
243. The "de" has been added in black ink.
244. "distribuido." Sometimes spelled "distribuydo" in the text.
245. Originally "el": the "d" has been added in black ink.
246. "presencia." Sometimes spelled "precencia" in the text.
247. "recoge."

de Yacapar segun[248] como llaman sus padrones terminado èsto parten las paradas hasta el lugar de "Mashca" y los funcionarios quedan en "Laco" con la alegría o/el[249] el canto de hualina con tódo[250] los aficionados de caballos una vez que las paradas estén en la loma de "Mashca" el Campo suspende la alegría y ordena a colocarse en órden al frente de la cruz a rezar un misterio ó algunas oraciones religiosas encomendandose[251] a los santos y santas de la corte del cielo para que por medio ellos los atienda nuestra divina providencia en preferencia resará[252] dos Padrenuestros[253] y dos Ave María para el patrón ("San Pedro")[254] y el patrón "San Antonio" de este [in the margin in red ballpoint: an arrow] pueblo.

Hecho estos actos religiosos el Sr. Alcaldo campo dara[255] la voz ¡que se preparen! los jugadores con sus caballos lo que han de entrar a la cancha.

Una vez (terminado) preparado llamará el Cam-

[f. 11r] -po a la formación a todos los aficionados de acaballos una vez dictado ésto partirá el Campo acabalgado a la oyada[256] plano a donde se forma y aviva[257] fuerza inpondrá[258] la órden[259] según el número que ocupan en la relación que el Concejo pasa,[260] será aliniado sobre una linia[261] recta vertical y el Campo dara[262] la voz si están[263] listos o no a lo que contestarán con sí ó con nó[264] para dar mas tiempo a fin que terminen.

---

248. "según." Sometimes written without an accent in the text.
249. The "o" replaces the original "el" here.
250. "todo."
251. "encomendándose."
252. "rezará." Sometimes spelled "resará" in the text.
253. The "p/P" here is both lowercase and capitalized, a possible instance of self-correcting by the original scribe.
254. Parentheses added by the same hand with the same ink. The quotation marks have been added in blue ink.
255. "dará."
256. "hoyada."
257. "a viva."
258. "impondrá."
259. The accent on the letter "o" has been added in black ink.
260. The comma has been added in black ink.
261. "linea."
262. "dará."
263. The accent has been added in black ink.
264. "no." Sometimes spelled with an accent in the text.

En este acto peligroso el Alcalde campo con las lagrimas[265] en los ojos[266] encargará a sus jugadores que a ningunos y ningunos de ellos sean atropellados o atropellen en el momento de la cancha o juego cumpliendo con todo estos deberes el Alcalde campo vuelve a revisar la linea recta de los caballos si están[267] bien colocados o nó repasará[268] tras de subir y bajar y despues se retira de tres a cuatro metros para la cruz y da la voz preventiva en voz alta contando con los números uno, dos, y tres prepararse vuelve a repetir otra vez con los mismos números uno, dos y tres, anunciando ya que esta última es la ejecutiva y termina con las mismas palabras un, dos y tres vayan con Dios al instante de esta partida el Alguacil[269] del Campo suena un[270] cuhete este es puesto por el Campo una vez pasado los jugadores la loma de Mashca entran las paradas y espectadores al camino; pero para entonces en todo[271] los lugares mas viciblis[272] y puntos fijos entonan los yaravíes las mayorales y mas aficionados según como vengan sevan[273] recogiéndose y si vienen hasta el pueblo con las tinyas y los cuatro Michcos hasta el casa del Teniente Gobernador estando estos en la tenencia sacuden las mantas los Michcos al público luego el Sr. Teniente ordena la suspensión e hasta el día siguiente en seguida los alferes de ambas paradas suplican al Sr. Teniente y a los mayores para sus paseos hasta las horas señaladas mientras tanto los aficionados se gustan en la casa del gana-

[f. 11v] -dor o del primer caballo con lo que se terminó los deberes y obligaciones del día (mientras) miercoles.

~Día Jueves~

Sus deberes y obligaciones

El Alcalde Campo, Rejedor mayor, Rejedor campo y Alguacil mayor prepararán un rico desayuno cada uno en sus casas hecho por sus Alguaciles y

---

265. "lágrimas."
266. The reader who went through the Entablo with a pencil, marking short vertical lines, focused on this section.
267. The accent has been added in black ink.
268. The accent has been added in black ink.
269. The original lowercase "a" has been replaced with a capital "A."
270. The article "un" has been added in black ink, squeezed into the line.
271. "todos."
272. "visibles."
273. "se van."

anunciará al pueblo con un cuhete, cada uno de ellos,[274] una vez terminado el desayuno saldrán los Michcos a recojer[275] las cocas de cada funcionario conforme[276] al día anterior en el mismo mate o collo, esto es cada funcionario; entregará a su relelo[277] o al Michco asi mismo pedirán sus cumplimientos de [neon pink highlighter place mark: —] entrada sentada movida y salida una vez terminado esto salen los Michcos dirijendose[278] al lugar de costumbre llamado "Taquina."

Encontrándose en este lugar o paraje los Michcos ejecutarán[279] las chichas a los camachicos así como también las banderas y cajeras de ambas paradas ésta[280] exijencia[281] será por los Michcos en voz alta y fuerte del lugar de "Taquina."

Encontrándose[282] los camachicos en el lugar donde están[283] los Michcos entregará los veinte cántaros o más a los Michcos.

El Michco mayor distribuirá a cada parada conforme el primer día y luego de ese lugar los Srs. Michcos irán[284] cada uno á sus tareas con sus respectivos trabajantes. El Michco mayor irá a la laguna de Chushgua. El Segundo irá á la laguna de Laclán y los dos menores "Ocusha" y "Yanapaccha" irá a la laguna de Hualhual cada uno de ellos al principio del trabajo

[f. 12r] dará su chaccha de la manta que mantiene en su poder.

Una vez estando por mitad del trabajo saldrán[285] los funcionarios[286] del lugar de "Taquina," dirijiéndose[287] al lugar de Chushgua a recibir los trabajos, dichos funcionarios entrarán hasta el estanque de la laguna a recibir el trabajo con la

---

274. The comma has been added in black ink.
275. "recoger."
276. "conforme."
277. "relevo."
278. "dirigiéndose."
279. The accent has been added in black ink.
280. "esta." The accent has been added in black ink.
281. "exigencia."
282. The accent has been added in black ink.
283. The accent has been added in black ink.
284. The accent has been added in black ink.
285. The accent has been added in black ink.
286. The "s" has been added in black ink.
287. "dirigiéndose." The accent has been added in black ink.

armonía de la cheremía[288] y su cantor, y hací[289] dichos funcionarios comensarán[290] a dar sus cumplimientos a todos los trabajantes todos los funcionarios hasta el último camachico: terminado el recibimiento del trabajo salen con un tiro de cuhete, una vez en el borde de la laguna darán una vuelta alegrando con el cántico de hualina yaravíes y la caja y en siguida[291] se derijerán al lugar de la laguna de "Laclan"[292] donde harán las mismas ceremonias y terminado el recibimiento con las mismas alegrías, se derigen al lugar de la laguna de "Huahual" donde darán el encuentro con los dos Michcos y entrarán a recibir el trabajo y donde principia los cumplimientos; terminado todo ésto,[293] salen los Michcos al lugar "Pampacocha," para entonces los funcionarios todos reunidos hasta el camachico se quedan en la laguna "Hualhual" entonando sus cánticas de hualina, y una vez los cuatro Michcos en la laguna de "Pampacocha" se dividen sus taréas[294] cada uno y comiensan[295] el trabajo todos los michcos como es, el mayor, ejecutaran[296] el agua el michco mayor pondran[297] el agua entregará el agua al Michco de "Cumau" a primera hora con su gente, el Michco de "Cumau" lebanta la toma o desagüe de la quebrada de "Huanaquirma" con su gente, el Michco de "Yanapaccha" lebanta el agua de la quebrada de "Olacocha" con su gente y el michco de "Ocusha" lebantará el agua de la quebrada de "Oculi" con su gente, y emposarán[298] el agua en la laguna de "Hualhual"[299] para el recibimiento ya sea antes del banquete o despues y en seguida salen los funcionarios con un tiro de cuhete a recibir el trabajo y continúan sus cumplimientos al recibir los trabajo[300] de cada michco hecho por sus trabajantes, en

[f. 12v] seguida el Sr. Teniente ordena á los funcionarios para suspender toda la armonia[301] y da la voz el Campo la suspensión a toda la gente de las armonías, y luego salen todos a la plazuela a tomar asiento[302] todos los hijos

---

288. "chirimía."
289. "así."
290. "comenzarán."
291. "seguida."
292. "Laclán."
293. "esto."
294. "tareas."
295. "comienzan."
296. "ejecutarán."
297. "pondrá."
298. "empozarán." The accent has been added in black ink.
299. The quotation marks have been added in black ink.
300. "trabajos."
301. "armonía."
302. The original spelling "aciento" has been corrected by another hand.

del lugar. el Campo o Regedor ordenará a los jóvenes[303] que recogen a las visitas y darán[304] asiento una vez terminado esto, el Rejedor da la voz á los dos camachicos que recojan las mesas paños o manteles preparados por las mujeres solas para las vecitas.[305] luego el Alcalde campo dará la voz a todas las mujeres[306] que se lebanten con la invitación para las vecitas hasta rellenarlas las mesa, en seguida dará la voz a las mismas mujeres[307] que se levanten con la carhuaymesa sus esposas y si en caso[308] se encontrará el párroco presente en la capilla con un[309] cruz que está conducido por el principal del pueblo, y en caso no hubiera el párroco se levantará una persona notable a dar[310] la vendición,[311] y dirá la vendición del Padre y del Hijo y del Espiritu[312] Santo y luego continuarán[313] el banquete una vez por mitad[314] el alimento lebantarán los camachicos con sus respectivos cumplimientos y dichos se pondra[315] una bolsa o shicra en el pecho donde los ciudadanos del lugar o de la mesa obsequiaran[316] unos viscochos donde apercibirán los camachicos con[317] buena voluntad de todas las mesas, terminado el banquete se levantarán todos los[318] jóvenes o recurrente[319] a resar[320] la vendición de la mesa el Campo o Rejedor dará la voz á las Sras. mujeres que se lebantan a recojer[321] la mesa y en seguida ará el recibimiento del agua con las [mayores?][322] alegrías[323] con unos tiros de cuhetes y cuhetecillos,[324] terminado ésto seguirá el padrón de los veinte cántaros.

---

303. The accent has been added in black ink.
304. The accent has been added in black ink.
305. "visitas." Sometimes spelled "vecitas" in the text.
306. This word has been emboldened in black ink.
307. This word has been emboldened in black ink.
308. The original spelling "casa" has been corrected in black ink.
309. "una."
310. The word has been emboldened in black ink.
311. "bendición." Sometimes spelled "vendición" in the text.
312. "Espíritu." The names of the Padre, Hijo, and Espíritu Santo were originally lowercased but have been capitalized by the same hand.
313. The accent has been added in black ink.
314. The "d" has been added in black ink.
315. "pondrá."
316. "obsequiarán."
317. The "c" has been emboldened in black ink.
318. The article "los" has been added in black ink, squeezed into the line.
319. "recurrentes."
320. "rezar."
321. "recoger."
322. The page is torn here, but other sections of the text make such superlative references.
323. The "s" has been added in black ink.
324. "cohetecillos."

Los Michcos entregarán los cántaros (que han recibido a su cargo una vez reunidos los dichos cántaros [note in the margin in red ballpoint: X] principiará el padrón[325] de las Sras. de Yañac[326] según[327] el padrón que les corresponden[328] terminado el padrón, el Campo

[f. 13r] dará la voz al camachico que entregen[329] la flor por dos mandados, es decir que los mandados deberán[330] ser los recién casados y que éstos[331] entregen una alforja de flores cada uno es decir flores como son shira shira, cumante[332] y serán distribuidos[333] en todos los concurrentes para entonces las paradas comensarán[334] con sus alegrías como són la caja, y en seguida los Srs. \ mayores tomaran[335] la santísima cruz y se [in the margin in red ballpoint: an arrow] partirán al pueblo cambiando uno en sus costumbre como ya es sabido, una vez llegado a la loma de "Otagaca" las paradas, el camachico sesante[336] se prepara con un cántaro o dos de chicha que ésto será por su obligación y será presenciado por una (vacija)[337] (m)[338] persona mayor que la vasija está llena y continuará á[339] preparar en la plaza chica un Santo Cristo una mesa cubierto con un paño de lo mejor y quedará uno en su lugar bijilando[340] y este dicho vijilante[341] se encontrará con un chicote o truenador, la chicha será disfrutada desde el lugar "Shamarume"[342] o "Gotogoto" hasta la plaza chica o el "Cuhuay" ante[343] toda la gente que hubiera, una vez reunidos los concurrentes, el Teniente Gobernador o el principal dará la voz al pueblo á que se sorprendan las armonías a continuación llamará a los cuatro Michcos para

---

325. The "X" in red ink here indicates interest in the *padrón* by a reader/ritual initiant.
326. The tilde on the "n" has been added in black ink.
327. The word has been emboldened in black ink.
328. The "n" has been added in black ink.
329. "entreguen." Sometimes spelled "entregen" in the text.
330. The "n" has been added in black ink.
331. "estos." The accent has been added in black ink.
332. This word has been emboldened in black ink.
333. Fresh dots above the "i"s in this word have been added in black ink.
334. "comenzarán."
335. "tomarán."
336. "cesante." Often spelled "sesantes" in the text.
337. "vasija."
338. The parentheses have been emboldened in black ink.
339. "a." The "á" has been added in black ink, squeezed into the line.
340. "vigilando."
341. "vigilante."
342. The toponym "Shamarume" has been emboldened in black ink.
343. "ante" has been emboldened in black ink.

que dea[344] término de sus mantas y lo que sacudirá a la vista del público y en seguida el Teniente llamará al Campo, y al micho mayor de "Carguayumac" para que dicho Michco haga su entrega de su manta un bastón/[345] un broche o prendador y un corredor y dirá el Teniente a los dos que se postren de rodilla y perdone por haber desempeñado dos días de remplazo en su fabor[346] del Campo, el Teniente ordenará que se perdone, hantes[347] de esto dará tres látigos no bromas sino legalmente de sufrir y en seguida el regidor y el michco de "Comao"[348] hacen la misma ceremonia ante dicho.[349] y en seguida continúa el Rejedor campo con dos látigos y perdona el Alguacil y el Micho "Ocusha" lo mismo hace la ceremonia hante[350] dicho.

[f. 13v] [in the margin: a red ballpoint place mark: —] Terminado estas costumbres el Teniente Gobernador dará la voz a los funcionarios que se levanten los alferes de ambas paradas con sus cumplimientos general, terminado esto cumplimiento el Teniente Gobernador dice[351] que suspenda la alegría y ordena que pase a la tenencia hambas[352] paradas a recebir[353] órdenes, llegando a la tencia[354] los alferes entrarán con sus cumplimientos a suplicar para continuar con sus placeres o alegrías, el Sr. Teniente y sus mayores les dá[355] el permiso a los dos paradas con una seria responsabilidad que no hayan[356] ninguna novedad, terminado la lisencia[357] el Teniente Gobernador ordena a los funcionarios que llamen a las dos paradas una vez reunido todos en la tenencia hacen suspencias[358] de las alegría,[359] y el Sr. Teniente sale a la puerta de su domicilio con el puño de plata, y luego dá[360] su decreto de descanso

---

344. "diere."
345. The forward slash has been added in pencil.
346. "favor."
347. "antes."
348. Originally spelled "Cumau": the "u" has been changed to an "o" in black ink.
349. The period has been added in black ink.
350. "ante."
351. "dice" has been added in black ink.
352. "ambas."
353. "recibir."
354. "tenencia."
355. "da."
356. "haya."
357. "licencia."
358. "suspensiones."
359. "alegrías."
360. "da."

asiendo[361] antecipación[362] que el día viernes tienen que atender todos los hombres a la cuenta terminado esto las juntas se retiran y queda el pueblo tranquilo, el Sr. Teniente y sus mayores autorizan a los alferes de las paradas que amanescan[363] con sus yaravíes y hualinas en la plaza chica como quien vijilando[364] al cristo con mucha órden como los camachicos sesantes estan[365] en esa vigilanza[366] que ninguna persona puede entrar al lado del cristo con sombrero o gorra y el individuo[367] (que)[368] que no está[369] sujeto[370] a esta[371] órden[372] el camachico largará el chicote sin responsabilidad, dichas paradas o juntas tomarán chicha caliente puesto por el camachico *precentes[373]* (.) hasta el amanecer una vez terminado esto el Alcalde campo o el Regedor hará suspención de las alegrías para seguir la cuenta de los hombres. [in black ink] Vale la palabra sesante entre lineas.[374]

* [in the margin in black ink by the same hand as the note above:] decir por el sesante no por el nuevo.*

[in green ink] Adición: Por olvido se hace presente que en esta noche del jueves pondrá la chicha el camachico presente y lo calentará el camachico sesante como quien vigilando al Cristo.

[f. 14r] ~ Día Viernes ~

Sus deberes y obligaciones. [wavy underlining]

En la mañana el Teniente llamará a los dos camachicos sesantes para antecipar[375] de sus obligaciones que les pertenecen por este día, el camachico

---

361. "haciendo."
362. "anticipación."
363. "amanezcan."
364. "vigilando."
365. "están." Sometimes spelled without an accent in the text.
366. "vigilancia."
367. Sections of this word have been emboldened with black ink.
368. The parentheses have been added in black ink.
369. The accent has been added in black ink.
370. Word emboldened in black ink.
371. Originally misspelled "este": the black ink editor has corrected the grammar.
372. The accent has been added in black ink.
373. "presente." Sometimes spelled "precente" in the text. Asterisks in green ink alert the reader to an entry below in dark ink: ("decir por el sesante no por el nuevo").
374. "líneas."
375. "anticipar."

sesante dara[376] por obligación una libra de coca, una botella de rón, y cántaro de chicha de ados y uno de real, cada uno estos serán[377] bien llenas y probadas por los mayores que deberán ser chicha de jora y continúa[378] las obligaciones de este día, el camachico precente pone una mesa grande [an "o" here has been crossed out] y tres bancos en la de "Cuhuay," y los camachicos sesantes ponen sobre la mesa un plato con su paño blanco una cruz de paja de "Huay-Shocsha" y una tinaja de barro para el diposito[379] de chicha también tapado con un paño y con una cruz lo mismo del interior.[380]

[in the margin: a red ballpoint arrow] Lo mismo el Alguacil mayor pondra[381] una mesa chica una vaticola[382] de huacura y una tigiera[383] y una soga de lana éstos materiales son para los castigos (cam) de los camachicos y los[384] camachicas dichos castigos son por los apoyos que hacieran[385] à[386] los ciudadanos de sus obligaciones los servicios comunales. En siguida[387] el Teniente Gobernador hará precente los deberes y obligaciones a los camachicos sesantes como són[388] dos vasijas de potos para que enviten[389] las chichas a todo[390] los que necesiten saciarse la sed ésto[391] será en el mismo sitio, que los camachicos sesantes a los que pidan los obligará que termine.

El Teniente Gobernador ordenará al Campo y al Rejedor que tomen asiento en órden de[392] ciudadanos divididos y conocidos por sus parcialidades;[393] los de Yacapar tomarán[394] el asiento hacia al Este,[395] y los de Yanac hacia el Oeste,

---

376. "dará."
377. The accent has been added in black ink.
378. The accent has been added in black ink.
379. "depósito."
380. "anterior."
381. "pondrá."
382. "baticola."
383. "tijera."
384. "las." The article has been added in black ink.
385. "hicieron."
386. "a." The accent has been added in black ink.
387. "seguida."
388. "son." The accent has been added in black ink.
389. "inviten."
390. "todos."
391. "esto." The accent has been added in black ink.
392. The "de" has been added in black ink, squeezed into the line.
393. The semicolon has been added in black ink.
394. The "n" has been added in black ink to correct the grammar.
395. The comma has been added in black ink.

los ciudadanos de ambos se sentarán[396] sobre la paja llamada[397] Huay-Shocsha, dichas pajas son mandados por los camachicos presentes

[f. 14v] a dos mujeres solas.

Una vez colocados[398] todos en sus respectivos asientos y puestos ordenará el Teniente a su Campo o Rejedor que[399] sigua[400] el padrón general de los hombres, terminado este nombrará cuatro personales para corregir los yerros o faltas de cada uno ésta reprención[401] será en los términos que sean útil y probechoso[402] para cada persona.

Terminado ésto ordenará que continúa[403] la chaccha general despúes de terminado ésto llama a la mesa al secretario puesto por los camachicos sesantes que dicho secretario principia a dar su chaccha a los señores como són[404] coca y rón de su fiambre para entonces el camachico sesante está preparando una mesita chica y una silla que esto será para su secretario, terminado el secretario con su cumplimiento los mayores piden la lista o planilla para aprobar los números de los cumplidos[405] o reveldes[406] y como en la planilla consta de los hombres (qy) originarios que són con el número 355 revelde o incumplido 355.___Con[407] el número 352 deve[408] dos __ con el número 351. deve uno. __ Con el número 12. cumplido u obidiente[409] con el número 5. pasado de hacer sus servicios ó (sinó)[410] ha sido muy obediente, una vez aprobado dicha planilla el secretario pasa a su asiento.

Terminado ésto el Teniente ordena a todos sus funcionarios que se pongan en planta para continuar la cuenta, los alguaciles [note in black ink: *] dará la voz y pasará a juntas de notables y principiarán el concejo por uno de ellos

---

396. The accent has been added in black ink.
397. The "o" in the original spelling "llamado" has been changed to an "a" in black ink.
398. The "s" has been added in dark ink.
399. The "que" has been added in dark ink, squeezed into the line.
400. "siga."
401. "reprensión."
402. "provechoso."
403. The accent has been added in dark ink.
404. "son." The accent has been added in black ink.
405. "cumplidos."
406. "rebeldes." Sometimes spelled "reveldes" in the text.
407. Originally spelled with a lowercase "c," this has been corrected to a capital by the same hand.
408. "debe."
409. "obediente."
410. The parentheses have been added in black ink.

de los notables. [in the margin: * menores oirá[411] al secretario el número que que menciona] El que toma la palabra hará vez al que está postrado todos sus faltas publicamente[412] especialmente con los deberes para con la Iglesia y para con sus obligaciones y administración para con su casa y otros deberes.

Terminado la represión, pasará al Consejo que se arrodillará de tres o cuatro metros á distancia de los mayores el quin[413] a[414] de dar su castigo preguntará a los concejeros cuales han sido sus culpabilidades u amorosidades y cuanto[415] orde-

[f. 15r] -na su castigo.

Entonces el quien (no) ha estado en la reprención[416] juzgando su falta se manifestará dise[417] uno, dos, tres o cuatro según como lo recae y al que no solamente a reprención una vez terminado este cuidano se levantará y dará las gracias a los mayores atravesandese[418] la mano de satisfacción esto lo recibin[419] con la mayor atrivusion[420] y respeto una vez que esté[421] por mitad el padrón llamará al descanso a todos[422] los concurrentes.

Y el sicretario[423] pasa a la mesa de la notabilidad que son los mayores a cuntinuar[424] con sus cumplimientos como son la coca, algunas cupitas de rón,[425] puesto por los camachicos sesantes.

La chicha será generalmente para todos los[426] ciudadanos. Una vez que se ha terminado ésto volverán a continuar hasta dar su término en las mismas formas.

---

411. "oirá."
412. "públicamente."
413. "quien."
414. "ha."
415. "cuánto."
416. "reprensión." Sometimes spelled "reprención" in the text.
417. "dice."
418. "atrevesándose."
419. "reciben."
420. "atribución."
421. The accent has been added in black ink.
422. The "s" has been added in dark ink.
423. "secretario."
424. "continuar."
425. The accent has been added in black ink.
426. The "los" has been added in black ink, squeezed into the line.

Los camachicos sesantes siendo ya de tarde llamará suspensión difinitiva[427] o dará la voz que se terminó.[428] Y para entonces se[429] retiran a[430] todos del lugar indicado y llama á[431] su casa a tomar un poco de comida que ellos lo prepararon con algunas restos que lo han sobrado de sus deberes antiriores[432] esta comida será generalmente.

Terminado ésto será asentada la merienda con un vaso de vino marca acequia o con una o dos botellas de rón.

[f. 15v] ~Día Sábado~ [wavy underlining]

Sus deberes y obligaciones. [wavy underlining]

En la mañana llamará el Sr. Teniente Gobernador a los dos camachicos sesantes y hará presentes de las obligaciones de este día como es de dos potos chayaneros y los camachicos llevarán[433] dichos chayaneros á la tenencia, y halla[434] aprobarán[435] con un pequeño cumplimiento (en seguida se preparan los camachicos sesantes) en seguida se preparan los camachicos sesantes con dos dictadores para seguir cobrando los chayanas.

En seguida el Sr. Teniente ordenará[436] a sus funcionarios a que notefiquen[437] a las paradas para continuar la costumbre del "Cuhuay" hacer cambios de los alferes mayoralas[438] y [in the margin: a red ballpoint arrow] cajeras de paradas; en cada parte los alferes tirarán un cuhete y los alferes prepararán dos timbladeras[439] o copas engasadas en una tiras de cinta como tambien cada parada en partes[440] sus banderas, y las armonías continuarán[441] de lo más alegres terminado esta obligación o costumbre ordenará[442] el Sr. Teniente

---

427. "definitiva."
428. The accent has been added in black ink.
429. The "se" has been added in black ink.
430. The "a" has been added in black ink.
431. "a." The accent has been added in black ink.
432. "anteriores." Sometimes spelled "antiriores" in the text.
433. This word has been added in black ink, squeezed into the line.
434. "allá."
435. The accent has been added in black ink.
436. The accent has been added in black ink.
437. "notifiquen."
438. Originally spelled "mayorales": an "a" added in black pen replaced the "e."
439. "tembladeras."
440. The "s" has been added in black ink.
441. The accent has been added in black ink.
442. The accent has been added in black ink.

suspensión[443] de juntas, y decreta que pasen à la tenencia y luego parten con sus banderas cada parada al ganarse unos à los otros, una vez llegado a la puerta de su domicilio el Sr. Teniente con el puño en la mano y manifiesta al público de las obligaciones y asistencia de este día notefica[444] a todos los[445] padres o guardadores de familia que asistan a la cuenta general de señoras originarías[446] y da lugar para el almuerzo oras[447] señaladas[448] en las paradas terminado el almuerzo ordena para continuar la cuenta todo como el primer día, los funcionarios ejecutan a la reunión de todas y a los hombres y mientras esto el camachico llaba[449] la lista o planilla como[450] el primer día para la aprobasión[451] de los números, y con sus cumplimientos una vez aprobado se ban[452] a la plaza chica o Cuhuay

[f. 16r] a seguir el padrón general de los hombres y mujeres dándoles[453] sus correcciones al que no asista a dicho padrón de dos latigos[454] para entonces hace llamar al camachico sesante para que entregen las obligaciones de una libra de coca y una botella de rón mientras los dos dictadores y enterinos[455] del camachico y su secretario continuarán el cobro de las chayanas con las mismas costumbres de entrada y salida.

El Teniente ordena que tomen asiento como el primer día dos de "Yañac"[456] y dos hombres de "Yacapar" como corrigedores[457] de dichas faltas; una vez terminado esto pone el camachico sesante coca, ron, y chicha en la mesa de los notables y en la misma vasija que se ha hecho en el día antirior y continúan la chaccha generalmente, los notables elige[458] a una persona que es el mas siguiente que desfrute de la chaccha y de todo el cumplimiento.

---

443. "la suspension."
444. "notifica."
445. The "los" has been added in black ink, squeezed into the line.
446. "originarias."
447. "horas."
448. The tilde over the "n" has been added in black ink.
449. "lava."
450. The "m" has been emboldened in black ink.
451. "aprobación."
452. "van."
453. Accent added in black ink.
454. "látigos."
455. "interinos."
456. There is already a tilde on the "n" which has been emboldened with black ink.
457. "corregidores."
458. "eligen."

El Sr. Teniente solecita[459] al elegido nuevo o electo para que tomen aciento[460] a su lado terminado la chaccha ordena el Teniente sesante reunidos[461] las Sras de ambas parcialidades y principian el padrón de las Señoras contando sus numeros[462] como cumplidos o rebeldes—como cumplido lleva el no. 11 __como pasado lleva el no. 15. Como rebelde lleba[463] el no. 365.

Los funcionarios o alguaciles dará[464] la voz a los notables luego el camachico descarga de sus inacistencia[465] o mal incumplimiento y luego principia el concejo o reprención por una persona notable haciendole[466] ver toda[467] sus faltas, terminado la reprensión dara[468] pase (d) al Concejo entonces se lebantan todos los hombres de las parcialidades a favorecer a las señoras como es costumbre de tiempos remotos. las señoras el que recibe[469] la reprención llevara[470] una manta doblada en tres partes o puntas y todas las señoras no llevaran nigunas[471] cosas (mensuales) manuales[472] con el fin de atender con el mayor orden la reprención y continúa, una vez por mitad el padrón llama al descanso y pasa el secretario (pasa) a la mesa de los notables con su cumplimiento y la chaccha general y continúa la chicha con los potos chayaneros, despues de las invitaciones, el que pide chicha dará

[f. 16v] con el chayanero hasta que termine con el látigo en la mano el Sr. Teniente Gobernador y notables ordena[473] que continúa la cuenta y el secretario pasa a su asciento[474] y continúa la cuenta o padrón, terminado ésto de todo cumplimiento, el Teniente Gobernador publica en álta[475] voz à los

---

459. "solicita."
460. "asiento."
461. The "re" has either been emboldened or added in black ink.
462. "números."
463. "lleva." Conjugated forms of "llevar" sometimes spelled with a "b" in the text.
464. "darán."
465. "inasistencias."
466. "haciéndole."
467. "todas."
468. "dará."
469. The syntax in this section suggests that it was a challenge to arrange the regulations in Spanish.
470. "llevará." Sometimes spelled without an accent in the text.
471. "ningunas."
472. This word has been written above the line.
473. "ordenan."
474. "asiento."
475. "alta."

nombrados electos desde el Teniente hasta el último Alguacil Mayor, para que el pueblo le guarden el debido respeto y consideración * (ojo) [in the margin: ojo pasa mas abajo donde indica ojo] en seguida el secretario del pueblo o cantor resará el rosario con todos los concurrentes hombres y mujeres, para entonces el camachico sesante lebantará al cristo y pondrá una candelija[476] y una cera, y continuarán el rosario. terminado el rosario, recoge el crusifijo[477] como todos los útiles de costumbre y luego se lebantan todas las Sras mujeres con sus cumplimientos y aperciben todos los Señores con el major agrado de haber desempeñado nuestra costumbre sin la menor novedad dando gracias a Dios continúan sus cumplimientos.

En seguida el secretario de los camachicos envitan[478] a los Sres la merienda propuesto por los camachicos como el primer día.

[in the margin: ojo aqui?-] Los notables llaman a los camachicos sesantes y el camachico ordena que que [sic] los amarren la mano hacia atrás y lo lleba ante la precencia de los notables y reciba su reprención por haber apollado[479] a ciertos ciudadanos o haber recargados en sus mandatos ù obligaciones, los notables ordena[480] que pase al concejo[481] y lo lleban a la mesa donde está la vaticola[482] y latiguera y luego sale una persona de entre el círculo de los notables a darles la correción[483] y tomo la tigera[484] y hace la ceremonia de pelarle como siempre las Srs son desobedientes le pelan a aparencia[485] y proceden con la vaticola a dar el castigo y luego se lebantan todas las señoras a defenderle y el notable atiende a las señoras y no lo corrige.

Como tambien en el primer día en el padrón de los hombres debe hacer lo mismo todo[486] estos castigos como queda dicha[487] en los antiriores.

---

476. This word was originally spelled "candelijo," but the spelling has been edited.
477. "crucifijo."
478. "invitan."
479. "apoyado."
480. "ordenan."
481. "consejo."
482. "batícola." Sometimes spelled "vatícola" in the text.
483. "corrección."
484. "tijera."
485. "apariencia."
486. "todos."
487. "dicho."

[f. 17r] ~Día Domingo~

Durante este día ambas paradas seguiran[488] sus cuentas de sus inseres[489] útiles y dinero que tengan cada uno lo que pasarán oficios al Sr. Teniente Gobernador al Síndico y mas autoridades para que le prestan las garantías auxilios y apoyos para los cumplimientos de los morosos.

Asi mismo cada parada pasará una relación ó nómina de los que asisten o estén presentes con sus servicios, y otra igual pasará los que no contribuyen y asisten ya séa[490] hombres y mujeres con sus cargos de tushmac y mayorala esta relación o nómina será derigida[491] ante la reunión de "Cuhuay" a las autoridades para que descubran o aclaren cuales[492] son sus motivos que no están, por cuanto es la vase[493] principal la fiesta de la champería de la acequia.

Tambien durante ésta cuenta entregarán los alferes los sacos de panes y cajones de chancaca a cada parada cada mayordomo ó alferes de cada parada, una vez entregado destribiuyirán[494] las mayoralas emposando cada uno de ellas su quinci[495] centavos.

En cuánto[496] a los hombres ya en este día deberán cancelar sus cuotas que cada parada les impone, quien recavarán[497] éstos como cobradores serán los mismos alferes que á cada individuo que pague tiene la obligación de dar los alferes una copo[498] de chacpacne[499]: durante el medio día o mas tarde irán los hombres con las mayoralas a coger un poco de leñas[500] al campo.

Una vez llegado seguirán sus cuentas.

---

488. "seguirán."
489. "enseres."
490. "sea."
491. "dirigida."
492. "cuáles."
493. "base."
494. "distribuirán."
495. "quince."
496. "cuanto."
497. "recabarán."
498. "copa."
499. "champaña."
500. "leña."

EL ENTABLO 193

[f. 17v] ~Día Lunes~ [wavy underlining]

Durante éste día todos los señores de ambas paradas terminarán sus cuentas y harán que legalise[501] y autorise[502] las autoridades del lugar sus libros.

Una vez hecho ó terminado esperarán reunidos alegremente para la noche llegado la hora once o doce de la noche se preparán[503] generalmente todos.

En primer lugar las paradas siguen con las armonías con el mayor órden ambas paradas llamarán a las autoridades para dar término al despacho con todas las ceremonias de viejos y viejas yaravíes y hualinas y las cajas se hará el despacho, primero llegarán a la plaza chica, y después a Ursno, la parada de Carguayumac irá adelante en seguida la parada de Cumao bien entonadas de chirimías y harán una forma de correrse y no irse como don Basilio Jimenez y otros demás, los viejos y viejas unos con la bandera y otros con la caja sevan[504] hasta "Gotogoto" y de ahí regresan con las banderas desarmadas y las cajas destempladas y regresan al pueblo cada uno à sus huaironas o paradas con una alegría muy distinta con lo que se dió[505] término la presente memoria de nuestras costumbres [a large period in blue ballpoint] desde los tiempos de su fundasión[506] que fue formado por los indigenas[507] y a la que hoy llevamos un recuerdo la constancia del ante pasado y queda para lo susecivo escrita lo que nos recordamos nosotros los dictadores que hemos alcanzado algunas partes lo que han sido exacto siendo así esta memoria dictado[508] o dirigida por los señores mayores [in the margin in red ballpoint: X] elegidos por el pueblo en primer lugar Don Vicente A. Reyes, Don Jacinto Bautista y Félix B. Chagua con lo que se terminó el precente recuerdo.

[f. 18r] El presente acuerdo (que queda escrita[509] [crossed out]) fué[510] discutida tres años atrás para la constancia del presente libro y por tal creemos

---

501. "legalice."
502. "autorice."
503. "prepararán."
504. "se van."
505. "dio."
506. "fundación."
507. "indígenas."
508. "dictada."
509. "escrito."
510. "fue." Sometimes spelled with an accent in the text.

que ningún ciudadanos[511] recidentes[512] en este pueblo desde el que nace se rehusarán en firmar y otorgar sus rublicas.[513]

Así mismo fué por el empeño de las autoridades precentes en primer lugar el Síndico Don Máximo Calistro el señor Teniente Cristoval Jimenez, Rejedor mayor Melecio Calistro, Campo Jose M. Salinas, Rejedor Campo Facundo Bautista, alguacil mayor Victor B. Miranda, alguaciles menores Cosme Obispo, Santos M. Obispo, Toribio Calistro y Benancio Rojas camachicos Concepción Olivares y Simeón Calistro sacrestan[514] Exaltación Jimenez, Fiscal Yaspar Salinas y el principal don Justo Salinas y como tambien acompañaron los camachicos sesantes Nicasio Salinas y Timoteo Rojas personas que han obtenido cargos obligatorios de nuestro pueblo.

Así mismo pasa el presente libro al Sr. Alcalde Municipal + [+ in margin: don Pascual Calistro] para su revisión y autorisacion[515] que componen el concejo también los Srs. Pascual Gonzales primer Rigedor[516] [in the margin: a red ballpoint arrow] segundo Regedor Felex B. Salinas síndico de rentas don Catalino Bautista y síndico de gasto Francisco Obispo despues de haber revisado y observado los señores miembros del concejo pasó al precente libro a la gobernación siendo Gobernador Don Nemesio Bautista quien tambien aprobo[517] y acepto[518] el règimen y reglamento de los deberes y sus obligaciones que todo[519] los ciudadanos del pueblo de Casta están sugetos[520] solamente a esta obligación.

No teniendo más que decir agregar ni obervar[521] devolvió a la cuminidad[522] para que lo firmen con sus propias rúblicas.[523]

---

511. "ninguno de los ciudadanos."
512. "residentes."
513. "rúbricas."
514. "sacristán."
515. "autorización."
516. This was originally spelled "Regedor."
517. "aprobó."
518. "aceptó."
519. "todos."
520. "sujetos."
521. "observar."
522. "comunidad."
523. "rúbricas."

El precente libro lo autorizará el Sr. Juez de Paz Don Cecilio Rojas y el primer axeso[524] Don Jorge Obispo.

[X X X X X][525]

[f. 18v] [All signatures]

Florencio Lopez

J. B. Olivares i Yaure

Silverio Miranedo [Miranda?]
Vicente O. y Reyes
Jose R. Gonsalez
(Camachico cesante) Catalino Bautista
Pascual Calistro
Eusebio Gonzáles
Andrés Calistro (alguacil menor)
J. Hildiberto O. Rodriguez [with a personalized stamp: J. Hildiberto O. Rodriguez. Sastreria Casta]

Marcelino Lopez

Ysidro R. Calistro [stamped: Sindicatura del pueblo de Casta]

J. Rojas y Salinas—Secretario de Casta

Celestino Salinas
Jacinto Bautista [nearly illegible]
Cecilio Rojas
Nemesio Bautista (Alcalde Campo)

Facundo Bautista (Regidor Mayor)
Victor Perez (Alguacil Mayor)
Nicolás Murrillo[?]
Diósdado López (Alguacil de Campo)

Estanislao Calistro
Prudencio Jimenez

[f. 19r] [All signatures]

Adolfo Salinas
Concepcion Cristóstomo
Bernardino Bautista
Vivancio Rojas

José M. Salinas
Toribio Calistro
Santos Obispo
Olipio Bautista

---

524. This was originally spelled "acceso."
525. The "end" of the document has been marked along the bottom margin with crosses, in blue (ballpoint?) ink.

Pedro Bautista Y.
Claro Jiménez

Victor Bautista
Silvestre Olivares
Braulio Flores (aficionado)
Doroteo Perez

Nazario Rojas
Pablo Olivares y Vásquez (camachico)
Juan Cl[?]Calistro
Cristóbal Jímenez
Tomas Perez

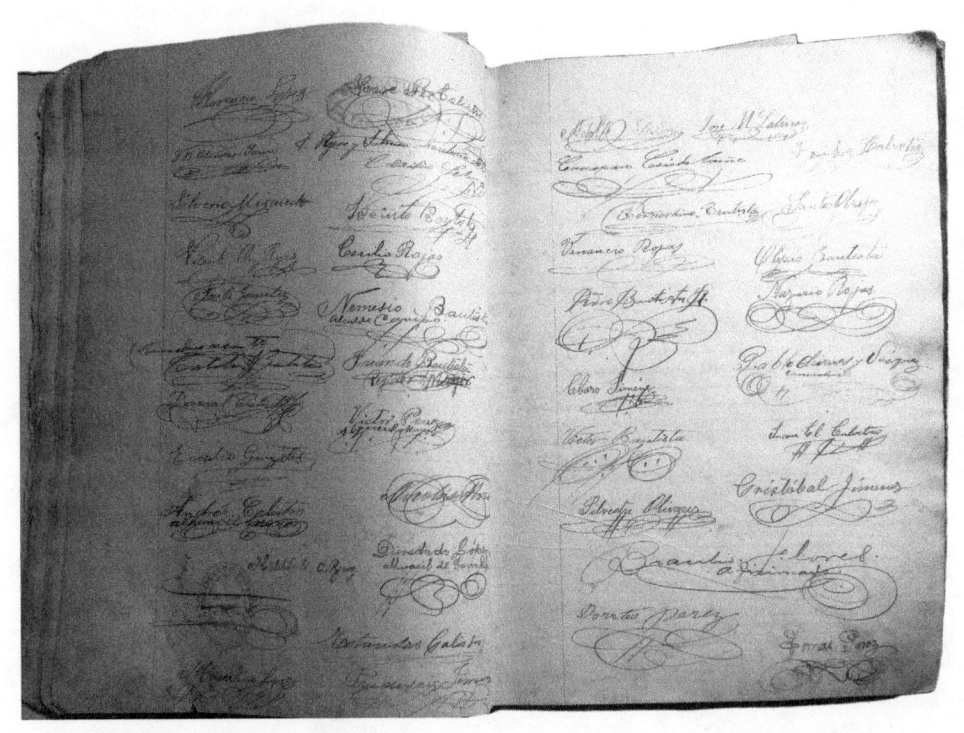

FIGURE 3.1. *Folios 18v and 19r.*

[f. 19v] [in the top margin a note in pencil:] no estoy de acuerdo.

Eusebio Olivares Antonio Bautista
Félix Bautista Chagua Gabino[?] Oyhorozco
Bautista Teodocio Exaltación y Bautista
Félix Calistro y Bautista Emiliano S. Saliermino

Esta celebración o fiesta de la Walla-Walla, tiene un atractivo cientifico[526] mitológico i[527] por ella sale o pierde aquella que relaciona con el alcohol mas bien en lugar de este va la chicha i coincide ademas[528] muchas leyes de la era arcaica i por estos lo firmo Miranda[?]

Vergilio Ríos y [?]
Bonifacio Salinas
Ruego mi salvador en lo que me pon-
cerra a mi parecer y firmo Máximo[?]
Rojas

(Camachico menor) M. E. Santos [?]

[f. 20r] Saturnino Bautista y.O. [?] Melecio Calistro

Bacilio Jimenez R. Salinas y Yayo [?]
Catalino Medina Félix Bautista y Salinas
Catalino Gonzales i B [?] Teofilo Huáman
Pedro Echuanqui [?] Cornelio [?] Salinas
Pedro Jiménez Gerónimo Crisostomó
Lorenzo Medina y C. Genaro [?] Salinas
Nicolas Salinas Wenceslao Olivares
Mario Calistro Ferruco [?] y Calistro
[illegible initials] Salinas C. Benicio[?] Salinas
 [illegible, in blue pen]

Hipolito Obispo [stamped: Comunidad Indígena de San Pedro de Casta Prov. de Huarochirí. Presidencia]

---

526. "científico."
527. "y." The text often has "i" instead of "y."
528. "además." Sometimes spelled without an accent in the text.

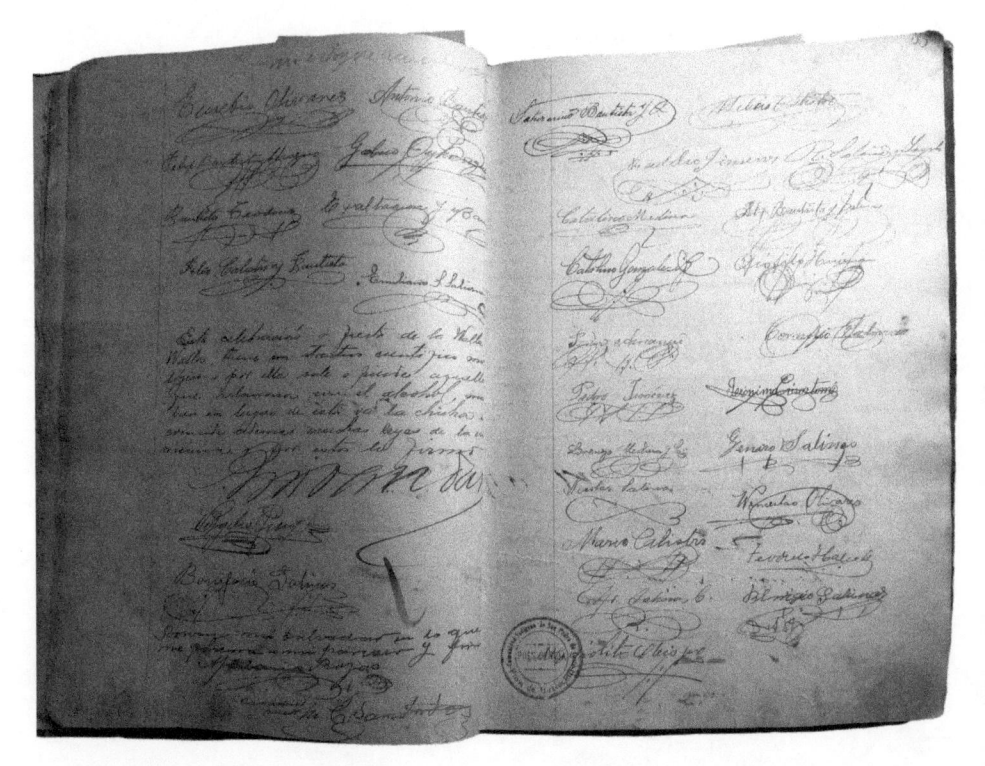

FIGURE 3.2. *Folios 19v and 20r.*

[f. 20v] [all green ink] Faustino Calistro

En el pueblo de San Pedro de Casta en diez días del mes de octubre del año mil novecientos veinte seis reunidos en el lugar de Coguay el día domingo como de costumbre, acordaron todos los notables que todas las personas en adelante darán chicha conforme indica en hojas anteriores o en cambio una botella de ron quedan suprimido[529] las botellas de cerveza i vino y para mayor cumplimiento firmamos.

Florencio Lopez	Faustino Calistro
Vicente O. y Reyes	Jose R. Gonzales
J. B. Olivares i Yaure	Pascual Calistro
Wenceslao Olivares	Jorge Obispo

---

529. "suprimidas."

Simeón Calistro   Eusebio Olivares
M. O. [illegible]   R. Bautista
Concepción Jimenez [?] Victor Perez
                        Hecterio Larjo[?]

[f. 21 is torn out]

[f. 22r] [all black ink]

Nazario Rojas

Ynocensio Obispo

Alejandro Jimenez

Selino P mancioetta [?]

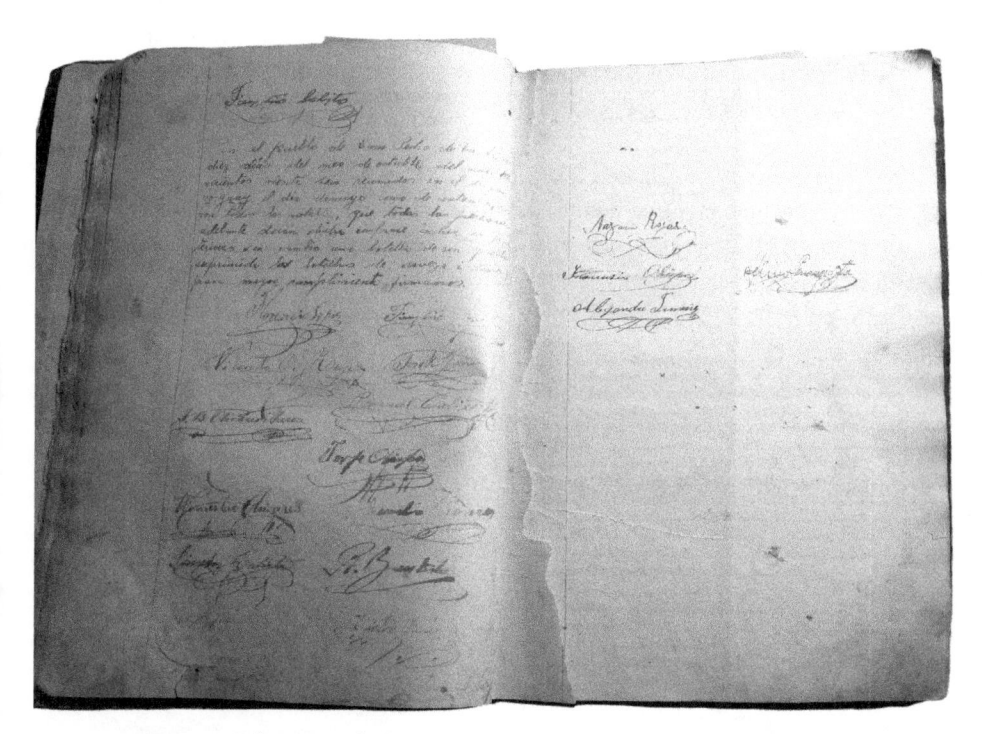

FIGURE 3.3. *Folios 20v and 22r.*

[f. 22v] [Black ink in a new hand in the main body of the page] [Note in the margin in dark blue ballpoint: ojo]

En el pueblo de San Pedro de Casta á los ocho días del mes de enero de mil novecientos treinta i nueve reunidos en el local de la comunidad la "Comisión" designada en asamblea comunal para la organización del reglamento interior en la fecha tres del presente. dicho comisión formamos los suscritos Presidente Cecilio Rojas Secretario Pedro R. Bautista, Pro-secretario Francisco Salinas, Vocales Pascual Calixtro. Vicente Obispo, Jacinto Bautista, Concepción Olivares, Man[uel?] Obispo, Dalmacio Salinas, Diósdado Lopez, Nemesio Bautista y Teófilo A. Crisostomo.

Despues de haber formulado un reglamento interior que será sometido a su estudio y provación[530] del Ministerio de Salud Pública, Trabajo y Previción[531] Social y haciendo constar en su artículo No. diesiocho[532] que además de los de[cret?]-us[533] mencionados en ello, tambien tienen obligaciónes secundarios que cumplir y que están estipulados en el libro del "Campo" y en el "Entablo" dejamos constancias que el libro denominado el "Entable" ha quedado reformado por sesión de junta general del trece de Enero de mil novecientos veinte que consta en los folios ochenta, seis, ochenta, siete, ochenta, ocho, ochenta, nueve, y noventa de dicho libro.

La junta presente acordamos unanimamente dejar constancias de las obligaciones secundarias que tienen los funcionarios comunales desde el mes de Enero á Diciembre tornando la copia literal del trece de Enero de mil novecientos veinte para que en este libro figure con las obligaciones y atribuciones en órden interno.

[f. 23r] Obligaciones i Atribuciones Secundarias de los Funcionarios comunales durante el año de Administración. Hacemos constar que los funcionarios comunales tal como el "Campo" Regidor "Mayor" "Regidor Campo," "Alguacil Mayor," todos presentes, en su período harán los gastos de obligación que les corresponde según ecepción[534] hecho en la forma siguiente.

---

530. "aprobación."
531. "Previsión."
532. "dieciocho."
533. "decretos"?
534. "excepción."

El comunero que pasa el cargo de Campo queda eceptuado[535] de Regidor Mayor i lo mismo el que pasa Regidor Campo no pasará Alguacil Mayor. cumpliendo las obligaciones que les corresponden á cada uno dando principio del día primero de Enero de cada año los funcionarios sesantes tienen la obligación de recibir las visitas de los nuevos funcionarios en compañia[536] de los comuneros. quedando descargado absolutamente las obligaciones de los funcionarios sesantes durante las reverencia[537] del pueblo de sementeras, de puna i de maquiyal[538] i fundo de Viquil que para los dos días ultimos de puna i maquiyal el síndico tesorero hará pronto los gastos con dinero de la caja comunal que fijará en el presupuesto.

Las Obligaciones en el Año Nuevo

[Note in the margin in light-blue felt-tip pen: ojo]

Para cumplir las costumbres secretas del pueblo, El Teniente Gobernador, Regidor mayor y Alguacil Mayor contribuiran[539] con sus obligaciones que corresponde[540] durante los días que ocupa[541] las seremonia á la que contribuirá el Campo i Regidor Campo por viéndose de acuerdo para que lo corresponde en las fiestas de "Carnaval" y la Limpia de Acequia de Octubre. i durante estas fiestas secretas el camachico tiene obligación debiendo estos los funcionarios en compañia de sus esposa[542] i familias asistiendo los alguasiles[543] menores sin obligación de

[f. 23v] gastos fin de[?] presentar sus curiosidades de labores que tiene deberes. i las mujeres de los funcionarios presentarán su conosidades[544] de todo genero[545] á una expresa titulada yachak quien esta[546] encargada revisar

---

535. "exceptuado."
536. "compañía." Sometimes spelled without an accent in the text.
537. "reverencias."
538. "maquial."
539. "contribuirán."
540. "corresponden."
541. "ocupan."
542. "esposas."
543. "alguaciles."
544. "conocidades/conocimientos."
545. "género."
546. "está."

i referir a los que no cumplen. despues, todo[547] juntos cumplir en medio de una alegría dicha fiesta con lo que termina en curco.

Fiestas de los Carnavales

[Note in the margin in light-blue felt-tip pen: ojo]

Para la fiesta de los carnavales según indica el Calendario Anual. se lleva a cabo una faena de limpia de Acequia, ordenada en la forma siguiente:

Día Viernes

Los funcionarios se reunirán en la casa del Campo en compañia del teniente i el principal para formar el acto de seremonia que es la víspera de la fiesta y el principal hará recuerdo a los funcionarios de sus obligaciones que le corresponde el día Sábado para esto si han contribuido en la costumbre de Enero el Campo, Regidor Campo, les deve[548] corresponder los de esa fiesta formando una mesa donde se exhibirá[549] los gastos de obligación, el padrón de comuneros representados por granos esto lo ejecutan desde los seis de la tarde hasta horas que terminan i continuan con una víspera nocturna al lugar de Hualhual. regresando al pueblo i descansan para el siguiente día de la faena.

Día Sábado

A las primeras horas se reunen[550] los funcionarios en la tenencia donde se encuentra el principal para pesar sus obligaciones de gastos. principado por los dos mayores "Campo" y "Regidor Mayor"

[f. 24r] como son una libra de coca una botella de ron una cajitilla[551] de cigarros i dos cuhetes de arranques i los menores "Regidor Campo" i Alguacil Mayor dará la mitad o sea ½ libra coca ½ botella de ron ½ cajitilla de cigarros i un cuhete la pesa para las obligaciones de coca será una romana típica[552] llamada "Huipi" despues de[553] terminado de presentar sus obligaciones en la

---

547. "todos."
548. "debe."
549. Originally spelled "exibirá" without an "h," which has been added in blue ballpoint.
550. "reúnen." Sometimes spelled without an accent in the text.
551. "cajetilla."
552. "típica."
553. "haber."

tenencia se dirijerán al lugar de "Cohuay" de donde el Campo llamará [note in the margin: a red ballpoint arrow]. à los comuneros à reunión o a la junta en seguida pasará padrón de hombres i mujeres que deben concurrir á la faena una vez reunidos los comuneros vuelven pesar los funcionarios sus obligaciones para que sepan el cumplimiento de cada uno i en seguida a voz de los comuneros los dos kamachicos presentan según la relación las chichas de obligación de las comuneras casadas, viudas i solteras i asi como de los hombres vuidos[554] ó solteros que tienen turno de agua compartiendo dicho cantaro consistente en una peseta ó (veinte centavos) para esé[555] dia i para el lunes. en ese acto el Síndico <u>tesorero dará un kilo de coca</u>[556] para los dos días de faena asi como el inspector del romano[?] terminada la exhibición de obligaciones el Campo vuelve repitir[557] á los jovenes que estén o no inscritos en el padron[558] comunal que son mandados de cruces para los lugares de costumbres que cumplan i nombrando en seguida cuatro mayordomos dos para los hombres i dos para mujeres; terminada la designación recurren los cuatro funcionarios con sus brindes[559] de buena voluntad que dice el "Fiambre." partiendo en seguida los comuneros sin distinción a Hualhual de donde dan principio la faena bajo la supervigilancia

[f. 24v] de los mayordomos despues de una lejira[560] chaccha otra parte de Huascuila en igual forma curan[?] el trayecto de los comuneros, los funcionarios que en el Cohuay en compañía de los comuneros mayores que se encargan à separar [reparar?] mejoras de los corrales de incierros,[561] potreros o el camino del Pueblo al lugar de Huayacocha. Del Cohuay se dirigen soltando un cuhete los funcionarios despues de haber dejado la obligación de un funcionario menor parte de chicha i del gasto de comisión[?] del inspector a chicra[?], al lugar de Hualhual tocando Pampacocha con su rispectivos[562] cumplimiento[563] donde corresponde. llegando a la toma que se

---

554. "viudos."
555. "ese."
556. This section has been underlined using a slightly lighter colored ink. This instance of editing makes it clear that the Entablo is used as a point of reference in clarifying the material contributions of the ritual functionaries.
557. "vuelve a repetir."
558. "padrón."
559. "brindis." Sometimes spelled "brindes" in the text.
560. "ligera." Sometimes spelled "lejira" or "ligira" in the text.
561. "encierros."
562. "respectivos."
563. "con sus respectivos cumplimientos."

dirije[564] a Maiguai tratan de una ligira seremonia[565] i continuan[566] recorriendo la acequia observando el estado que deja los comuneros hasta alcanza con los cumplimientos despues con los brindes de sus "Fiambres" los cuatro funcionarios y los camachicos con la chicha i siguen pasando hasta el lugar de Huayacocha dando aviso por medio de un cuhete de Oclu-guiron[?]. para que los que fueron limpiando de Huascuila siguen en la laguna de Huayacocha donde entrarán los funcionarios con alegría entonada por aficionados de la "Chirimia" á dar sus brindes de fiambres en seguida todos juntos salen al sitio de costumbre para continuar con las observaciones de "Huallquis" "Eshkupuros" i cascabillos [cascabeles?] los jovenes aficionados terminada poseen descanso apercibiendo una ligira merienda. en seguida continua[567] participar los obligaciones mostrados[568] en el Cohuay i siguen otra vez el trabajo hasta terminar i se reunen otra vez en unión

[f. 25r] de los mayores i teniente que llegan a la hora de padron. donde el de campo [termine?] que todos atienden su padrón i dá[569] principio llevando el secretario una lista de los inasistentes, terminado el padrón de comuneros, entra en el de chicha o cantaros que dan cuenta los "Kamachicos" en este momento el Campo en compañia de uno de los funcionarios sacando[?] cruces á los lugares de costumbres del día lunes á los jovenes como de costumbre. despues de terminarlo regresarán al pueblo con alegría brindando las chichas en lugares de costumbre Ocluguirron[?] Paxxaguirma[?] lleno i el Cabildo retirandose[570] todos a su[571] domicilios tratando en seguida los funcionarios de reunirse en casa del Campo para organizar la fiesta del domingo.

Dia Domingo

En este dia los funcionarios de lo más temprano se reunen en casa del campo para seguir curiosamente con las costumbres que está obligado.[572] continuan[573] formado la mesa en la mejor forma que desea, para esto están reunidos[574]

---

564. "dirige."
565. "ceremonia."
566. "continúan."
567. "continúa a."
568. "mostradas."
569. "da."
570. "retirándose."
571. "sus."
572. "están obligadas."
573. "continúan."
574. "reunidas."

sus esposas i familias para la cocina i aperciben un comite[575] extra en este los Kamachicos están cobrando las chichas para el día lunes i además preparando los toros i menu[576] incaica para el almuerso[577] del dia lunes de todo[578] los comuneros. despues de esto, todo[579] juntos disponen la ida á Maiguai. quedando un camachico prepararando[580] los útiles de cocina i envitando[581] à las mujeres viudas i solteras para su ayuda en la cocina de la noche: en el trayecto à maiguai lo practican todo lo que debe de hacer el lunes tocando el lugar de "Cueca" un lijero descanso i en

[f. 25v] [in the margin in blue ballpoint: an arrow] seguida el "Campo" expone la costumbre de la carrera de ese punto à Bailana Pastos de tres alguasiles[582] menores i un Kamachico practicamente[583] en seguida dando la voz de partida con un cuhete i continuan[584] à tras[585] todos casi en silencio al sitio donde esperan los de la carrera despues de un brindes de todos i continuan a la toma donde tambien practican las seremonias secretas. i siguen tocando en chacchadera cumpliendo entre todos las observaciones de los objetos de Huallqui Eschcupuros etc i jugando los carnavales con <u>pinturas naturales</u> que [illegible] en ese sitio continuando à maiguay para la visita de este caserio[586] manda un <u>alguasil para que los que habitan en este, se—oculten un rato.</u> <u>tocando en seguida "Ñamuc"</u> lejeramente[587] pasan á la laguna de Lecas [?] que lo efectúan las ceremonias con mucho respeto moralidad donde sedan[588] las curiosidades de los Alguaciles menores sea las (Tacllas) i regresan à ñamuc continuan con las costumbres i obligación que lo efectua[589] el lunes en presencia de los comuneros, en seguida el Campo"[590] en compañía de un alguasil se constituyen à las casas de los que habitan allí a notificar sobre el cupo[?] de "Piso" que estan obligados a satisfacer segun la extención que poseen en

---

575. "comité."
576. "menú."
577. "almuerzo."
578. "todos."
579. "todos."
580. "preparando."
581. "invitando."
582. "alguaciles." Sometimes spelled "alguasiles" in the text.
583. "prácticamente."
584. "continúan." Sometimes spelled without an accent in the text.
585. "atrás."
586. "caserío."
587. "ligeramente."
588. "se dan/le dan"?
589. "efectúa."
590. There is no opening quotation mark for this quotation.

propiedad y en seguida regresan al pueblo con alegrias[591] de Chirimia i a la llegada al pueblo recojen sus cosas[592] que llevan á la cerremonia[593] retirándose à sus domicilios i en este instante los Kamachicos[594] organizan la cocina en medio de distracciones con sus aficionados de cualquier instrumento musical.

[f. 26r] continuan la cocina todo[595] la noche para la mañana del día lunes.

Dia Lunes

El dia lunes en las primeras horas harán las misma[596] del dia sábado i despues del almuerzo en el camachico i el respectivo desayuno en la casa del campo se derijirán[597] todos juntos con las mismas obligaciones de[598] costumbre hasta llegar al sitio de "queca" espescionando,[599] que en las peanas i lugares de costumbre hayan cumplido los mandado de cruz en ponerlo i arreglar las peanas. tomando nota para su respectivo castigo o en la llegada a la tarde en el cavildo[600] [written above, by the same hand: en caso no cumplirlo] i despues de un ligeró[601] descanso el campo llamará la atención a los aficionados en la carrera efectuandola[602] conforme lo hace los funcionarios en el día anterior hasta llegar a la toma de mayhuay donde se sientan los faeneros en orden de edades para presentar las obligaciones corespondientes,[603] habiendo dejado un funcionario sus obligaciones para los mayores la cual ellos dispondran[604] en seguida el campo hará la señal de partida al trabajo despues de haber repartido sus obligaciones i dando a los mayordomos de mujeres su gasto proporcional partiendo al trabajo con señal de un cuete [in the margin in blue ballpoint: ojo]. se quedan por un momento hasta que los faeneros habancen[605] alcansándole[606] en el lugar de Chacchadera para una nueva reunión i donde participan

---

591. "alegrías." Sometimes spelled without an accent in the text.
592. This section has been underlined with a blue ballpoint pen.
593. "ceremonia."
594. Originally spelled "Camachicos": a "K" has replaced the "C."
595. "toda."
596. "lo mismo."
597. "dirigirán."
598. Originally written as "del," but the "l" has been scribbled out in the same black ink.
599. "inspeccionando"?
600. "cabildo." Sometimes spelled "cavildo" in the text.
601. "ligero."
602. "efectuándola."
603. "correspondientes."
604. "dispondrán."
605. "avancen."
606. "alcanzándole."

las obligaciones i fiambre de los funcionarios. en seguida se hace la rebición[607] a los faeneros que presenten los huallques, escopuros[608] i cascabeles a todos los faeneros lo mismo que el mayordomo del trabajo a los funcionarios lo mismo que los camachicos con su repartición de chicha recabado de las comuneras i señoras de comuneros despues de un baile[,] alegres i con señal de cuete se teriran[609] dejando en el mismo chacchadera a los faeneros. dirigiendose[610] los funcionarios todos juntos al lugar de "Pacsa" i que despues de recibir el

[f. 26v] trabajo i reunidos la señoras faeneras se hace un brinde de participarán de cada funcionario las mencionadas i mayordomo. del mismo modo los camachicos repartirán la chicha i fiambre, regresando en seguida a la laguna [in the margin in blue ballpoint: ojo and an arrow] "Lecas" donde encuentran ya en trabajo los faeneros dejad[os?] en "chachadera" i despues de un ligero repartimiento de fiambre de los funcionarios i camachicos se derigen[611] al lugar "Ñamuc" llamandole[612] por medio de un alg[uacil?] a los mayordomos de hombres como de mujeres al padrón que su gente se reuna[613] a dicho lugar reunidos todos los funcionarios dan el ultimo brindes de sus obligaciones mostrando el agotamiento de la ultima gota de ron y con la ultima hoja de coca para que los faenero[614] acrediten haberse terminado la obligacion en el trabajo i toman cuenta de los pisos obligados su complimiento, que es para la misma gente i los no cumplidos hacerlo cumplir. despues de todo el campo hará el padron respectivo para saber de los asistentes i inasietentes.[615]

Del mismo modo hacerse presente la partida i juego de carnabal[616] que no sea en contra de la salud. veniendo[617] todos juntos al lugar de Shamashama. donde el camachico consume[618] un cántaro de chicha o segun la proporción de la gente continuando a "Taloc" i de alli[619] a "Puntangal" haciendo los

---

607. "revisión."
608. "eshcupuros."
609. "tirarán."
610. "dirigiéndose." Sometimes spelled without an accent in the text.
611. "dirigen."
612. "llamándole."
613. "reúna."
614. "faeneros."
615. "inasistientes."
616. "carnival."
617. "viniendo."
618. Originally written "cosume"; the scribe added the "n" above the line.
619. "allí."

camachicos las mismas obligaciones del [día?] anterior i los funcionarios repartiendo su fiambre si lo hay. donde se desarrolla un juego simpatico[620] por los faeneros. dirigiendose al sitio "Pacsagumo" en donde esperan los mayores de la comunidad i autoridades[621] pasando a el lugar de negro que es notable por su historia de juego Carnabalesco[622] llegados a Pacsagumo. [crossed out: se hace] Los mayores esperan anciosos[623] a saber la noticia malo o bueno de los funcionarios como de los faeneros i en seguida de la noticia los funcionarios camachicos hacen brindes a los mayores i los faeneros del mismo modo con

[f. 27r] racimo[624] de flores del campo, en señal de memoria del día de trabajo reverencia i respeto. dirigiendo en seguida todos al lugar de "Uhsno" donde se detienen por un momento i el camachico reparte de nuevo la chicha seguiendo[625] al cabildo en medio de alegres juegos i musica[626] de Chirimia[627] en orden de los funcionarios, Autoridades i mayores dejando a libertad la entreda[628] al cavildo al bando triunfante en el juego por los aficionados para el flanco de su estandarte de triunfo. Despues de un momento de distraccion[629] el Sr Teniente Gobernador hace que sese[630] por un momento el bullido i hace observación si hasido[631] correcto el cumplimiento de los funcionarios con sus obligaciones i los faeneros con el trabajo tanto en la asequia[632] como en la laguna que mencionamos. donde termina los camachicos con la reparticion[633] de chicha. En seguida para dar sueño a los costumbres que anotamos salen por orden gerarquico[634] de las autoridades i mayores a paseo en cada uno de los funcionarios anotados. ordenando al Sr Teniente Gobernador recojerse despues para no molestar el orden publico.[635]

---

620. "simpático."
621. "i autoridades" has been added in the margin.
622. "Carnavalesco."
623. "ansiosos."
624. "racimo."
625. "siguiendo."
626. "música."
627. "chirimía."
628. "entrada."
629. "distracción."
630. "cese."
631. "ha sido."
632. "acequia."
633. "repartición."
634. "jerárquico."
635. "público."

Obligaciones de lo empledio eclesiasticos

Los mayordomos de Yglesia en los dias de maytines,[636] dotrinas, Santo Rosario y domigo[637] si hubiera misa tienen obligacion de poner media libra de ceras cada uno tomando en cuenta que es desde el miercoles de Zenisa[638] al día domingo. de Resurección.[639] i ademas insienso[640] en las misas i maitines si fuera necesario en la semana Santa el día domingo (miercoles)[641] de Ramos. ponen dos palmas en rama entendiendo que es uno por cada uno. con cooperación del regedor mayor que por medio de mandados a los jovenes pondrán olivos para la selebración[642] necesaria y el día lunes hacer llavado[643] de paños i manteles de la Yglesia con las Sñras solas poniendo el mayordomo todo lo necesario para el lavado. Martes Santo. X. Miercoles Santo Entrega a las seras[644] en total segun consta en el libro de la

[f. 27v] Yglesia todos floridos i hace arder una media libra de cera de su obligación Dia Jueves Santo.

Desde la hora de misa hace arder constantemente una libra de cera cada uno hasta el día domingo de Resurrección entendiendo que las seras en centellas y sirios[645] hace arder segun proporcion[646] desde este dia al domingo resurrección a cuidado de ellos. Día Viernes Santo. pondrá algodon[647] a la proporción de la habitación general para su reparto i del mismo el regedor mayor pondrá agua de florida uno o dos pomo[648] segun sea necesario que saldrá de caja o pasará en su cuenta. Tambien anotamos que el dia miercoles de Zenisa cuando haya misa prepararán la senisa[649] de palma i olivo i en el maitines des-visarán un belon[650] de a dos libras cada uno de los mayordomos, teniendo en cuenta

---

636. "maitines."
637. "domingo."
638. "Ceniza."
639. "Resurrección."
640. "incienso."
641. The word "miercoles" has been written beneath "domingo."
642. "celebración."
643. "lavado."
644. "ceras."
645. "cirios."
646. "proporción."
647. "algodón."
648. "pomos."
649. "ceniza."
650. "velón."

que los cama chicos pondrán el monumento[651] consistentes en los mejores frutos como tributo al Sr. el día jueves Santo i recojiendo[652] papas de cada comunero harán cambio de flores de muerto para que entregen mas[653] las ramas de romero por su cuenta para adornar el santo cepulcro.[654] i capillas. para el deposito[655] del Señor.

Atribuciones del fiscal.

Durante la cuaresma, hace resar[656] los dias miercoles, viernes i domingo cuando no hay cura en las horas de dotrina.[657] mandar arco de flores naturales a las solteras para el Santo Rosario. como también mandar i recoger flores deshoyados[658] de las mismas, para los dias de maitines i Santo Rosario en caso haya prosesión[659] i a los jovenes solteros mandar masetas de flores para el sr. crusificado[660] en los días mismas. El dia Sabado[661] Santo hacer emflorar[662] con las solteras el coro, el altar i son obligaciones del sacristan,[663] hacer arder la sera en la sacristia[664] en los dias de maitines Santo Rosario i doctrinas una sera como estar al tanto de las fiestas de funerales, dotrinas y demas[665] para el toque de campana estar

[f. 28r] también en atención del cura cuando el enteresado[666] lo solicite i tocar la señal de oración todas las tardes desde el primero de enero en adelante.

El cantor de la comunidad.

Tiene obligación de asistir a la Yglesia hacer Santo Rosario en los días de costumbre durante la cuaresma i acompañar a los difuntos desde el muerto

---

651. "monumento."
652. "recogiendo."
653. Originally written "a" in place of "mas" (más), which has been added in the margin.
654. "sepulcro."
655. "depósito."
656. "rezar."
657. "doctrina."
658. "desollados."
659. "procesión."
660. "crucificado."
661. "Sábado."
662. "enflorar."
663. "sacristán."
664. "sacristía."
665. "demás."
666. "interesado."

que deja de existir hasta sus funerales en parte llano. i durante la semana santa, visperas[667] i oficios en compañia del cura si lo hay i sinó en compañia de sus compañeros vien[668] organisado.[669] estando de acuerdo con el Sr. Principal o concejo comunal i demas eclesiasticos. Por adicion,[670] se hace constar que el dia 31 de diciembre por la tarde se hace visita por los sesantes de la junta comunal alos[671] nuevos o entrantes. dejando un pequeño cumplimiento.

[In the margin in red ink: Viene de la F6. Reforma—]

—Reforma—

Por obserbación[672] del, Alcalde Campo Don J. Hildiberto Obispo: tomandose[673] en consederación[674] qué,[675] los menores alguaciles constituido con motivo a las costumbres de Octubre y Carnabal.[676] están obligados a llevar sus fiambres por su cuenta como una cuarta de Pisco, coca y sigarros, por alcansar[677] beneficio de la comunidad, de lo que, queda; aprovado[678] para lo sucecibo.[679]

También se deja constancia que desde epocas[680] remotas, en el mes de Diciembre del 26 al 30. los funcionarios, como, el Campo, el Rejedor, el Rejedor Campo y el alguacil mayor. dictaran[681] faenas para que los caminos se limpian del pueblo a Chauca y del pueblo a San Antonio; por los comuneros, con el control del Campo.

[f. 28v] del pueblo a Huachupampa. con el control del Rejedor Campo, y el Rejedor Mayor hacer el aseo de la población, de las entradas y salidas. con las señoras solas. que lo acompañará el alguacil Mayor.

667. "vísperas."
668. "bien."
669. "organizado."
670. "adición."
671. "a los."
672. "observación."
673. "tomándose."
674. "consideración."
675. "que."
676. "Carnaval."
677. "alcanzar."
678. "aprobado."
679. "sucesivo."
680. "épocas."
681. "dictarán."

Con los días del año, nuevo, durante las reserencias, El Rejedor Mayor, entregará la población b-[?]-cuado y con sus respetivos, cruz,⁶⁸² que le corresponden hacer poner. para que lo entrega al nuevo funcionario. y así mismo el papal; [?] En seguida el Campo el dia 4 de Enero, juntamente con el Rejedor Campo, eran⁶⁸³ al cerro de Rairay⁶⁸⁴ entregar los—deros, a los nuevos: el Campo de Rairay, Chacc-saygua, Moya, Shirapamku y Pitic con respetivos, cruces. y demarcaciones y lo legales.⁶⁸⁵

Así mismo el Rejedor Campo, de Racray, a Racraquiron, la Punta de Bitama, Carhuachayco, Namanlilpa de ahí a Zambo y Carema, Todos los reserencieros regresaran⁶⁸⁶ al pueblo con la mayor aligria:⁶⁸⁷ qué,⁶⁸⁸ el Señor Rejedor hara⁶⁸⁹ preparar una comelona, con los mujeres solas.

El día 5 de Enero, seguira⁶⁹⁰ la reserencia de Pitic Santa María. Tomesilla, a Tandari⁶⁹¹ por comuneros, el Campo, recorrera⁶⁹² la ascequia⁶⁹³ de Mayguay constandose⁶⁹⁴ los palos de arboles.⁶⁹⁵ como sause,⁶⁹⁶ a-[ba?]-jo deintro⁶⁹⁷ la ascequia que se dará cuenta de la Toma hasta Matoca; llegada⁶⁹⁸ al pueblo el Campo nombrará un perito para lo necesario del pueblo de "Mayguay," dado que este en desordenes ó no estan con sus deberes. procederá al Campo a castigarlos en el sitio de "Ñamoc." de ahi partiran⁶⁹⁹ todos juntos, a Santil y al fundo de Santo Domingo. donde serán reunidos los arren

---

682. "respectivas cruces."
683. "irán."
684. "para/a."
685. "legal."
686. "regresarán."
687. "alegría."
688. "que."
689. "hará."
690. "seguirá."
691. "Tandarí."
692. "recorrerá."
693. "acequia." Sometimes spelled "ascequia" in the text.
694. "constándose."
695. "árboles."
696. "sauce."
697. "dentro."
698. "llegado."
699. "partirán."

[f. 29r] darios[700] y Vecinos de Callahuanca. en el lugar del limites,[701] que el Campo con su alguacil ará[702] poner una cruz, y nombrar peritos, para ver la Huerta de Chirimoyas. y el estado del fundo; despues de un detenido rato, el Sindico[703] Personero el Tesorero y demas comuneros, detenidamente tomaran[704] un vaso de cerveza como quien entonando. con la "Chirimia." En seguida continuarán con los peritos, tocando Huamanshanca, Viquil donde se reunira[705] en la cruz. para las cuentas de los comeciones.[706] luego terminado, se vendrán el Caserio[707] de Cumpe, tocando con las Autoridades, el Campo nuevo prosederá[708] las vecitas del caserio, y se hubiere desabandono procedera[709] el corrigimiento; despues se pasará al Caserio "Huinco y seará[710] las mismas obserbaciones:[711] despues de un rato con las autoridades del Caserio, se regresará al pueblo trayendo ramas de plantas para el niño "Jesus."[712] y viendo en las pianas[713] la cruz que el Campo sesante entregara[714] al nuevo. *llegada* al sitio de piedra, rastro el pueblo, resivira[715] con Vayles[716] de. Doctores, que los reserencieros. entregarán flores de amancaes, a las autoridades y personas mayores; en seguida se enfresca al pueblo con repiques de Campanas, hasta el Cabildo donde se dará cuenta todo lo conserniente[717] a la reserencia. y castigos a los sesantes como al Campo, y el Rejedor Campo, que recorre de caracoma a Toro Puche y la vesita del fundo de "Opica."

También dejamos constancia que los gastos desde el desayuno hasta el último será puesto, por el Sindico Tesorero según los entablos, de presupuesto.

Nosotros los autoridades comunales dejamos

---

700. "arrendador"?/"arrendatario"?
701. "límite."
702. "hará."
703. "Síndico." Sometimes spelled without an accent in the text.
704. "tomarán."
705. "reunirá."
706. "comisiones."
707. "Caserío." The accent is omitted throughout this section.
708. "procederá."
709. "procederá."
710. "se hará."
711. "observaciones."
712. "Jesús."
713. "peanas."
714. "entregará."
715. "recibirá."
716. "bailes."
717. "concerniente."

[f. 29v] constancia con todo[718] los comuneros para que en todo tiempo, hasta la última[719] generaciones se respeta como recuerdo. inperecedero[720] y firmamos hoy en San Pedro de Casta a 15 de Noviembre del año 1947; Otro, que durante las cuentas, el Campo, entregará la alegría del pueblo hasta Carhuayumac y el Regidor Campo de Pampacocha hasta Huayacocha, cada uno entre los nuevos y sesantes llevarán sus gastos y la alegría de <u>Chirimia</u>.

Todo estos[721] se deja constancia por no existir en este libro honroso. Y firmamos.

Benito Flores	Diosdado Lopez
[stamped: Comunidad Indígena de San Pedro de Casta Prov. de Huarochirí. Presidencia]	
	Tiburcio Rojas
Cecilio Rojas	Antonio Bautista [stamped: Comunidad Indígena San Pedro de Casta. 1er. Vice-Presidente]
M. Agapito Medina	Campo C [illegible]
Catalino Gonzales i R [illegible]	Campo Juan H Obispo
Juan Jimenez	
Gabino Rojas	
	Vivancio O.[?]

[f. 30r] Refacción de la ascequia de "Carhuayumac"

En el local de la comunidad a los cinco días del mes de mayo del año de 1947 Reunidos[722] todas los autoridades comunales presente:[723] se deja constancia del proyecto anterior del Funcionario Alcalde Campo Don Juan Hildiberto Obispo y sus compañeros que, vistos los muchos años de la acequia de Carhuayumac a Pampacocha, no ha tenido refacciones se dio[724] por el interes[725] de hacerlo, con los corralajes de los meses que le corresponde con cargo de

---
718. "todos."
719. "hasta las últimas."
720. "imperecedero."
721. "Todo esto."
722. "reunidos."
723. "presentes."
724. "se dió."
725. "interés."

facilitar erramientas[726] como barrenas, puntas, explosivos gastos para los trabajadores, del que fue cumplido.

Pues nosotros las autoridades dejamos constancia en unión con los comuneros. y firmamos.

Benito Flores

[stamped: Comunidad Indígena de San Pedro de Casta Prov. de Huarochirí. Presidencia]

Cecilio Rojas

Catalino Gonzales R. [illegible]

Campo Juan H Obispo

Diosdado Lopez

Tiburcio Rojas

M. Agapito Medina

Juan Jimenez

Gabino Rojas

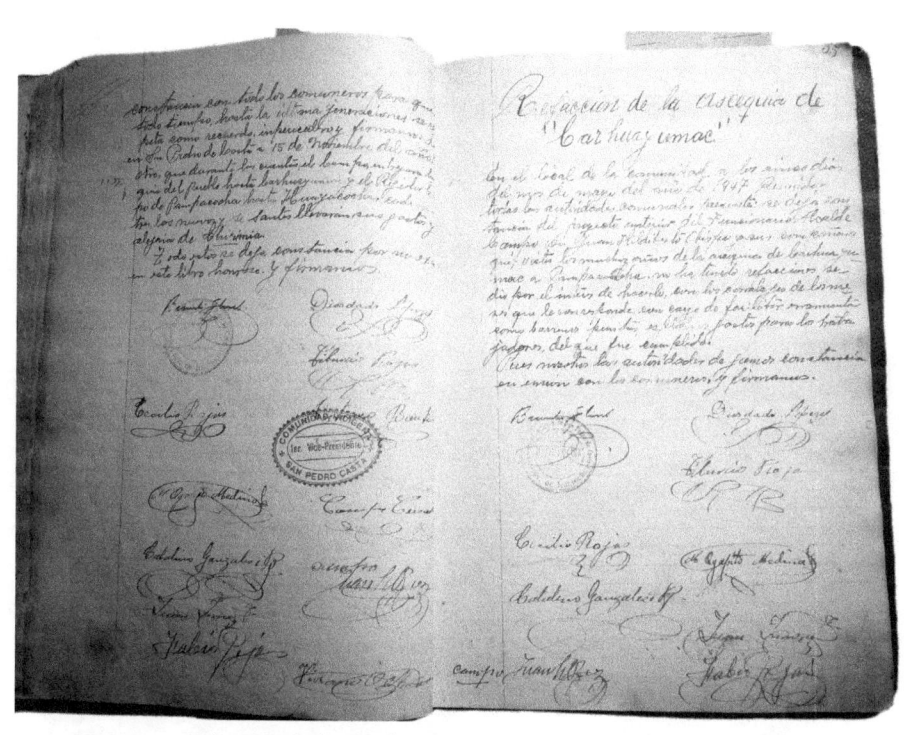

FIGURE 3.4. *Folio 30r, which records maintenance work carried out on the Carhuayumac irrigation canal in 1947 (on the right page).*

726. "herramientas."

[f. 30v] 1952

[In the top margin in blue ballpoint: 27 hojas en libro del entablo]

En la fecha siete de Enero de mil novecientos cincuentidos habiendo tomado en cuenta las costumbres antiguas i supersticiosas se ha venido á inventuar los objetos secretos que sirven como fokclore. tal es una piedra redonda que significaba el pueblo i sus habitantes en masa, una pequeña piedra en forma triangular con un color marrón que significaba el <u>Sami dios</u>. un objeto de metal que significaba la riquesa[727] del pueblo. i una figura piedra largata que significaba la persona del curador o brujo, una porción de algodón o lana blanca que significaba la niebla para avisar si había o no lluvias, la chicha sin dulce que sirvía[728] como licor para los trabajos entre el cura i el yachak. se deja constancia que entrega[?] el Sr. Gabino Obispo i Juan Obispo como presidentes.

Juan Ho. Juez   Gabino Obispo

[ff. 51–52 have been torn out]

[f. 53r] [a note in pencil:] Como dueño que soy de este libro que obseque[729] soy

[signature, with flourish below:] Notario S C

[f. 103r] [in black ink script, a sheet of plain paper attached with tape at the back of the notebook reads:]

Lista de los animales y dueños q:: [que] pagaran de Carcilajo q:: [que] va a caja de la comunidad. Siguientes:

---

727. "riqueza."
728. "servía."
729. "obsequié."

EL ENTABLO 217

Dueños	día	Febrero	Vacas	buey	Bulero	llamas	bestias	Chancho	Precio
Nemecio B	2	"	"	1	"	"	"	"	010
Juan O.V.	3	"	2	"	"	"	"	"	080
Mario C	4	"	1	"	"	"	"	"	050
Marcelino L.	6	"	1	"	"	"	"	"	030
Estanceslao C.	6	"	1	"	"	"	"	"	040
Hipolito O.	6	"	"	"	"	"	"	2	040
Catalino B.	7	"	1	"	"	"	"	"	040
José M.S.	7	"	1	"	"	"	"	"	020
Paula G.	8	"	1	"	"	"	"	"	050
Rafaela S.	8	"	"	"	1	"	"	"	050
Nemecio B.	9	"	3	1	"	"	"	"	140
Santas G.	14	"	1	"	"	"	"	"	030
Santas S.	14	"	"	"	"	1	"	"	040
Petronela P.	14	"	2	"	"	"	"	"	080
Eucebia Ch.	15	"	1	"	"	"	"	"	030
Gabina B.	17	"	1	"	"	"	"	"	050
Paula S.	18	"	1	"	"	"	"	"	040
Cecilio	"	"	1	"	3	"	"	"	140
Paula G.	17	"	1	"	"	"	"	"	040

[In the bottom margin of the animal inventory grid, Jesús Salinas Rojas, the 1990–1993 secretary, has written in blue ballpoint:]

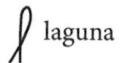

laguna

Secretario de 1990–1993

Jesús Salinas Rojas

[in black ink script matching the handwriting of the 1939 scribe:]

Gastos el 2 de Febrero 1,50 [¿1.50 *soles de oro*?] y más dos soles al [?], fecha 7 del presente y en faena se gasta 1,75 [¿1.75 *soles de oro*?] y peones—20 coca 40 sigarros 80 gastos en el camino el 19 de febrero 1,40 para la faena de la laguna Huayacocha.

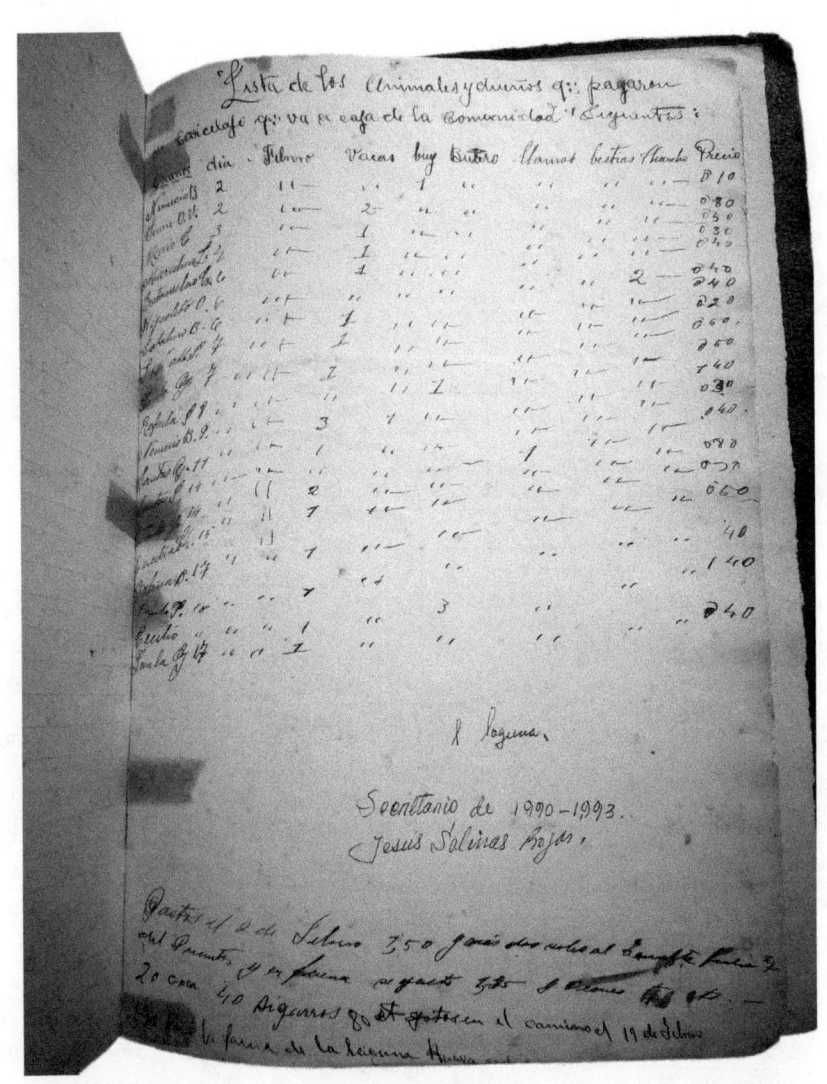

FIGURE 3.5. *Folio 103r, an attached plain sheet of paper used to record grazing fees from livestock owners. The handwriting matches that of the 1921 scribe Don Máximo Calistro.*

ACKNOWLEDGMENTS

This book is the product of nearly four years of work, so I would like to thank many people who all helped in different ways during that time. First, Abel Traslaviña Arias, Rosaleen Howard, Patricia Oliart, Sabine Dedenbach-Salazar Sáenz, Bill Hyland, Meg Hyland, Zoila Forss-Crespo Moreyra, Carlos Orozco García, and Lee-Ann Birse. I am indebted to two colleagues who generously shared some beautiful photographs of the Casta *champería*: Luis Miguel Silva-Novoa Sánchez, who attended in 2010, and Julio Erhart, who has visually documented the ceremony since the 1970s. Julio's 1979 image featured in this book is almost certainly one of the earliest photographic records of the *champería*.

The Orihuela García family, Silvia Soriano and family, and Cesar Urrutia and family generously provided lodgings, meals, logistical support, and good company in Lima. I benefited from the collegial support and friendship of many colleagues at the University of St. Andrews, including Adriana Wilde, Camilla Mørk Røstvik, Stephanie Yardley, Raluca Roman, Jonathan Alderman, and Christine Lee. I am grateful for the support and encouragement of Mette High, Catriona Harris, Nina Laurie, and Mark Harris. I also wish to extend my thanks to Daniel Knight for the sage publishing advice.

I wish to thank Sabine Hyland for her trust and encouragement over these past four years. I would like to express my gratitude to the Leverhulme Trust, which funded my fellowship position, and the University of St. Andrews, which covered the costs of my fieldwork and the commissioned map artwork featured in this book. I am very grateful for an Impact and Innovation Fund award from the University of St. Andrews. This funding enabled me to visit Casta in 2022 in order to share my published research on Casta and a summary of this book with the Comunidad Campesina de San Pedro de Casta. The Research Innovation Services team at the University of St. Andrews also provided valuable support.

I am indebted to the two reviewers of this book, one of whom (Frank Salomon) waived anonymity. To both reviewers, I extend a big thank you for their respective detailed readings of the book and for their helpful suggestions to expand on some topics in greater depth. I consider myself lucky to have had my first book reviewed by two scholars with such in-depth knowledge of Andean landscape traditions. Since my days as an undergraduate student in Sabine Dedenbach-Salazar Saénz's module on the Huarochirí Manuscript at the University of Stirling in 2007, Salomon's work has played a significant role in stimulating my enthusiasm for and academic interest in Huarochirí.

I need to thank Kathy Lewis for the diligent and brilliant copyediting. I also wish to express my deepest gratitude to Casey Kittrell, Lynne Ferguson, and the rest of the University of Texas Press team for their enthusiasm, impeccable work, and support.

I am indebted to the authorities of the Comunidad Campesina de San Pedro de Casta, who generously granted me permission to access and write about their sacred community archive. I also thank my collaborators in Casta for supporting this research with their insights, expertise, and valuable time. I am especially indebted to Catalina Olivares, Anselma Bautista Pérez, and Luzmila Salinas Bautista for sharing so much of their time and knowledge with me and to the late Dometila Calixtro for her kindness.

I need to say thank you to my parents, Graham and Ginny Bennison, for their support and encouragement. Finally, I would like to express my gratitude to Ehsan Jorat, whose constant support made any daunting tasks feel much more achievable and much less lonely.

This book is dedicated to my son, Alfred, who accompanied me as a baby to Huarochirí a decade ago and endured my absences on subsequent trips.

GLOSSARY

ayllu (Quechua): Andean kin group of common descent.
cargo (Spanish): an obligatory duty required of members of peasant communities and their earlier manifestations, including Indigenous communities.
champería (hispanicized Quechua term): annual irrigation canal-cleaning ceremony of the Lima highlands involving elaborate ancestor-focused rituals and traditional song and dance.
chancaca (hispanicized Nahuatl): solidified raw sugar syrup.
chicha (Spanish): fermented maize beer.
cómputo (Spanish): account through which to calculate changeable data sets for the organization of sacred events.
comunidad campesina: legally recognized peasant community in Peru.
costumbre (Spanish): ancestral law, customary law, obligatory ritual.
cura (Spanish): ritual expert and traditional healer, usually male, who leads ritual ceremonies alongside the *yachak* in Casta.
Entablo/entablo (Spanish): 1921 set of Spanish-language ancestral water ritual laws in San Pedro de Casta/khipu board or community account.
eshcupuro (escopuro, eshcupuru, ishcopuro) (Quechua): small gourd container in which the alkaline lime powder used for chewing coca leaves is stored.
faena (Spanish): obligatory communal labor event.
fiambre (Spanish): alcohol, food, or snacks carried to consume during a work break.
huaca (waka) (Quechua): powerful ancestral being, usually considered to own, inhabit, or manifest a location such as a site in the landscape.
hualina (warina) (Quechua): traditional water song of the Santa Eulalia valley in the Huarochirí province of Lima.
huallque (huallqui, wallki, wallqui) (Quechua): small bag for storing the stimulative items needed for work (coca leaves, lime, and cigarettes), worn around the neck by men at the *champería* and other community labor events.

huayrona (Quechua): annual January accounts ceremony at the ancestral assembly site of Cuhuay in Casta; also the assembly premises of Casta's two *parcialidades*, Yañac and Yacapar.

huipi (Quechua): small wooden Andean balance scale for measuring the ritual submissions of coca leaf at the *champería*.

kashwa (qachwa, kashua) (Quechua) ritual work songs.

khipu (Quechua): Andean fiber-based recording device.

khipu board: colonially derived hybrid recording device using alphabetic writing and khipu cords.

mayores (Spanish): community elders who are supreme authorities within the hierarchical Andean community organization system, also referred to as *notables*.

michco (hispanicized Quechua term): traditional water authority of Casta's *champería* who leads a *parada* (work group).

paccha (Quechua): waterfall, stream, or other site where water flows or descends quickly and audibly.

padrón (Spanish): community census or tribute list; khipu board recording the performance of participants in the Casta *champería*.

padroncillo (Spanish): possibly a khipu and/or a khipu board recording the performance of participants in the Casta *champería*.

parada (Spanish): work group in Casta's *champería*.

parcialidad (Spanish): sector; name given to the Yacapar and Yañac moieties in Casta.

pirwa (pirua, pirhua) (Quechua): granary; storehouse for harvested crops; annual rainy-season ritual relating to the planting of crops in Casta, attended by functionaries and the *yachak* ritual specialist.

Pro-Secretario (Spanish) Vice Secretary or Clerk.

puchka (pushka) (Quechua) distaff—instrument used for preparing fleece for spinning.

puchkar (Hispanicised Quechua) to spin a *puchka*.

qallapa (Quechua) synonymous with *puchka*, distaff—instrument used for preparing fleece for spinning.

sacsanero (hispanicized Quechua term): ritual functionary who monitors the performance of work at the *champería*.

sami (Quechua): vital energy conducive to fertility and the successful execution of skills that is derived from the ancestors.

shicra (shigra) (Quechua) net bags made from plant fibers produced using a manual looping technique.

Síndico de Gastos (Spanish) Expenses Trustee.

Síndico de Rentas (Spanish) Income Trustee.

teniente gobernador (Spanish): functionary of the Peruvian state, lieutenant to the district-level governor, who plays a central role in maintaining order during key ancestral ceremonies in Casta.

Vocal (Spanish) Committee Member.

walla-walla: an alternative name for Casta's *champería*.

Yacapar: one of Casta's two *parcialidades*, associated with lower-altitude lands.

yachak (yachaq) (Quechua): "knower," ritual expert.

Yañac: one of Casta's two *parcialidades*, associated with higher-altitude lands.

yaraví (hispanicized Quechua term): genre of melancholic ritual songs deriving from the Inca era.

REFERENCES

Abercrombie, Thomas A. 1998. *Pathways of Memory and Power: Ethnography and History among an Andean People*. Madison: University of Wisconsin Press.

Adelaar, Willem F. H. 1994. "La procedencia dialectal del manuscrito de Huarochirí en base a sus características lingüísticas." *Revista Andina* 23: 137–154.

Adelaar, Willem, F. H., and Pieter C. Muysken. 2004. *The Languages of the Andes*. Cambridge Language Surveys. Cambridge: Cambridge University Press.

Alberti, Giorgio. 1972. "Educación y movilización colectiva." In *Aspectos sociales de la educación rural en el Perú*, ed. Giorgio Alberti and Julio Cotler, 97–124. Lima: Instituto de Estudios Peruanos, 1972.

Allen, Catherine J. 2002. *The Hold Life Has: Coca and Cultural Identity in an Andean Community*. 2nd ed. Washington, DC: Smithsonian Institution Press.

Allen, Catherine J. 2016. "The Living Ones: Miniatures and Animation in the Andes." *Journal of Anthropological Research* 72(4): 416–441.

Andrade Ciudad, Luis. 2016. *The Spanish of the Northern Peruvian Andes: A Sociohistorical and Dialectological Account*. New York: Peter Lang.

Apaza, Dimas, Roberto Arroyo, and Andrés Alencastre. 2006. *Las Amunas de Huarochirí: Recarga de acuíferos en los Andes*. Gestión Social del Agua y Ambiente en Cuencas (GSAAC). Lima, Peru: Embajada Real de los Países Bajos y IICA-Perú.

Arguedas, José María. 2002. "Puquio: A Culture in Process of Change." In *Yawar Fiesta* (original Spanish version 1956), trans. Francis Horning Barraclough, 149–192. Long Grove, IL: Waveland Press.

Arnold, Denise Y., and Juan de Dios Yapita. 1998. *Río de vellón, río del canto: Cantar a los animales, una poética andina de la creación*. La Paz: ILCA and UMSA.

Arnold, Denise Y., with Juan de Dios Yapita. 2006. *Metamorphosis of Heads:*

Textual Struggles, Education and Land in the Andes. Pittsburgh: University of Pittsburgh Press.

Bacigalupo, Ana Mariella. 2022. "Subversive Cosmopolitics in the Anthropocene." *Climate Politics and the Power of Religion*: 176.

Bauer, Arnold J. 1983. "The Church in the Economy of Spanish America: *Censos* and *Depósitos* in the Eighteenth and Nineteenth Centuries." *Hispanic American Historical Review* 63(4): 707–733. https://doi.org/10.2307/2514902.

Belleza Castro, Nelly. 1995. *Vocabulario jacaru-castellano castellano-jacaru (aimara tupino)*. Cusco, Peru: Centro de Estudios Regionales Andinos "Bartolomé de las Casas."

Bennison, Sarah. 2016. "Who Are the Children of Pariacaca? Exploring Identity through Narratives of Water and Landscape in Huarochirí, Peru." PhD dissertation, Newcastle University, UK.

Bennison, Sarah. 2019. "Waqay: A Word about Water and the Andean World in a Twentieth-Century Spanish Manuscript of Huarochirí Peru)." *Anthropological Linguistics* 61(4): 459–490.

Bennison, Sarah. 2022. "The Record Keepers: Maintaining Irrigation Canals, Traditions and Inca Codes of Law in 1920s Huarochirí, Peru." In *The Social and Political Life of Latin American Infrastructure: Meanings, Values, and Competing Visions of the Future*, ed. Jonathan Alderman and Geoff Goodwin, 223–251. London: University of London Press.

Beyersdorff, Margot. 2005. "Writing without Words/Words without Writing: The Culture of the Khipu." *Latin American Research Review* 40(3): 294–311.

Bolin, Inge. 1998. *Rituals of Respect: The Secret of Survival in the High Peruvian Andes*. Austin: University of Texas Press.

Burns, Kathryn. 2010. *Into the Archive: Writing and Power in Colonial Peru*. Durham, NC: Duke University Press.

Butterworth, James. 2014. "Andean Divas: Emotion, Ethics and Intimate Spectacle in Peruvian Huayno Music." PhD dissertation, Royal Holloway, University of London.

CCSPC (Comunidad Campesina de San Pedro de Casta). 1711–1808. "Auto redondo." Copy of a manuscript transcription (1988) obtained from Archivo Colonial, Títulos de Comunidades, legajo 4, cuaderno 47, Archivo General de la Nación, Lima.

CCSPC (Comunidad Campesina de San Pedro de Casta). 1921. "Entablo comunal." Archive of the Comunidad Campesina de San Pedro de Casta, Lima.

Coloma Porcari, César. 2010. "La comida traditional del Perú en la obra de Ricardo Palma." Centro Nacional de Información Cultural, Instituto Nacional de Cultura. http://repositorio.cultura.gob.pe/handle/CULTURA/224.

Contreras, Carlos, and Patricia Oliart. 2014. *Modernidad y educación en el Perú*. Lima: Ministerio de Cultura. http://repositorio.cultura.gob.pe/handle/CULTURA/31.

Course, Magnus. 2018. "Words beyond Meaning in Mapuche Language Ideology." *Language & Communication* 63: 9–14.

CSSD (Centro Social San Damián). 1957. *La Voz de San Damián* Lima: CSSD.

Curatola, Marco, and José Carlos de la Puente Luna. 2013. "Contar concertando: Quipus, piedritas y escritura en los Andes coloniales." In *El quipu colonial*, ed. Marco Curatola and José Carlos de la Puente Luna, 193–244. Lima: PUCP.

Cushman, Gregory T. 2015. "The Environmental Contexts of Guaman Poma: Interethnic Conflict over Forest Resources and Place in Huamanga (Peru), 1540–1600." In *Unlocking the Doors to the Worlds of Guaman Poma and His "Nueva Corónica,"* ed. Rolena Adorno and Ivan Boserup, 87–140. Copenhagen: Museum Tusculanum Press.

Dalton, Jordan. 2020. "Excavations at Las Huacas (AD 1200–1650): Exploring Elite Strategies and Economic Exchange during the Inca Empire." PhD dissertation, University of Michigan. http://hdl.handle.net/2027.42/162930.

Dargent Chamot, Eduardo C. 2017. "Historia del azúcar y sus derivados en el Perú." Universidad Ricardo Palma: Informes de Investigación 37. https://www.urp.edu.pe/pdf/id/20926/n/historia-del-azucar-y-sus-derivados-en-el-peru.pdf.

Dedenbach-Salazar Sáenz, Sabine. 2017. "Deities and Spirits in Andean Belief: Towards a Systematization." *Anthropos* 112(2): 443–453. https://www.anthropos.eu/anthropos/journal/abstracts/1122/03.php.

de la Cadena, Marisol. 1989. "La institucionalización de la cooperación y las necesidades técnicas de la producción." In *Cooperación y conflicto en la comunidad andina: Zonas de producción y organización social*, ed. Enrique Mayer and Marisol de la Cadena, 77–113. Lima: Instituto de Estudios Peruanos.

de la Cadena, Marisol. 2000. *Indigenous Mestizos: The Politics of Race and Culture in Cuzco, Peru, 1919–1991*. Durham, NC: Duke University Press.

de la Cadena, Marisol. 2010. "Indigenous Cosmopolitics in the Andes: Conceptual Reflections beyond Politics." *Cultural Anthropology* 25: 334–370.

de la Cadena, Marisol. 2015. *Earth Beings: Ecologies of Practice Across Andean Worlds*. Durham, NC: Duke University Press.

de la Puente Luna, José Carlos. 2019. "Calendars in Knotted Cords: New Evidence on How Khipus Captured Time in Nineteenth-Century Cuzco and Beyond." *Ethnohistory* 66(3): 437–464.

de la Puente Luna, José Carlos, and Renzo Honores. 2016. "Guardianes de la real justicia: Alcaldes de indios y justicia local en los Andes." *Histórica* 40(2): 11–48.

Del Solar, María Elena. 2011. *Las shicras de casca: El arte del tejido anillado en la sierra de Lima*. Lima: MINCETUR.

Dransart, Penelope (ed.). 2006. "Introduction: Terrains of Significance in the Andes" in *Kay Pacha: Cultivating Earth and Water in the Andes*, ed. Penelope Dransart. British Archaeological Reports International Series 1478, 1–18. Oxford: BAR.

Drinot, Paulo. 2011. *The Allure of Labor: Workers, Race, and the Making of the Peruvian State*. Durham, NC: Duke University Press.

Drzewieniecki, Joanna. 1995. "Indigenous People, Law, and Politics in Peru." Conference paper: Meeting of the Latin American Studies Association, Washington, DC (September 28–30, 1995).

Durston, Alan. 2007. "Notes on the Authorship of the Huarochirí Manuscript." *Colonial Latin American Review* 16(2): 227–241. doi: 10.1080/10609160701644516.

Durston, Alan. 2018. "Quechua-Language Government Propaganda in 1920s Peru." In *Indigenous Languages, Politics, and Authority in Latin America: Historical and Ethnographic Perspectives*, ed. Alan Durston and Bruce Mannheim, 161–180. South Bend, IN: University of Notre Dame Press.

Duviols, Pierre. 1973. "Huari y Llacuaz: Agricultores y pastores, un dualismo prehispánico de oposición y complementaridad." *Revista del Museo Nacional* (Lima) 39: 153–191.

Echeandia Valladares, J. M. 1981. *Tecnología y cambios en la comunidad de San Pedro de Casta*. Lima: Universidad Nacional Mayor de San Marcos, Dirección Universitaria de Proyección Social, Seminario de Historia Rural Andina.

Ediciones Flora Tristán and CENDOC-Mujer. 2002. *Hijas de Kavillaca: Tradición oral de mujeres de Huarochirí*. 2002. Lima: Ediciones Flora Tristán y CENDOC-Mujer.

Emery, Irene. 1994. *The Primary Structures of Fabrics: An Illustrated Classification*. Washington, DC: Thames and Hudson/Textile Museum.

Escalante, Carmen. 2010. "Derechos colectivos en la gestión del agua en la Asociación Pata." In *Lo colectivo y el agua: Entre los derechos y las prácticas*, ed. Rocío Bustamente, 233–254. Lima: Instituto de Estudios Peruanos.

Fernández, Patricia. 2003. "Las hualinas de San Pedro de Casta: Construcción de identidades locales a través de canciones tradicionales." In *Tradición oral y culturas peruanas*, 133–146. Lima: Universidad Nacional Mayor de San Marcos.

Fernández Osco, Marcelo. 2000. *La ley del ayllu: Práctica de jach'a justicia y jisk'a justicia (justicia mayor y justicia menor) en las comunidades aymaras.* La Paz: Fundación PIEB (Programa de Investigación Estratégica en Bolivia).

Fernández Osco, Marcelo. 2001. "La ley del ayllu: justicia de acuerdo." *Tinkazos: Revista Boliviana de Ciencias Sociales* 9: 11-28.

Gelles, Paul H. 1984a. "Agua, faenas y organización comunal en los Andes: el case de San Pedro de Casta." Master's thesis, Pontificia Universidad Católica del Perú (Lima).

Gelles, Paul H. 1984b. "Agua, faenas y organización comunal: San Pedro de Casta—Huarochirí." *Anthropológica del Departamento de Ciencias Sociales* (Pontificia Universidad Católica del Perú) 2(2): 305-334.

Gelles, Paul H. 2000a. "Introduction: Channels of Power, Fields of Contention." In *Water and Power in Highland Peru: The Cultural Politics of Irrigation and Development*, 1-25. Brunswick, NJ: Rutgers.

Gelles, Paul H. 2000b. *Water and Power in Highland Peru: The Cultural Politics of Irrigation and Development.* Brunswick, NJ: Rutgers University Press.

Gentille Lafaille, M. E. 1977. "Los Yauyos de Chaclla: Pueblos y ayllus (siglo XVIII)." *Bulletin de l'Institut Français d'Études Andines* 6(3-4): 85-107.

Gonçalez Holguín, Diego. (1608) 1952. *Vocabulario de la lengua general de todo el Perú llamada Quichua o del Inca.* Lima: Ediciones del Instituto de Historia, Imprenta Santa María.

Gose, Peter. 1994. *Deathly Waters and Hungry Mountains: Agrarian Ritual and Class Formation in an Andean Town.* Toronto: University of Toronto Press.

Gow, Rosalind, and Bernabé Condori. 1976. *Kay Pacha: Tradición oral andina.* Cusco, Peru: Biblioteca de la Tradición Oral Andina.

Guaman Poma de Ayala, Felipe. 1615/1616. "El primer nueva corónica y buen gobierno." Royal Danish Library, Copenhagen, GKS 2232.

Guevara-Gil, Armando. 2006. "Official Water Law versus Indigenous and Peasant Rights in Peru." In *Water and Indigenous Peoples*, ed. R. Boelens, M. Chiba, and D. Nakashima, 130-147. Knowledges of Nature 2. Paris: UNESCO.

Guevara-Gil, Armando, and Rutgerd Boelens. 2010. "Derechos colectivos al agua en los países andinos: Una reflexión regional." In *Riego campesino en los Andes: Seguridad hídrica y seguridad alimentaria en Ecuador, Perú y Bolivia*, ed. J. M. C. Vos and E. R. Rap, 23-50. Agua y Sociedad: Sección Concertación, No. 14. Lima: Instituto de Estudios Peruanos (IEP).

Guevara Pérez, Edilberto. 2015. "Evolución histórica de la legislación hídrica en el Perú." *Derecho Ambiental* 15: 319-334.

Günel, Gökçe, Saiba Varma, and Chika Watanabe. 2020. "A Manifesto for Patchwork Ethnography." Member Voices, *Fieldsights*, June 9. https://culanth.org/fieldsights/a-manifesto-for-patchwork-ethnography.

Gushiken, José. 1972. "La extirpación de idolatrías en Santiago de Carampoma." *Boletín del Instituto Riva-Agüero* (Lima) 9: 151–165.

Haboud de Ortega, Marleen. 1980. "La educación informal como proceso de socialización en San Pedro de Casta." *Debates en Sociología* 5: 71–114.

Hall, Ingrid. 2014. "Compter les journées de travail, classer les individus et ordonner la société dans une communauté des Andes sud-péruviennes." *Ethnologie et Mathématiques* 29. https://www.ethnographiques.org/2014/Hall.

Hamilton, Andrew James. 2018. *Scale and the Incas*. Princeton, NJ: Princeton University Press.

Hardman, Martha J. 1966. *Jaqaru: Outline of Phonological and Morphological Structure*. The Hague: Mouton.

Harris, Olivia. 2000. *To Make the Earth Bear Fruit: Ethnographic Essays on Fertility, Work and Gender in Highland Bolivia*. London: Institute of Latin American Studies, University of London.

Harrison, Regina. 1989. *Signs, Songs, and Memory in the Andes: Translating Quechua Language and Culture*. Austin: University of Texas Press.

Harrison, Regina. 2015. "Guaman Poma: Law, Land, and Legacy." In *Unlocking the Doors to the Worlds of Guaman Poma and His "Nueva Corónica,"* ed. Rolena Adorno and Ivan Boserup, 141–162. Copenhagen: Royal Library, Museum Tusculanum Press.

Harvey, Penny, and Hannah Knox. 2015. *Roads: An Anthropology of Infrastructure and Expertise*. New York: Cornell University Press.

Hornberger, Esteban, and Nancy Hornberger. 2008. *Diccionario trilingüe quechua de Cusco: Qhiswa, English, castellano*. Cusco, Peru: Centro Bartolomé de las Casas.

Howard, Rosaleen. 2002. "Yachay: The Tragedia del fin de Atahuallpa as Evidence of the Colonization of Knowledge in the Andes." In *Knowledge and Learning in the Andes: Ethnographic Perspectives*, ed. Henry Stobart and Rosaleen Howard, 17–39. Liverpool: Liverpool University Press.

Howard, Rosaleen. 2012. "Shifting Voices, Shifting Worlds: Evidentiality, Epistemic Modality and Speaker Perspective in Quechua Oral Narrative." *Pragmatics and Society* 3(2): 243–269.

Howard, Rosaleen, Luis Andrade Ciudad, and Raquel de Pedro Ricoy, 2018. "Translating Rights: The Peruvian Languages Act in Quechua and Aymara." *Amerindia: Revue d'Ethnolinguistique Amérindienne* 40(1): 219–245.

Howard, Rosaleen, Françoise Barbira-Freedman, and Henry Stobart. 2002. "Introduction." In *Knowledge and Learning in the Andes: Ethnographic Perspectives*, ed. Henry Stobart and Rosaleen Howard, 1–13. Liverpool Latin American Studies, New Series 3. Liverpool: Liverpool University Press.

Howard-Malverde, Rosaleen. 1990. *The Speaking of History: "Willapaakushayki" or Quechua Ways of Telling the Past*. Institute of Latin American Studies Research Papers No. 21. London: Institute of Latin American Studies.

Huber, Ludwig. 2002. *Consumo, cultura e identidad en el mundo globalizado: Estudios de caso en los Andes*. Lima: IEP, Colección Mínima.

Hyland, Sabine. 2016. "How Khipus Indicated Labour Contributions in an Andean Village: An Explanation of Colour Banding, Seriation and Ethnocategories." *Journal of Material Culture* 21(4): 490–509. https://doi.org/10.1177/1359183516662677.

Hyland, Sabine. 2017. "Writing with Twisted Cords: The Inscriptive Capacity of Andean Khipus." *Current Anthropology* 58(3): 412–419.

Hyland, Sabine. 2021. "Festival Threads: Khipu Calendars and Mercedarian Missions in Rapaz, Peru (c. 1565–1825)." *Catholic Historical Review* 107(1): 119–147. Project MUSE, doi:10.1353/cat.2021.0004.

Hyland, Sabine, Sarah Bennison, and William P. Hyland. 2021. "Khipus, Khipu Boards, and Sacred Texts: Toward a Philology of Andean Knotted Cords." *Latin American Research Review* 56(2): 400–416. doi: http://doi.org/10.25222/larr.1032.

Hyland, Sabine, Gene A. Ware, and Madison Clark. 2014. "Knot Direction in a Khipu/Alphabetic Text from the Central Andes." *Latin American Antiquity* 25(2): 189–197.

Isbell, Billie Jean. 1978. *To Defend Ourselves: Ecology and Ritual in an Andean Village*. Long Grove, IL: Waveland Press.

Itier, César. 2013. *Viracocha o el Océano, naturaleza y funciones de una divinidad andina*. Lima: Institut Français d'Études Andines/Instituto de Estudios Peruanos.

Kemper Columbus, Claudette. 1998. "Parientes no-humanos: Filiaciones entre el cordón umbilical, la casa y la piedra." In *Gente de carne y hueso: Las tramas del parentesco en los Andes*, ed. Denise Y. Arnold, 439–460. La Paz: CIASE ILCA.

Kuss, Malena. 2004. *Music in Latin America and the Caribbean: An Encyclopedic History*. Austin: University of Texas Press.

Lara, Jesús. 1971. *Diccionario Qhëshwa-Castellano/Castellano- Qëshwa*. La Paz and Cochabamba: Los Amigos del Libro.

Larson, Brooke. 2004. *Trials of Nation Making: Liberalism, Race, and Ethnicity in the Andes*. Cambridge: Cambridge University Press.

Lira, Jorge A. 1945. *Diccionario Kkechuwa-Español*. Tucumán, Argentina: Universidad Nacional de Tucumán.

Llanos, Oliverio, and Jorge P. Osterling. 1982. "Ritual de la Fiesta del Agua en San Pedro de Casta, Perú." *Journal of Latin American Lore* (UCLA Latin American Center) 8(1): 115–150.

Mackenzie, Ian. 2017. "The Linguistics of Spanish." https://www.staff.ncl.ac.uk/i.e.mackenzie/index.html.

Mackey, Carol. 2002. "The Continuing Khipu Tradition: Principles and Practice." In *Narrative Threads: Accounting and Recounting in Andean Khipu*, ed. Jeffrey Quilter and Gary Urton, 320–348. Austin: University of Texas Press.

Mannheim, Bruce. 2015a. "All Translation Is Radical Translation." In *Translating Worlds: The Epistemological Space of Translation*, ed. Carlo Severi and William F. Hanks, 199–219. Chicago: University of Chicago Press.

Mannheim, Bruce. 2015b. "What Kind of Text Is Guaman Poma's Warikza Arawi?" In *Unlocking the Doors to the Worlds of Guaman Poma and His "Nueva Corónica,"* ed. Rolena Adorno and Ivan Boserup, 211–232. Copenhagen: Museum Tusculanum Press.

Mannheim, Bruce, and Guillermo Salas Carreño. 2015. "Wak'as: Entifications of the Andean Sacred." In *The Archaeology of Wakas: Explorations of the Sacred in the Pre-Columbian Andes*, ed. Tamara Bray. 46–72. Boulder: University Press of Colorado.

Martínez Céspedes, Jimmy. 2016. "'Cristóval Choquecassa' y la extirpación de las idolatrías: Una aproximación a la autoría del Manuscrito Quechua de Huarochirí (1577–1637)." *Tiempos* 11(11): 21–78.

Matos Mar, José. 1958a. "Introducción." In *Las actuales comunidades indígenas de Huarochirí en 1955*, ed. José Matos Mar, 11–44. Lima: UNMSM.

Matos Mar, José (ed.). 1958b. *Las actuales comunidades indígenas de Huarochirí en 1955*. Lima: UNMSM.

Mayer, Enrique. 1989. "Zonas de producción." In *Cooperación y conflicto en la comunidad andina: Zonas de producción y organización social*, ed. Enrique Mayer and Marisol Cadena, 15–76. Lima: Instituto de Estudios Peruanos.

Mayer, Enrique. 2002. *The Articulated Peasant: Household Economies in the Andes*. Boulder, CO: Westview Press.

Medrano, Manuel, and Gary Urton. 2018. "Toward the Decipherment of a Set of Mid-Colonial Khipus from the Santa Valley, Coastal Peru." *Ethnohistory* 65(1): 1–23. doi: https://doi.org/10.1215/00141801-4260638.

Nuckolls, Janis B. 2010. *Lessons from a Quechua Strongwoman: Ideophony, Dialogue, and Perspective*. Tucson: University of Arizona Press.

Nuñez Palomino, Pedro Germán. 1995. "Law and Peasant Communities in Peru (1969–1988)." Thesis, Wageningen University, the Netherlands.

Olivas Weston, Rosario. 1983. *Marcahuasi: mito y realidad*. Lima: Talleres de Litográfica Multicolor.

Ortiz Rescaniere, Alejandro. 1980. *Huarochirí, 400 años después*. [Lima:] Pontificia Universidad Católica del Perú, Fondo Editorial.

Padilla Deza, Fernando. 2018. "El concepto y la representación de lo indio en la propuesta política de Julio César Tello Rojas (1917–1929)." Master's thesis, Pontificia Universidad Católica del Perú, Fondo Editorial, Lima.

Paulson, Susan. 1990. "Double-Talk in the Andes: Ambiguous Discourse as Means of Surviving Contact." *Journal of Folklore Research*, 27(1/2): 51–65. https://www.jstor.org/stable/3814458.

Pearce, Adrian J. 2001. "The Peruvian Population Census of 1725–1740." *Latin American Research Review* 36(3): 69–104.

Pérez Galán, Beatriz. 2004. *Somos como Incas: Autoridades tradicionales en los Andes*. Madrid: Iberoamericana Vervuert.

Pérez Galán, Beatriz. 2008. "Alcaldes y kurakas: Origen y significado cultural de la fila de autoridades indígenas en Pisac (Calca, Cuzco)." *Bulletin de l'Institut Français d'Etudes Andines* 37(1): 245–255.

Pimentel, Nelson. 2014. "De qué y cómo 'hablan' los khipu etnográficos aymaras." In *Sistemas de notación inca: Quipu y Tocapu: Actas del simposio internacional, Lima 15–17 de enero de 2009*, ed. C. A. Hoffman, 177–196. Lima: Ministerio de Cultura, Museo Nacional de Arqueología, Antropología e Historia del Perú, 2014.

Platt, Tristan. 2002. "'Without Deceit or Lies': Variable 'Chinu' Readings during a Sixteenth-Century Tribute-Restitution Trial." In *Narrative Threads: Accounting and Recounting in Andean Khipu*, ed. Jeffrey Quilter and Gary Urton, 225–265. Austin: University of Texas Press.

Platt, Tristan. 2018. *Defendiendo el techo fiscal: Curacas, ayllus y sindicatos en el Gran Ayllu Macha, Norte de Potosí, Bolivia, 1930–1994*. Biblioteca y Archivo Histórico de la Asamblea Legislativa Plurinacional, Vice-Presidencia del Estado, La Paz, Bolivia.

Polia, Mario 1989. "'Contagio' y 'pérdida de la sombra' en la teoría y práctica del curanderismo andino del Perú septentrional: Provincias de Ayabaca y Huancabamba." *Anthropologica* 7(7): 195–231. https://revistas.pucp.edu.pe/index.php/anthropologica/article/view/2070.

Ráez Retamozo, Manuel (director). 1995. *La Fiesta del Agua*. Video. Lima: Pontificia Universidad Católica del Perú, Instituto de Etnomusicología.

Ráez Retamozo, Manuel. 2001a. "Jerarquía y autoridad comunal: Los varayos y la Fiesta del Agua de la comunidad campesina de Llachaqui, Canta." In *Identidades representadas: Performance, experiencia y memoria en los Andes*, ed. Gisela Cánepa Koch, 331–368. Lima: Fondo Editorial PUCP.

Ráez Retamozo, Manuel. 2001b. "Introduction," in *Traditional Music of Peru 7: The Lima Highlands*, ed. Raul R. Romero, 1–25. Washington, DC: Smithsonian/Folkways.

Ramírez Villacorta, Yolanda. 1980. "La penetración capitalista en una comunidad campesina: El caso de San Pedro de Casta, Huarochirí." *Debates en Sociología* 5: 39–70.

Real Academia Española. (1726–1732) 2014. *Diccionario de autoridades*. https://apps2.rae.es/DA.html.

Real Academia Española. (1780) 2014. *Diccionario de la lengua española*, 23rd ed.: https://dle.rae.es.

Rengifo de la Cruz, Elías. 2018. *Al canto del agua: Poesía, testimonio y libro de la Comunidad Andina de San Pedro de Casta, Huarochirí*. Huancayo, Peru: Silbaviente Ediciones.

Robles Mendoza, Román, and Raquel Jackelyne Flores Yon. 2016. "La chirisuya andina: Diáspora de la cultura árabe al Perú." *Alma Máter* (Lima, UNMSM) 3(4): 103–120.

Romero, Raúl. 2001. *Debating the Past: Music, Memory, and Identity in the Andes*. Oxford: Oxford University Press.

Rösing, Ina. 1995. "Paraman Purina—Going for Rain: 'Mute Anthropology' versus 'Speaking Anthropology': Lessons from an Andean Collective Scarcity Ritual in the Quechua-Speaking Kallawaya and Aymara-Speaking Altiplano Region (Andes, Bolivia)." *Anthropos* 90: 69–88.

Rösing, Ina. 2003. *Religión cotidiana en los Andes: Los diez géneros de Amarete*. Frankfurt/Madrid: Iberoamericana/Vervuert.

Rösing, Ina. 2010. *White, Grey and Black Kallawaya Healing Rituals*. Frankfurt/Madrid: Vervuert/Iberoamericana.

Rostworowski de Diez Canseco, María. 1978. *Señoríos indígenas de Lima y Canta*. Lima: Instituto de Estudios Peruanos.

Salas Carreño, Guillermo. 2018. "On Quechua Relatedness to Contemporary and Ancient Dead." In *Non-Humans in Amerindian South America: Ethnographies of Indigenous Cosmologies, Rituals and Songs*, ed. Juan Javier Rivera, 197–223. New York: Berghahn Books.

Salomon, Frank. 1991. "Introductory Essay: The Huarochirí Manuscript." In *The Huarochirí Manuscript: A Testament of Ancient and Colonial Andean Religion*, 1–38. Translated from the Quechua by Frank Salomon and George L. Urioste. Austin: University of Texas Press.

Salomon, Frank. 1998. "Collquiri's Dam: The Colonial Re-voicing of an Appeal to the Archaic." In *Native Traditions in the Post-Conquest World*, ed. Elizabeth Hill Boone and Tom Cummins, 265–293. Washington, DC: Dumbarton Oaks.

Salomon, Frank. 2002a. "¡Huayra huayra pichcamanta!: Augurio, risa y regeneración en la política tradicional (Pacota, Huarochirí)." *Bulletin de l'Institut Français d'Études Andines* 31(1): 1–22.

Salomon, Frank. 2002b. "Unethnic Ethnohistory: On Peruvian Peasant Historiography and Ideas of Autochthony." *Ethnohistory* 49, no. 3: 475–506. muse.jhu.edu/article/11827.

Salomon, Frank. 2004. *The Cord Keepers: Khipus and Cultural Life in a Peruvian Village*. Durham, NC: Duke University Press.

Salomon, Frank. 2013. The Twisting Paths of Recall: Khipu (Andean Cord Notation) as Artifact. In *Writing as Material Practice: Substance, Surface and Medium*, ed. K. E. Piquette and R. D. Whitehouse, 15–43. London: Ubiquity Press. doi: http://dx.doi.org/10.5334/bai.b.

Salomon, Frank. 2016. "Long Lines of Continuity: Field Ethnohistory and Customary Conservation in the Sierra de Lima." In *A Return to the Village: Community Ethnographies and the Study of Andean Culture in Retrospective*, ed. Francisco Ferreira and Billie Jean Isbell, 169–198. London: University of London Press.

Salomon, Frank. 2018. *At the Mountains' Altar: Anthropology of Religion in an Andean Community*. New York: Routledge.

Salomon, Frank. 2019. "The Long Afterlives of Central-Peruvian Khipu Patrimonies." Conference paper: Khipus: Writing Histories in and from Knots, the Mr. and Mrs. Raymond J. Horowitz Book Prize Symposium (February 1, 2019).

Salomon, Frank, Carrie Brezine, Reymundo Chapa, and Víctor Falcón Huayta. 2011. "Khipu from Colony to Republic: The Rapaz Patrimony." In *Their Way of Writing: Scripts, Signs, and Pictographies in Pre-Columbian America*, ed. Elizabeth Hill Boone and Gary Urton, 353–378. Washington, DC: Dumbarton Oaks Research Library and Collection.

Salomon, Frank, and Mercedes Niño-Murcia. 2011. *The Lettered Mountain: A Peruvian Village's Way with Writing*. Durham, NC: Duke University Press.

Salomon, Frank, and George L. Urioste. 1991. *The Huarochirí Manuscript: A Testament of Ancient and Colonial Andean Religion*. Translated from the Quechua by Frank Salomon and George L. Urioste. Austin: University of Texas Press.

Sherbondy, Jeanette E. 1998. "Andean Irrigation in History." In *Searching for*

Equity: Conceptions of Justice and Equity in Peasant Irrigation, ed. Rutgerd Boelens and Gloria Dávila, 210–214. Assen, the Netherlands: Van Gorcum.

Skar, Sarah Lund. 1994. *Lives Together, Worlds Apart: Quechua Colonization in Jungle and City.* Oslo: Scandinavian University Press, distributed by Oxford University Press.

Soler, Eduardo. 1958. "La comunidad de San Pedro de Huancaire." In *Las actuales comunidades indígenas de Huarochirí en 1955*, ed. José Matos Mar, 169–257. Lima: UNMSM.

Soto Flores, Froilán. 1950. "Los kipus modernos de la comunidad de Laramarca." *Revista del Museo Nacional* 19–20: 299–306.

Spalding, Karen. 1984. *Huarochirí: An Andean Society under Inca and Spanish Rule.* Stanford: Stanford University Press.

Spalding, Karen. 2012. *El diario de Francisco de Melo: El levantamiento de Huarochirí.* Lima: Centro Peruano de Estudios Culturales.

Spica, M. A. 2018. "Pluralism with Syncretism: A Perspective from Latin American Religious Diversity." *Open Theology* 4(1): 236–245.

Stobart, Henry. 2001. "La flauta de la llama: Malentendidos musicales en los Andes." In *Identidades representadas: Performance, experiencia y memoria en los Andes*, ed. Gisela Cánepa Koch, 93–113. Lima: Fondo Editorial de la Pontificia Universidad Católica del Perú.

Stobart, Henry. 2006. *Music and the Poetics of Production in the Bolivian Andes.* Aldershot, UK: Ashgate.

Taylor, Gerald. 1974. "Camay, Camac et Camasca dans le manuscrit quechua de Huarochirí." *Journal de la Société des Américanistes* 63: 231–244.

Taylor, Gerald. (ed.). 1987. *Ritos y tradiciones de Huarochirí: Manuscrito quechua de comienzos del siglo XVII, versión paleográfica, interpretación fonológica y traducción al castellano.* Lima: Instituto de Estudios Peruanos/Institut Français d'Études Andines.

Taylor, Gerald. (ed.) 2008. *Ritos y tradiciones de Huarochirí.* Lima: Instituto Francés de Estudios Andinos.

Tello, Julio C. n.d. [1922]. "Socta Curi y Huambo. Marka Wasi / Números de Kipus." Cuaderno 30, Paquete 21: "Textos originales." Archivo Tello, Casona Cultural, Universidad Nacional Mayor de San Marcos, Lima, Peru.

Tello, Julio C. 1923. "Wira Kocha." *Inca* (Lima) 1: 93–320.

Tello, Julio C., and Próspero Miranda. 1923. "Wallallo: Ceremonias gentílicas realizadas en la región cisandina del Peru central." *Revista Inca* 1(2): 475–549.

Thomas, Werner. 2001. *Los protestantes y la Inquisición en España en tiempos de Reforma y Contrarreforma.* Leuven, Belgium: Leuven University Press.

Topic, John R. 2015. "Final Reflections: Catequil as One Wak'a among Many." In *The Archaeology of Wak'as: Explorations of the Sacred in the Pre-Columbian Andes*, ed. Tamara L. Bray, 369–396. Boulder: University Press of Colorado.

Trawick, Paul B. 2001. "Successfully Governing the Commons: Principles of Social Organization in an Andean Irrigation System." *Human Ecology* 29: 1–25.

Trawick, Paul B. 2002. "Comedy and Tragedy in the Andean Commons." *Journal of Political Ecology* 9: 35–68.

Tschudi, Johann Jakob von. 1847. *Travels in Peru, during the Years 1838–1842: On the Coast, in the Sierra, across the Cordilleras and the Andes, into the Primeval Forests*. London: D. Bogue.

Urbano, Henrique. 1997. "Introducción: La tradición andina o el recuerdo del futuro." In *Tradición y modernidad en los Andes*, ed. Henrique Urbano, vii–l. 2nd ed. Cusco, Peru: Centro de Estudios Regionales Andinos. "Bartolomé de las Casas."

Urioste, George L. (ed.). 1983. *Hijos de Pariya Qaqa: La tradición oral de Waru Chiri (Mitología, ritual y costumbres)*. 2 vols. Latin American Series No. 6, No. 1. Syracuse, NY: Foreign and Comparative Studies Program.

Urton, Gary. 2017. *Inka History in Knots: Reading Khipus as Primary Sources*. Austin: University of Texas Press.

Urton, Gary, and Carrie J. Brezine. 2005. "Khipu Accounting in Ancient Peru." *Science* 309(5737): 1065–1067.

Vaughan, Jill, and Ruth Singer. 2018. "Indigenous Multilingualisms Past and Present." *Language & Communication* 62: 83–196.

Vera Delgado, Juana Rosa. 2011. "The Ethno-politics of Water Security: Contestations of Ethnicity and Gender in Strategies to Control Water in the Andes of Peru." PhD dissertation, Wageningen University, the Netherlands.

Vera Delgado, Juana, and Margreet Zwarteveen. 2008. "Modernity, Exclusion and Resistance: Water and Indigenous Struggles in Peru." *Development* 51: 114–120.

Villar Córdova, Pedro Eduardo. 1935. *Las culturas prehispánicas del Departamento de Lima: Arqueología peruana*. Lima: Tall. Gráf. de la Escuela de la Guardia Civil y Policía.

Wallis, Christopher N. 1975. "Some Considerations on Social Classification in the Inca Empire, the Concept of Viracocha, and Its Response to the Spanish Invasion." PhD dissertation, Durham University. Available at Durham E-Theses Online: http://etheses.dur.ac.uk/9945.

Whyte, William F. 1969. "Integración y desintegración en dos comunidades serranas." In *Dominación y cambios en el Perú rural: La micro-región del valle del Chancay*, ed. Giorgio Alberti, Oscar Alers, Julio Cotler, Fernando Fuenzalida, José Matos, Lawrence Williams, and William Whyte, 162–222. Lima: Instituto de Estudios Peruanos.

Williams, Patrick Ryan, Donna J. Nash, Joshua M. Henkin, and Ruth Ann Armitage. 2019. "Archaeometric Approaches to Defining Sustainable Governance: Wari Brewing Traditions and the Building of Political Relationships in Ancient Peru." *Sustainability* 11(8): 1–16.

INDEX

Page numbers in italic type indicate information contained in images or image captions.

Abercrombie, Thomas A., 52
abuelos (ancestors), 6n10, 106n64
acto (ceremony), 113n94
Adelaar, Willem F. H., 58
Agrarian Reform of 1969 (Peru), 31
agua más bravo (wildest waters), 61–62n63
alcalde campo ("Campo," rural mayor), 94n5; assignment of *paradas*, 109; book of (*libro del campo*), 138; duties and roles, highlights, 40, 60, 93–94, 138; maintenance and punishments, oversight of, 150–152; material obligations, distribution of, 98, 101–103, 109–110; New Year duties and obligations of, 139–146; as overseer of horse race, 116–117
alcaldes (magistrates), 33
alcohol use in *champería*, 68–71, 100–101n43, 136n168. See also chicha (maize beer); rum obligations, examples
alfereces (standard bearers), 15, 111, 117, 121–122, 127, 131
alforja (woven bag carried over shoulder), 120
alguacil (constable), 11
alguaciles menores (assistant constables), 40, 85, 125, 144, 149
alguacil mayor (chief constable), 40, 41, 109, 110, 139, 140

Allauca (earlier ayllu, ethnic group), 72, 97n26
Allen, Catherine J., 61, 72, 154n222
amancaes flowers, 151
añaz (Andean skunk), 72
ancestor-focused customs and rituals, overviews, xiii, 1–2, 3–7, 30–31, 37–38, 46–52
"ancestral wedding" (*matrimonio gentílico*) sexual game of *champería*, 132n161
ancha ñawpa pacha (very ancient times), 26n29
Anchelia Llata, Eugenio, 7, 51–52
Anchucaya (Santiago de Anchucaya District), 13n15, 22, 39, 54
Andean Spanish, 57–58, 60
Andrade Ciudad, Luis, 57–58
annual canal-cleaning rituals, overviews, 3–9. See also *champería/walla-walla/warina/walina*, overviews
apus (sacred mountain spirits), 46–47, 53
arawi/harawi narratives (song, poetic form), 27, 66, 67. See also *yaravíes* (melancholy songs)
Arguedas, José María, 43, 59n58, 61, 62
Arnold, Denise Y., 67, 104n57, 121n119
arroba (archaic unit of weight), 99, 105, 107

239

INDEX

Atagaca site. *See* Otagaca/Atagaca site
aukis/awkis/auqis (sacred ancestors), 50
Auto Redondo manuscript, 48
autoridades de vara (staff-holding authorities), 42. See also *varayoc/varayuq/varayoq* (staff-holding authorities)
ayllus (ethnic/kin/clan social units), 10–11, 14, 72–73, 73n74. See also *huayronas/huayrunas*; *parcialidades* (ayllus, ethnic groups)

Bacigalupo, Ana Mariella, 29n33
bailes sociales (social dances, modern), 68
balance economico (account settlement ceremony), 45
Bautista, Luzmila, xv, 15n16, 87, 139n175
Bautista, Nemesio (governor), 4, 35, 45, 87, 96, 133
Bautista Pérez, Anselma, 15n16, 45, 143n186
bells in *champería* rituals, 63–64, 68, 111, 114, 145
Beyersdorff, Margot, 27, 126n139
Binquiguamo (earlier ayllu, ethnic group), 72–73
biscocho/bizcocho (sweet bread), 115, 120
blood sacrifices, 97nn26–27, 133n164
Boelens, Rutgerd, 21
Bolin, Inge, 46, 84n81
book of the "Campo" (*libro del campo*), 138
Botada de Parada. *See* maize kernels used in labor or obligations computations
braided cords in ceremonial use, 15, 23
bulero (pardoner), 155n226
Burns, Kathryn, 19–20n25

Cabildo (town council or town hall), 142, 146
cajeras (women who sing and play *tinya* drums), 65, 113, 117–118, 127

Calistro, Máximo, 4–5, 96
Calistro, Pascual, 35
callapa (ceremonial distaff), 139n175
callpa (ritual energy, vital force), 50
camachicas (female law enforcers), 123
camachicos (law enforcers): duties and roles, highlights, 13, 40, 97; obligations of outgoing officers, 122–125, 126–128; punishments of outgoing officers, 123, 129–130
camay (Quechua concept regarding obligations), 18, 102n50, 123n129, 130n153
Campo. See *alcalde campo* ("Campo," rural mayor)
canal system: intake at Carhuayumac River, 76, 81, 95, 106, 113, 143; origins and etymology around, 38–39; path overview, 76–78
cántaros (pitchers), 69, 118n107
canterito (little jug), 62n64
cantor (religious functionary), 109, 149
capitalism. *See* modernization, impacts of
Carampoma (village), 56–57, 78, 104n58
Carapongos and Lunaguaná/Lunahuaná (local brewed drinks from), 68, 114
cargos (functionary roles/duties), 8, 123n128, 130
carhuaymesa (banquet of yellow foods), 119
Carhuayumac/Carguayumac (*parada*), 43, 71, 73, 81
Carhuayumac/Carguayumac (principal canal), 76, 95n14
Carhuayumac River, 76
carismanta/carishmanta/kalashmanta/calashmanta (rectangular carry cloth), 41, 50
Carnival Season events and rituals. *See* New Year and Carnival Season events and rituals

cascabeles (bells in *champería* rituals), 63–64, 68, 111, 114, 145
Casta (San Pedro de Casta, Huarochirí): community organization of, 39–42; and creation of "El Entablo," 1–2, 16–19, 28–31, 35; importance of water supply to, 3–9
Catholicism: elements of in *champería*, 57; *entablo* use in, 16–17; influence of on youth behavior, 55; khipus in, 27, 34; material obligations of ecclesiastical functionaries, 147–149. See also Christianization of Indigenous; Christian practices or aspects of *champería*
Cauqui/Jaqaru (an Aymara language), 56–57, 58–59, 60
centellas (church candles), 147
chaccha (coca-chewing interval/ceremony), 99, 105, 124, 128, 141
Chacchadera/Chacchana site, 78, 106, 143, 145
Chakian branch of canals, 76, 78
chakitaqlla (foot plow), 144n190, 155n224
champería/walla-walla/warina/walina, overviews: annual scheduling of, 70n71; codifying and recording of in Entablo, 3–6; impact of COVID-19 on, 89; work scheduling, 79–81
chancaca (solidified sugar syrup), 131
Chaupi Ñamca/Chaupi Ñamoc (female huaca), 143–144n188
chayanas (resting/drinking place), 127–128
chayaneros (earthenware jugs), 126–127, 129
chicha (maize beer): *chicha de jora* (made from black maize), 99, 105, 123; distribution and serving of (examples), 99, 102, 112–113, 118, 123–124, 129, 141–142; obligations for *champería*, 65, 68–69, 71–72, 74
chicha caliente (coffee), 122n124

chicra. See *shikra/shicra/chicra* bags (ritual coca pouches)
chirimía/chirisuya (indigenized oboe used in *champería*), 63–65, 100, 102, 114, 132, 144, 152
chonta (palm shoot), 111
Christianization of Indigenous, 18, 32–34, 73n74
Christian practices or aspects of *champería*: Holy Season, 147–149; hymns during canal-cleaning rituals, 118–119; overview, 57; prayers at Hualhual reservoir, 119–120; prayers at Mashca site, 115–116, 116n102; rosary recitation and thanksgiving at Saturday *padrón*, 129; vigil for Christ at conclusion of *champería*, 122–123
ch'ullu (knitted hat with earflaps), 41
Chuqui Suso (huaca of Cupara people), 18, 69–71
Chuswa/Chuscwa/Chusgua/Chushgua/Chushwa reservoir, 61n62, 73, 74, 76, 78, 81, 103, 118
cigarettes as part of material obligations, 51, 69n70, 98n32, 101, 104, 140, 149
ciudadanos (citizens), 5
clothing. See dress and clothing traditions/rules
coca-chewing, 78n80, 80, 98n31, 99, 113, 115. See also *chaccha* (coca-chewing interval/ceremony)
coca leaf obligations, 8, 13, 41, 79–80, 98, 99, 100, 107, 117
Código de Aguas, 31
cofradías (religious confraternity), 73, 108
Coguay, 136. See also Cuhuay/Coguay/Cohuay site
collo/qollo (bowl-shaped object), 117
colonial influences, 1, 17–19, 32–34, 56–60. See also Catholicism
colors of *paradas*, 75, 103n55
Comaopaccha *parada*, 73n75, 74

Communist ideologies, 53, 54
community law and standards: cohesion and conflict management, 6–7, 9–13, 15–16; and collective decision-making, 95n16; *entablo* agreement process, 94n8; organization and hierarchy of authority, 39–42; statutes, 24–25. *See also* national/state law in conflict with community law
competitive spirit of *champería*, 74–75
compliances (obligatory material goods), 108n78, 121n121. *See also* material obligations, highlights
cómputos (calculation), 108
comuneros (community members), 8, 95n12. *See also padrón comunal* (community census/register)
comunidad (community), 4
comunidades indígenas (Indigenous communities), 35
Concha people, San Damián, Huarochirí, xiv, 48–49, 63, 68, 97n26
Condori, Bernabé, 53
conflict management, importance of, 6–7, 9–13, 15–16, 99n36. *See also* intergenerational conflict; *justicia de acuerdos* (agreement justice) system
conopas (small objects that transmit power), 154n222
constancia (official record/durable knowledge), 21, 95n15, 132n162
Constitution of the Republic of Peru (1920), 2, 28–36
conteo. *See* maize kernels used in labor or obligations computations
conversion to Christianity, resistance to, 18
corredor (runner), 110, 121
corrigedores (correctors), 128
corrigedores de indios (provincial magistrates to exercise royal law and collect tributes), 33
costumbres (ancestral law, obligatory ritual), 1, 9, 26

cotton for ritual/religious activities, 147–148n202, 154–155
COVID-19 pandemic, impact of, 89–90
Crispín, Mario, 27–28
crying in ritual practices, 57, 66–67. *See also waqay/huajay* (to weep, wail, or cry out)
Cuenta General de Señoras Originarias (General Account of the *Originaria* Women), 127
cuentas (accounts), 100n41, 107, 125, 129n151. *See also padrones* (registers or census accounts)
Cuhuay/Coguay/Cohuay site, 14–15, 28, 78, 99; Friday rituals, 123–126; New Year *faena*, 141; Saturday rituals, 126–130; Sunday secret ceremony, 109n79; Wednesday events and rituals, 111
Cumau/Comao/Cumao Waterfall, 61–62, 63–64, 65, 76, 106, 114
Cumau/Cumaopaccha (*parada*), 71, 73, 74, 81, 114
cumbia (modern music form), 68
cumplimientos (obligatory material goods), 108n78. *See also* material obligations, highlights
Cunya spring, 76
Cupara people, 18, 69–70
cura (ritual specialist), 7, 64, 109n79
curacas (elite native lords/nobles), 33, 34
curanderos (ritual experts and healers), 7, 25
curco/curcucha (rainy season ritual dance), 139
curiosidades (skilled crafts, traditional handicrafts), 50, 101–102, 139, 143n184
Cushman, Gregory T., 46
Cuswa reservoir. *See* Chuswa/Chuscwa/Chusgua/Chushgua/Chushwa reservoir

Dalton, Jordan, 141n178
dancing in *champería*, 42

INDEX 243

deberes (duties), 102n50
"debt" scores and punishments, 44–45
December obligations, 85, 149–150
de-Indianization goal, 86
de la Cadena, Marisol, 25, 29n33, 30, 42–43, 53
de la Puente Luna, José Carlos, 33, 34
Diccionario de autoridades (Real Academia Española), 16, 19n24
Doctor Dances, 151
Dransart, Penny, 61
dress and clothing traditions/rules, 15, 41–42, 122, 128–129
Drinot, Paolo, 53n47
drums. See *tinya drum* (traditional Andean drum)
dualism themes, 66–67
dynamite in rituals, 114

Easter rituals, 147–148
Echeandía Valladares, J. M.: on civic responsibilities for water distribution, 5; on ethnic group names, 72n72; and *huipi* use, 13; on importance of material obligations to ritual, 50; on languages, 57, 59; on messengers delivering tasks to urban villages, 104n58; on record-keeping methods, 140n177; on ritual stones, 154n220; on role/work of *yachak*, 155n224
El Diario, 11–12
entablar, definitions and interpretations, 16–18, 30
Entable (previous manuscript), 138n172
Entablo, *17*; 1939 changes and additions, 33, 62, 85, 137–149; 1947 reforms to, 33, 85, 149–154; 1952 changes and additions, 85, 154–156; 1990–1993 addendum, 86, 156; approval/authorization of, 131–133; community grazing fees entries, 85–86, 155–156; contents overview, 84–87; creation of, overviews, 1–2; language of, 1, 56–60; loss/misplacement of, 90–91, 94n10; motivation for and authorities over, 3–6; notations and markings, 87–88; as support for community laws and traditions, 5–7, 37–38; syncretic nature of, 33–34; transcription and translation of, challenges and procedures, 81–84
entablos/entables, 16, 17, 18–19
equipos (khipus), 22–23, 75–76. See also khipus (string recording devices)
Escalante, Carmen, 9
eshcupuros (gourd for storing lime), 145n194
estatuto comunal (community statute), 24–25

faena/faeneros (communal work/workers), 8, 74, 95n13, 140, 145
fairness, focus on, 96n22
faltas/falta de costumbre (failures of ritual), 44, 46, 50–51, 125n135
February obligations, 85
fee/tax/monetary contribution paid during *champería*, 74, 95n13, 103, 131
Fernández Osco, Marcelo, 10–11, 68, 84n81
fiambres (provisions), 100–101n43
Fiesta del Agua ("Yakuraymi," Water Fiesta), 3n4. See also *champería/walla-walla/warina/walina*, overviews
filming of *champería* for rumored Netflix documentary, 90
fireworks in rituals, 114, 120
flags, ceremonial, 65
flares, ceremonial (examples), 79, 98, 100, 105, 106, 107
Florida water (scented cologne), 148
flourishes, handwritten/drawn, 19–20, 95n11
flowers in *champería*, 111, 120, 146, 147, 148, 151
"folklore" (certain ritual objects), 154
Friday events and rituals, 45, 81, 123–126, 139–140

funcionarios (functionaries), 6, 39–40, 50–51, 138. See also *cargos* (functionary roles/duties); material obligations, highlights

Gelles, Paul H.: on carnival games, 146n197; on Casta, 3; on cooperation and reciprocity of communal work, 8; on faena labor tax, 74n76, 95n13; on music of the *champería*, 63; on ritual stones/paraphernalia, 154n220; on roles of *michcos*, 80–81; on signature section of Entablo, 135n166
gendered ritual activities, 13, 55, 69, 99n35
generational issues. See intergenerational conflict
gobernador (governor), 4
Gose, Peter, 11, 107n68
Gow, Rosalind, 53
gran audiencia (high court), 13
grazing records/fees for community, 85–86, 155–156
Guallacocha (earlier ayllu, ethnic group), 72
Guaman Poma de Ayala, Felipe, 18, 30
guardia (state police officer), 51
Guevara-Gil, Armando, 21, 29, 30, 34
guinea pigs used in rituals, 97n26, 97n27, 98n29, 106n64, 143n185
Gushiken, José, 56–57, 73

Hall, Ingrid, 14, 35, 39, 99n35, 102n52, 104n57
hamawt'a (philosophers), 27
harawikuq (poets), 27
Hardman, Martha J., 58
herding and grazing khipus, 85–86
Honores, Renzo, 32n36, 33, 34
horse race during *champería*, 75, 79, 111–112, 116–117
Howard-Malverde, Rosaleen, 53–54, 98n28

huacas (sacred beings), 6–7, 18, 47–48, 69–71, 114n98, 133n164, 143–144n188, 154n222
huacho/wachu (obligation hierarchy), 39
huacura (strap made from sheep's wool), 123
huajay. See *waqay/huajay* (to weep, wail, or cry out)
Hualhualcocha (*parada*). See Ocshayco/Ocusha/Ucucha/Uchucha/Hualhualcocha (*parada*)
Hualhual reservoir, 73, 81, 118–119, 140, 141
hualinas/walinas/warinas (water songs, cheerful songs), 38, 63–65, 66–68, 89–90, 111, 114, 131
huallques/huallkis/huallquis (ritual pouches worn by men), 32n35, 50, 51, 143
Huanaquirma Waterfall, 76, 114
Huanca-Acequia reservoir, 76, 80, 98, 99
Huanca-Shilca/Wanka Ilka/Huankailka site, 76, 103, 106, 113, 114
huanca/wanka standing stones, 98n28
Huancayo, Peru, 90
huaris (Wari/Huari ethnic group), 38, 72
Huarochirí Manuscript (1608): on importance of rituals, 10, 46; language of, 1, 58; overviews, 1–2, 36–38; and superficial religious conversion, 18
Huarochirí Province, 36, 38–39, 58
huatru/wachu (furrow, rank file), 38–39
Huayacocha site, 141, 142
huaynos (songs of rainy season), 61, 67
huayronas/huayrunas: annual accounting ceremony, xvii, *14*, 38, 45, 85; meeting places for ayllus or *paradas*, 38, 72, 132, 132n160
huayruro seeds, 139n175
huipis (balance scales), 13, 99n36, 105n61, 140–141n178
Hyland, Sabine, 13n15, 23, 52

illas (objects that transmit power), 154n222
Inca cultural continuity: codes of law and 1920 National Constitution, 30; concept of scale, 24; khipu-like devices of, 12, 14, 18, 22, 27, 126n138; ritual practices and customs, 57, 66–67, 70n71, 126n139; social organization and governance, 42
Indigenous, recognition of, 137–138n170
"Indigenous cosmopolitics," 29n33, 97n24
industrialization. *See* modernization, impacts of
intergenerational conflict, 42–43, 53–56, 62, 67–68
interlanguage concepts, 58, 60–61, 62, 67n68
irrigation system configuration and landmarks, 76–78
ishcopuro (gourd for storing lime), 51

Jaqaru/Cauqui (an Aymara language), 56–57, 58–59, 60
Jimenez, Basilio, 132
jugar carnavales ("playing carnival"), 143n187, 146, 146n197
junta directiva (board of directors, community), 39
justicia de acuerdos (agreement justice) system, 10–11, 15, 19, 31. *See also* proportionality principle

Kaha Wayi (treasury house), 52
Karwayuma. *See* Carhuayumac/Carguayumac *(parada)*
kashwas (songs), 67n68
Kemper Columbus, Claudette, 154n220
khipu boards (hybrid khipu-text devices), 2, 12, 18–19, 27–28, 31–32. *See also* "washing" (unknotting) of khipu boards
khipu cosecha (harvest khipu), 27–28

khipukamayuq (experts on khipu records), 27, 32
khipus (string recording devices), xiv, 11–12, 15, 20n25, 21–23, 34, 75–76, 86. *See also* khipu boards (hybrid khipu-text devices)
Kishka K'umo branch, 76, 78
Komau *(parada)*. *See* Cumau/Cumaopaccha *(parada)*
kuimeres (law enforcers), 13n15
Kuri Pata Hill, 76
Kuway. *See* Cuhuay/Coguay/Cohuay site

labor/moral debts, 12–13, 13n15, 15, 44–45, 52, 121n118, 125n134
Laclán reservoir, 73, 78, 81, 118
Laco site, 76, 101, 102, 107, 112, 115–116
lakes (reservoirs), 81. *See also individual reservoirs*
Lalancaria branch group (married women), 78, 80
lamperos (spade workers), 101, 103, 107
landscape (ancestral) as animate, 29n33, 30
language: of Entablo, 1, 56–60; of Huarochirí Manuscript, 1, 58; legal considerations for record-keeping, 62; modernization and stigma of Indigenous languages, 57, 59, 62; Quechua, xiii–xiv, 35–36, 56–63; transcription and translation challenges, 81–84; written *vs.* oral/unwritten, 1–2, 6, 31–33
La Quinta Internacional, 53
lashes. *See* whippings (punishments)
Latin language, 56, 59–60
Latour, Bruno, 30
Leguía, Augusto B., 35, 53n48
Lent, rituals for, 148–149
Ley General de Comunidades Campesinas of 1987, 25
liberalized thinking and social change, 53, 54–55

libro del campo (book of the "Campo"), 138
lime powder for coca activation, *51*, 98n31, 145n194
liquor obligations, examples, 100, 103. *See also* pisco (grape brandy); rum obligations, examples
livestock and grazing records/fees for community, 85–86, 155–156
llacuazes (Llacuaz ethnic group), 38, 72, 144n188
llampu (red ceremonial powder), 61
Llanos, Oliverio, 8, 56, 103n54, 109n79, 122n122
llanquis (moccasins), 15n16
Luzmilla, Doña. *See* Bautista, Luzmila

Mackenzie, Ian, 58, 60
Mackey, Carol, 12
maize kernels used in labor or obligations computations, 73, 97n25, 108, 140
Mama Capiama (female huaca), 114n98
Mannheim, Bruce, 23–24, 66–67
manta tarmeña (brown poncho worn as formal attire), 110, 117, 121, 128
manteles (embroidered cloths), 119
"manual (monthy) items," interpretation of, 128–129n149
Marcahuasi plateau (popular tourist site near Casta), 76
María Cascanti. *See* Juan Rojas and María Cascanti (canal-dwelling ancestors at Oculi appeased in ritual)
Martínez Céspedes, Jimmy, 32, 32n35
Mascha/Mashca/Mashka/Machca site, 76, 78, 105, 112, 115–116
masqayoq/masqay/maskay (ritual specialist, "seeker"), 78–79
mate (gourd drinking cup), 101n43, 110, 117
material obligations, highlights: ecclesiastical, 147–149; functionaries, 39, 138–141, 145; married men and women, 103, 105; overviews, 8, 50, 98–100; recording/scoring of fulfillment, 8, 12–13, 22, 32, 75. *See also* chicha (maize beer); cigarettes as part of material obligations; coca leaf obligations; *individual functionary designations*
Mayer, Enrique, 26–27, 42, 53, 108n77, 109n79
Mayguay/Maiguai/Maiguay/Mayhuay (village), 142, 143, 150
mayoralas (women stewards), 15, 67, 113
mayordomos (auxiliaries), 41, 80, 99, 141
mayores (elders or notables), 39–40
memoria (memory), 27
memory (elder/ancestral), importance of in *champería* ritual, 16, 26–27, 37, 52, 109n79, 132
men, organization and duties of, 80, 97n27, 104, 105, 141
menores (Menores). *See alguaciles menores* (assistant constables)
Mercedarians (religious order), 27, 38
mesas (tables used in ritual activities), 119–120, 140, 148n202
mesas paños (tablecloths), 119
"mestizo cosmopolitics," 29n33
mestizo cultural identity, 29n33
michcos/michicos/michikuy (functionary-elects and *parada* leaders), 15, 41–42, *43*, 65, 80–81, 110–111. *See also varayoc/varayuq/varayoq* (staff-holding authorities)
Ministerio de Salud Pública, Trabajo y Previsión Social (Ministry for Public Health, Work, and Social Security), 85, 137
Miranda, Próspero, 135n166
modernization, impacts of: and burgeoning capitalism, 10; and clothing/dress rules for *champería*, 15; on community record-keeping methods, 29–30; and decline of traditional practices, 3–5, 44–46, 67–68; declining khipu use, 23; on languages, 57, 59, 62; nation-building and govern-

mentalization of Indigenous, 35; social change and intergenerational conflict, 7, 8, 42–43, 53–56, 62
Monday (first) events and rituals, 98–100; canal cleaning groups assigned, 80; clearing of road for horse race, 79; end of *champería*, 65–66; naming of *notables* (experts), 25–26; Padrón General de los Asistentes a la Faena (General Padrón of the Work Party Attendees), 74
Monday (second) events and rituals, 131–132
Monday New Year and Carnival season events and rituals, 144–147
Montes, Melecio, 52
monthly items, 128–129n149
morality: and ancestral code of justice, 5, 9–10, 35, 49, 56, 81, 121; policing of, 6, 32, 42, 52, 55n51, 125nn136–137. See also labor/moral debts
multilingualism, 58, 59–60
music as part of *champería*, 63–68. See also songs/singing in *champería*
músicos (musicians), 15

Ñamuc/Ñamoc site, 143–144, 145, 151
national/state law in conflict with community law, 10, 28, 37–38. See also Constitution of the Republic of Peru (1920)
ñawpa ("in front") and importance of past, 26n29, 37
New Year and Carnival Season events and rituals, 55n51, 85, 105n61, 139–147, 150–151. See also *pirwa* (rainmaking ritual)
Niño-Murcia, Mercedes, 56, 93n1, 95n15, 154n219
nómina (roster), 28, 50, 130–131
notables (individuals that fulfilled all community obligations in their lifetime), 25–26, 27, 31, 39–40
Nueva Corónica (Guaman Poma chronicle), 18, 30

numeric values: five (numeric symbolism of), 125n134; scores for performance of assigned duties and tasks, 12–14, 44, 125, 128; three (numeric symbolism of), 121n118
Nuñez Paolmino, Pedro Germán, 1n1, 25

Obispo Bautista, Kedwin, 61–62, 90
Obispo Rojas, Eufronio, 16, 22, 97n26, 114n98, 123n127
obligations/*obligaciones*. See material obligations, highlights
Ocshayco/Ocusha/Okshaiko/Ucucha/Uchucha site, 76, 114–115
Ocshayco/Ocusha/Ucucha/Uchucha/Hualhualcocha (*parada*), 71, 73–74, 81
Oculi site, 78, 103, 106, 119
oficio divino (Catholic liturgical prayer), 149
Olacocha reservoir, 76, 78, 101, 102, 106
Olivares, Catalina (Yachak): on appearance of khipus, 22–23; on color of ritual guinea pigs, 97n26; on foot plows, 144n190, 155n224; on huaca Suqta Kuri, 47–48; on Juan Rojas and María Cascanti, 106n64; on New Year offerings and obligations, 139n175; on *parada* assignments, 73–74; performing *hualina* for documentary, 90; pledge to perform complete *champería* for 2022 (post-pandemic), 90; *puchka* of, 88; on sexual game of *champería*, 132n161
Olivares Bautista, Carlos Alberto, 89, 154n220, 154n223
oral *vs.* written record-keeping systems, 1–2, 6, 31–33
originarios (natives), 13, 124
Osterling, Jorge P., 8, 56, 103n54, 109n79, 122n122
Otagaca/Atagaca site, 67, 75, 102, 105, 111, 120

paccha/paqcha (waterfall), 61, 114
Pachamama (earth deity), 43

Pacsagumo (site), 142n182, 145, 146, 146n197
padroncillo (register with khipu cords), 22, 23
padrón comunal (community census/register), 23, 24–25, 140n177, 141
padrón/cuenta (census/register/account), 19. See also khipu boards (hybrid khipu-text devices)
Padrón de Comuneros (Padrón of Community Members), 140. See also *padrón comunal* (community census/register)
Padrón de Huallque y Poronguitos Labrados (Padrón of Huallque Bags and Decorated Drinking Gourds), xiv–xv, *19*, 50, 74, 101
Padrón de las Señoras (Padrón of the Married Women), 128
Padrón de las Señoras de Yañac (Padrón of the Yañac Women), 120
Padrón de los Veinte Cántaros (Padrón of the Twenty Pitchers), 71, 112n92, 120
padrones (registers or census accounts), 14, 17, 32n35, 35. See also *cuentas* (accounts); *padrón comunal* (community census/register)
Padrón General de los Asistentes a la Faena (General Padrón of the Work Party Attendees), 74, 103, 105n59
Padrón General de los Asistentes al Trabajo (General Padrón of the Work Attendees), 74, 105, 106
Padrón General de los Hombres (General Padrón of the Men), 124, 130
Padrón General de los Hombres y Mujeres (General Padrón of the Men and Women), 14, 127, 141
palangana (clownish, foolish) functionaries in ritual, 114
Pampacocha reservoir, 73, 78, 81, 98, 102, 118–119

panzón tayta ("papa potbelly," nickname for *michcos*), 42
paper *v.* khipus for record-keeping, 22, 54
paradas (kin work groups), 28, 73–74, 75, 80–81, 103n55
parcialidades (ayllus, ethnic groups), 32n35, 67, 73, 132n160. See also ayllus (ethnic/kin/clan social units); *huayronas/huayrunas*
Pariacaca (mountain ancestor deity), 10, 46
"Pariapungo" (grotto of ancestor, ceremonial site), 113
pasar cargos (undertaking functionary roles/duties), 8. See also *cargos* (functionary roles/duties)
Paulson, Susan, 18
Pearce, Adrian J., 22
pebble-based division of labor enumeration, 26–27, 108n77, 109n79
pena (penalty, shame), 15
Pérez Galán, Beatriz, 34, 37
personero/personería (State-recognized municipal authority), 4–5, 96n21, 141
Pimentel, Nelson, 27–28, 55n52
pirúa (storeroom for potatoes and corn), 57n55
pirwa (rainmaking ritual), 57, 61n61, 67n68, 85, 154n220
Piscatambo site, 115
pisco (grape brandy), 49, 101n43, 149
pishca/pichca (oracular dice game), 146n197
pitchers (*cántaros*) as standard measure, 118n107
Pitic Gorge, 76
planilla (name chart), 13–14, 44, 124–125, 127
Platt, Tristan, 35–36, 109n79
"playing carnival," 143n187, 146, 146n197
Pokle "Lake" reservoir, 78
policías (police officers), 42
poronguito (drinking gourd), 101–102

INDEX   249

potos chayaneros (earthenware jugs), 126–127, 129
principal (maximal community authority for *champería*), 40, 99n36
proportionality principle, 12–13, 14–15, 43–44. *See also* reciprocity principle
puchka (ceremonial distaff), 88, 139n175
puchu/putu/potito/mate (drinking gourd), 101n43
puna (high-elevation grasslands), 38, 72, 138
punishments for ritual failures: calculation of and administration of, 13–15, 124–126; droughts as, 7; and reciprocity principle, 12; reprimands, 126, 128; whippings, 45, 120–122, 123, 127–130. See also *faltas/falta de costumbre* (failures of ritual); proportionality principle
puño de plata (silver fist), 122n122, 127n144
Puquio (Lucanas Province), 43
purification ceremony, 45
Purpito Mama (progenitor stone), 85

qollo/collo (bowl-shaped object), 117
Quechua language, xiii–xiv, 35–36, 56–63, 67
Quinual site, 78, 102–103

Ráez Retamozo, Manuel, 42
rain, invocation of, 18n23, 147–148n202
Rapaz (Oyón Province, Lima region), 21–22, 52
Real Academia Española, 124n131
rebellions: and community dissonance, 53–56; eighteenth century, 34; khipus used in, 31–32
reciprocity principle, 8, 10, 12, 43. *See also* proportionality principle
recoger la leña (collecting the firewood), 132n161
recordatorios (reminders), 12
record-keeping of community laws and traditions, 1–2, 6, 29–30, 31. *See also* community law and standards
red color, meanings, 97n27
regidor campo (rural regulator), 40, 97, 98–99
regidor mayor (village regulator), 40, 97
reglamento (set of regulations), 16
relación (written report from data analysis, payment), 108n74, 130–131
religion. *See* Catholicism; Christianization of Indigenous; Christian practices or aspects of *champería*
Rengifo de la Cruz, Elías, 9, 94n8
reproduction, moral policing of, 55, 125n137
reserencias (New Year work), 150n210
reservoirs/lakes, 81. *See also individual reservoirs*
respect in cultural frameworks, 84n81
revisitas. *See visitas* (tributes, or inspections monitoring tributes)
reynas/reyes (queens and kings), 6n10
Ríos, Gregorio, 90
road maintenance/cleaning obligations, 79, 107, 149–150
Rojas, Juan, and María Cascanti (canal-dwelling ancestors at Oculi appeased in ritual), 106n64
Rojas, Timoteo, 133n164
Rojas Obispo, Eloy Tomás, 4n6, 16
Roman Catholic Church, influence of. *See* Catholicism
Rösing, Ina, 10, 12, 148n202
Rostworowski de Diez Canseco, María, 58
rum obligations, examples, 98–100, 104, 109, 126

sacred objects, 154
sacrifices: animal, 97nn26–27; human, 133n164
"sacrificial debt," 12–13
sacsaneros (supervisors, ones to be satisfied), 60, 102, 105

Salinas Bautista, Ishmila. *See* Bautista, Luzmila
Salinas Obispo, Jorge, *64*
Salinas Rojas, Jesús, 86
Salomon, Frank: on ayllu rivalries, 75; on *constancia*, 95n15; on inventorying community archive, 93n1; on khipu uses, 15, 28, 86; on local archive audits, 154n218; on modernization of record-keeping, 30; on Quechua to Spanish language shift, 56; on Rapaz khipu, 52
sami (vital energy), 61, 154n222
Sami Dios (Sami God), 85, 154
San Andrés de Tupicocha. *See* Tupicocha (Huarochirí, Lima region)
San Damián, Huarochirí, xiv, 7, 58, 67–68, 122n123
San Pedro de Casta (Casta), Huarochirí. *See* Casta (San Pedro de Casta, Huarochirí)
San Pedro de Huancaire, Huarochirí, 4, 43, 54–55, 73n74
Saturday events and rituals, 81, 126–130
Saturday New Year and Carnival season events and rituals, 140–142
scholarship on, 8–9
scores for tasks. *See* numeric values
seafoam in ritual use, 61–62n63
secret customs/rituals, 8, 61n61, 98n29, 109n79, 113, 114, 116n102
sexual/courtship games of *champería*, 132n161, 146n197
Sherbondy, Jeanette E., 10
shikra/shicra/chicra bags (ritual coca pouches), 115, 120, 139n175
shokurqur (punish by inflicting harm), 106n64
shouting. *See* vocalizing, shouting/crying out in *champería*
signatures for binding agreement, 19–21
Silguerito site, 114
Simancaria/Semankaria branch, 78, 80

síndico comunero/síndico personero (highest ranking local authority), 4–5
síndico tesorero (municipal treasurer), 141
singing. *See* songs/singing in *champería*
social media participation in pandemic-affected *champerías*, 89
Soculún (settlement), 76
Soculún site, 113
Soler, Eduardo, 54–55, 73n74, 84n81
songs/singing in *champería*, 57, 59, 61, 63–68, 78. See also *cajeras* (women who sing and play *tinya* drums); Taquina (Singing Place) ritual site
Spanish, Andean, 57–60, 83
staff-holding authorities. *See varayoc/varayuq/varayoq* (staff-holding authorities)
state/national law in conflict with community law, 10, 28, 37–38. *See also* Constitution of the Republic of Peru (1920)
Stobart, Henry, 63
stones, ritual, 154
Sunday events and rituals, 97, 98n29, 103n55, 109n79, 130–131
Sunday New Year and Carnival season events and rituals, 143–144
Suqta Kuri/Suqta Curi (rain/lightning huaca, rapist), 47–48, 133n164, 154n222

tacllas/taqllas (plows), 144
taleguita/taleqa/talega (bag to hold bottles of alcohol), 101
Tangor, Peru, 26–27, 42, 108n77, 109n79
Taquina (Singing Place) ritual site, 65, 66, 78, 112, 117–118
Taylor, Gerald, 58, 143–144n188
Tello, Julio C., 23, 46–47, 58, 132n159
Tello and Miranda: on appropriate dress for *champería*, 15n16; on *huipi* use, 13, 140–141n178; image of khipu

board, *19*, 23; on irrigation configuration and landmarks, 76; on languages, 57, 59; on principal deity honored in *champería*, 47, 48; on Saturday punishment rulings, 13; and "secret" ceremonies, 8, 98n29; on secret ritual at Mashca site, 116n102; on singing rituals of *champería*, 67
teniente gobernador (lieutenant governor), 40, 104, 107, 117, 121–122
Thursday events and rituals, 15, 81, 117–123
timbladeras (drinking vessels), 15n19, 127
time/clock-time, 58–59
tinya drum (traditional Andean drum), 65n67, 68, 113, 131
toma (intake from river to canal system), 95, 113
toros/toritos (small guinea pigs), 97n26, 143
traditions of past, honoring and preserving, 26–27, 37
Trawick, Paul B., 12
tribunal de los ancianos (jury of the elders), 13
tribute and labor obligations of native population, 33. *See also faena/faeneros* (communal work/workers); labor/moral debts; *visitas* (tributes, or inspections monitoring tributes)
truenador ("thunderer," whip), 120n117. *See also* whippings (punishments)
Tschudi, Johann Jakob von, 67, 86
Tuesday events and rituals, 74, 80, 104–109
Tupicocha (Huarochirí, Lima region): community archive, 93n1; effects of modernization in, 30; khipu use in, xiv, 15, 20n25, 21–22, 28, 75–76, 86
turno de agua (ration of irrigation water), 108n73

tushmac (duties for preparation of *tushmada*), 130–131n156
tushmada (Friday meal with all paradas), 130–131n156
tutelary rights (protective rights), 10

Ucusha/Uchucha/Hualhualcocha (*parada*). *See* Ocshayco/Ocusha/Ucucha/Uchucha/Hualhualcocha (*parada*)
unañcha/uñancha/unanchay (indicators/reminders), 12, 14, 126n138
Urioste, George L., 18
Urno/Ursno/Uhsno branch, 78
Ursno branch work group (married men), 80, 97n27

varayoc/varayuq/varayoq (staff-holding authorities), 26–27, 42, 73, 108n77, 109n79. *See also michcos/michicos/michikuy* (functionary-elects and *parada* leaders)
vasija (jug, drinking vessel), 120
Vendelhombre (community khipu guardian), 52
Vera Delgado, Juana, 32–33, 97n27, 148n202
village cleaning and maintenance obligations and inspections, 150–152
Villar Córdova, Pedro Eduardo, 64–65
visibility concept and cultural preservation, 36–37
visitas (tributes, or inspections monitoring tributes), 72, 119, 124n133, 138, 151
vocalizing, shouting/crying out in *champería*, 42, 57, 66–67, 78, 111, 112. *See also* songs/singing in *champería*

wachik/wachiq (ritual authority), 59, 98n29
wachu/huacho (obligation hierarchy), 39
Wallallo/Huallallo (Inca deity), 3, 78–79, 116n102

walla-walla (Wallallo song), 67
wallkis (ritual pouches). See *huallques/huallkis/huallquis* (ritual pouches worn by men)
Wamani (mountain deity), 43
Wanka-Acequia. See Huanca-Acequia reservoir
Wanka Ilka. See Huanca-Shilca/Wanka Ilka/Huankailka site
waqachiku (rain), 18n23
waqay/huajay (to weep, wail, or cry out), 57, 67, 111, 112
Wari/Huari (canal creator, water deity), 38, 46–47
warina/walina. See *champería/walla-walla/warina/walina*, overviews
Wari Runa (annual accounting procedure/event), 13, 38. See also *huayronas/huayrunas*
wari runa (Wari people), 38. See also *huayronas/huayrunas*
"washing" (unknotting) of khipu boards, 13–14, 15, 127n145
water: ancestral traditions and laws, 3–4, 5–7, 12; centrality and importance of, 2–3; *hualinas/walinas/warinas* (water songs of *champería*), 38, 63–65, 66–68, 89–90, 111, 114, 131; irrigation system configuration and landmarks, 76–78; rights and ancestral claims, 9–10, 32, 62; state management and legislation, 30–31, 37; Wari/Huari (canal creator, water deity), 38, 46–47. See also canal system; Cumau/Comao/Cumao Waterfall
waxay. See *waqay/huajay* (to weep, wail, or cry out)
Waya Kocha branch, 78
Wednesday events and rituals: chicha and food distribution and consumption, 68–71; Cumau Waterfall offering, 61–62; Entablo text on, 109–117; formation of *paradas* and ritual cleaning of reservoirs/lakes, 80–81; horse race and running race, 75, 81, 116–117; music after waterfall offering, 63–64; ritual crying, 67
Wellington boots, 41
whipping of water, 42, *43*
whippings (punishments), 45, 120–122, 123, 127–130. See also punishments for ritual failures
widows and widowers, water rights of, 99n35
Williams, Patrick Ryan, 67
wipis. See *huipis* (balance scales)
women, organization and duties of, 40, 80, 103, 105, 119, 119n115, 120, 128, 141

Yacapar (ayllu, ethnic group), 72–73, 112, 115, 124, 128, 132n160
yachak/yachaq (ritual expert, knower), 22, 47, 73, 139, 155n224. See also Olivares, Catalina (Yachak)
Yañac (ayllu, ethnic group), 72–73, 120, 124, 128, 132n160
Yanapaccha (*parada*), 71, 73–74, 81, 114
yancas (priests), 13
Yapita, Juan de Dios, 67, 104n57, 121n119
yaravíes (melancholy songs), 66–67, 113, 117, 131
young men, *champería* duties of, 99n35, 102n52, 104, 132n161
young people and social change. See intergenerational conflict
Yunca people, 46
yunsa (*cortamonte*, game), 146n197
yupanas (counting devices), 141n178

Zwarteveen, Margreet, 32–33